Church of England Record Society

Volume 4

BRETHREN IN ADVERSITY

BISHOP GEORGE BELL,
THE CHURCH OF ENGLAND AND
THE CRISIS OF GERMAN PROTESTANTISM

1933–1939

Throughout the middle years of the twentieth century George Bell, bishop of Chichester 1929–57, was deeply involved in the ecumenical movement and the political life of Europe. His sustained commitment to German affairs was demonstrated by his ten visits to Germany, between 1928 and 1957. These were documented in extensive travel 'diaries', some of them purely personal and others circulated confidentially to fellow church leaders at the time. Through these and other related sources, we receive extraordinary insights into the struggles of the German churches during the Third Reich. Equally, we see the profound difficulties which English Christians faced in coming to terms with a very different protestant Christianity, and a disturbingly violent political culture.

The volume revolves around material in the Bell archive at Lambeth Palace, but also includes documents from different collections written by other figures in the Church of England who shared Bell's concern with the Christian life of Germany.

G.K.A. BELL (1883–1958), BISHOP OF CHICHESTER
(Lambeth Palace Library, Bell Papers, 357, fo. 187)

BRETHREN IN ADVERSITY

BISHOP GEORGE BELL,
THE CHURCH OF ENGLAND AND
THE CRISIS OF GERMAN PROTESTANTISM
1933–1939

EDITED BY

Andrew Chandler
Director, George Bell Institute
Queen's College, Birmingham

THE BOYDELL PRESS

CHURCH OF ENGLAND RECORD SOCIETY

First published 1997

A Church of England Record Society publication
Published by The Boydell Press
an imprint of Boydell & Brewer Ltd
PO Box 9, Woodbridge, Suffolk IP12 3DF, UK
and of Boydell & Brewer Inc.
PO Box 41026, Rochester NY 14604–4126, USA

ISBN 0 85115 692 4

ISSN 1351–3087

Series information is listed at the back of this volume

A catalogue record for this book is available
from the British Library

The paper used in this publication meets the minimum requirements
of American National Standard for Information Sciences –
Permanence of Paper for Printed Library Materials, ANSI Z39.48–1984

Set by Rowland Phototypesetting Ltd
Bury St Edmunds, Suffolk

Printed in Great Britain by
St Edmundsbury Press Ltd, Bury St Edmunds, Suffolk

In Churches, when the'infirmitie,
Of him which speakes, diminishes the Word,
When Magistrates doe mis-apply
To us, as we judge, lay or ghostly sword,
When plague, which is thine Angell, raignes,
Or wars, thy Champions, swaie,
When Heresie, thy second deluge, gaines;
In th'houre of death, the'Eve of last judgement day,
Deliver us from the sinister way.

John Donne (1572–1631)
The Litanie

For Melanie Barber

CONTENTS

Acknowledgments   viii
Introduction   1
The text   33
A note on editorial principles   35
List of letters   36

1933   39

1934   68

1935   94

1936   104

1937   119

1938   142

1939   153

Biographies
  England   159
  Germany   162
  The international ecumenical movements   175
Selective bibliography   177
Index   181

ACKNOWLEDGMENTS

To begin: all scholars who have worked on the Bell Papers will know that a basic debt is owed to Melanie Barber, deputy librarian and archivist at Lambeth Palace Library, who has devoted many years to the thousands of letters and documents in the collection. Because of her labours one of the most impressive and important archives in the history of the Church of England is now accessible to scholars of Anglican, ecumenical, political, and international history. I also owe much to my editor, Dr Stephen Taylor of the Department of History at Reading University, for his meticulous advice and editorial skills, and his forbearance and kindness.

I am grateful to the archbishop of Canterbury's secretary for ecumenical affairs, the Rev. Dr Richard Marsh, for permission to publish material from the Archbishop of Canterbury's Council on Foreign Relations; to Lambeth Palace Library for permission to publish documents from the Bell archive; and to the Karl Barth-Archiv for permission to publish a letter by Karl Barth. Permission has been sought for all other material.

I wish to thank those who have given me academic guidance and personal friendship over the years in which I have been working in this area, in particular Mr Richard Gutteridge, Dr David M. Thompson of Fitzwilliam College, Cambridge, Professor J.A.S. Grenville of the University of Birmingham and Professor John S. Conway of the University of British Columbia. I am grateful to Mrs Elsie Duncan-Jones for making available a letter written by her father-in-law, A.S. Duncan-Jones, an act of kindness which illustrates a very splendid friendship. I also acknowledge gratefully the advice of colleagues in the School of History at the University of Birmingham, and the generosity of the Arts Faculty there for a grant to assist with the costs of the work.

The publication of this book has been assisted by a grant from The Scouloudi Foundation in association with the Institute of Historical Research, whom I would also like to thank.

My parents, Eric Chandler and Janet Chandler, have been a continuing and invaluable support. My wife, fellow historian Fiona Terry-Chandler, has sustained me while I have ploughed on with my transcriptions, writing and referencing, with all their attendant confusions, and my debt to her is inestimable.

INTRODUCTION

THE ECUMENICAL CENTURY

It was Thomas Cranmer's wish that there should exist a union of the Reformed churches of Europe. In 1530 he had travelled as Henry VIII's ambassador to a number of German states, and in Nuremberg he had married the niece of the Lutheran theologian Andreas Osiander. As archbishop of Canterbury, Cranmer later invited a succession of protestant scholars from the Continent to England, among them Martin Bucer, and he continued to press for a closer relationship between their churches and his own. But such a vision was not to endure. The European Reformation fractured the face of Christian Europe; its Reformed churches had secured their freedom from the Pope by framing alliances with political states and seeking to confirm the emergent identities of new nations. Protestantism embraced, and was an integral part of, the national argument which now gave Europe its form and set it on its hectic course. Each church now spoke a different language and each developed the different forms of doctrine and self-government they inherited from their founders. Rarely did they communicate with each other.

At the onset of the twentieth century this was set to change. Protestant ecumenism broke out with all the splendid vitality and confidence of an enthusiasm, and those who committed themselves to serve the new ideal did so with excitement. Journals were printed; conferences were held; books were published and reports submitted. In a popular phrase, Archbishop William Temple spoke of the ecumenical movement as the 'great new fact' of Christian life.[1] In England church leaders believed that a new, sustained dialogue between Christian churches would restore the unity of purpose which faithful Christians in all countries now sought. In a divided world, meanwhile, the churches together could work for peace and concord where there was distrust and fear. Ecumenism was an idea whose time had come. There were trains, aeroplanes and motor cars to bring churchpeople together, and there were prophets in each land to inspire a following. The World Missionary Conference of 1910 sounded the first blast of the ecumenical trumpet and inaugurated a new era in the Christian world. The movement was soon institutionalized in the forms of two bodies: Faith and Order, which addressed questions of doctrine and sought reunion, and Life and Work, which devoted itself to the Church's relationship with the world. The bishops of the Church of England embraced these grand enterprises and endeavoured to play their part. Many others, clergy and laity, joined their councils or their conferences.

George Kennedy Allen Bell was born on 4 February 1883.[2] His father was

---

1 F.A. Iremonger, *William Temple, archbishop of Canterbury: his life and letters* (London, 1948), p. 387.
2 The standard life of Bell is R.C.D. Jasper, *George Bell, bishop of Chichester* (London, 1967).

vicar of Hayling Island, when his first son was born, but soon led his family to a succession of vicarages in Southampton, Pershore in Worcestershire, Birmingham and then Wimbledon. In 1896 the young Bell won a scholarship to Westminster School where he worked hard and did well. In 1901 he was rewarded with a scholarship to Christ Church, Oxford. Here he secured a first class result in his 'Moderations' and narrowly missed another in 'Greats' in 1905. But he also won a prestigious award for poetry, the Newdigate Prize, and became the general editor of a series of poetry anthologies. He met William Temple, the son of an archbishop of Canterbury and already a star rising towards the Oxford firmament, who was a student at Queen's College. Bell was destined for the Church, and in 1906 he went to Wells Theological College. Here he was influenced by Tissington Tatlow, secretary of the Student Christian Movement, and in the college he organized a weekly service of intercession for the unity of the Christian Church. In June 1907 he was ordained deacon in Ripon Cathedral, and he moved to Leeds. He was admitted to priest's orders in its parish church in September 1908. Although he returned to Oxford as a clerical student in 1910 his time in the north had left its mark, and over the next four years he brought small bands of students from Oxford to glimpse the urban realities of industrial life there. He was able to renew his friendship with Temple, now a fellow at The Queen's College, and he met the new regius professor of divinity, Henry Scott Holland, who had become a canon of Christ Church. Then a turning point in Bell's life occurred. In the summer of 1914 he was invited to Lambeth Palace in London to take his place as chaplain to the archbishop of Canterbury, Randall Davidson.

On the night that Bell went to Lambeth the British government declared war on Germany. Now he found himself at the very nexus between church and state; he confronted the intricacies of ecclesiastical diplomacy and organization; he observed what had become an important partnership between Davidson and the far younger archbishop of York, Cosmo Gordon Lang. His understanding of what Christian authority meant in this new century matured, his awareness of the world grew, and his perception sharpened.

One episode which may well have influenced Bell's development as an ecumenist occurred almost as soon as he assumed his responsibilities. On 1 August 1914 Davidson had written to the chief court chaplain to Wilhelm II, Dr Ernst Dryander, 'War between two great Christian nations of kindred race and sympathies is, or ought to be, unthinkable in the twentieth century of the Gospel of the Prince of Peace.'[3] But the next day he heard Sir Edward Grey speak to the house of commons and returned convinced that there was no alternative to the course chosen by the British government. Then early in September a letter from Germany, an 'Appeal to Evangelical Christians abroad', arrived at Lambeth. It was the work of the leading lights of the Anglo-German Movement for Friendship between the Churches, an ecumenical group which had assembled at Lake Constance only days before the outbreak of war to found the World Alliance for Promoting International Friendship through the Churches. Here were the signatures of the theologians Adolf Harnack and Adolf Deissmann, the educationalist and philanthropist Friedrich von Bodelschwingh and Dryander himself. Together they denied German guilt and talked of the 'sacred legacy' of the 1910 Edinburgh

3 G.K.A. Bell, *Randall Davidson, archbishop of Canterbury* (London, 1952 edn.), pp. 732–3.

World Missionary Conference. If this new fellowship was broken now, the responsibility lay not with German Christians, but with Christians abroad: 'With the deepest conviction we attribute it to those who have long secretly and cunningly been spinning a web of conspiracy against Germany, which now they have flung over us in order to strangle us therein.'[4] Davidson replied with 'amazement' at such ideas, and emphasized 'the paramount obligation of fidelity to the plighted word, and the duty of defending weaker nations against violence and wrong'. The very principles of truth and honour were at stake.[5] The archbishops of Canterbury, York and Armagh, and the Free Church leaders put their names to the letter, and sent it back to Berlin.[6] Later, when the new archbishop of Uppsala, Nathan Soderblom, sought to bring Christians of warring nations together with an appeal for unity – 'The strife of nations must finally serve the dispensation of the Almighty, and all the Faithful in Christ are one' – Davidson found that he could not sign the document. A 'fundamental moral principle' was at stake.[7] The Christian churches of Germany prayed for victory and preached that God was on their side. The Christian churches of Britain did the same.

The experience of war shattered Europe and declared the fatal bankruptcy of inherited traditions. Humane, liberal minds saw that nationalism led to suspicion, hostility and conflict. If the world was to move forward in peace and with hope such values must be repudiated. The great work of the new internationalists was begun with the creation of the League of Nations. Bell himself had lost his two younger brothers within days of each other in the last year of the war. For him, and for many other Christians of his generation, political disaster and personal grief deepened his commitment to the ecumenical vision. In the friendship of the churches lay hope for the reconciliation of nations. The powerful strands which brought Christians in England to confront the crisis of German protestantism between 1933 and 1939 were already apparent.

The leaders of the World Alliance for Promoting International Friendship through the Churches met at Oud Wassenaar in Holland on 30 September 1919. Bell was present, and saw for himself how the conference was almost destroyed by the insistence of French representatives that the German delegation condemn the violation by their government of Belgian neutrality in 1914. But the ecumenical idea remained alive, and the new decade offered many encouragements. In 1920 the recently installed regius professor of divinity at Oxford University, Arthur Cayley Headlam, gave his Bampton lectures on *The doctrine of the church and christian reunion*. They were published the day after the last was given, with an eye on the approaching Lambeth Conference that summer. The book soon sold out. It was a panoramic view of Christian history, and a powerful argument for reunion. A reviewer in the *Church Quarterly Review* observed, 'the argument marches relentlessly over ground strewn with the debris of eighteen centuries of debate to its inevitable and triumphant close'.[8] For Headlam it was the purpose of God that all Christians be brought together in one church. Division was the consequence of sin. Like all such works the book was acknowledged

---

4 Ibid., pp. 740–1.
5 Ibid., p. 741.
6 Ibid., pp. 741–3.
7 Ibid., pp. 743–4.
8 Cited by R.C.D. Jasper, *Arthur Cayley Headlam, life and letters of a bishop* (London, 1960), p. 140. The reviewer was C.H. Turner.

to have weaknesses – not least because the author appeared quite uninterested in contrary arguments or recent studies which might have modified views long ago adopted. But it was a controversial success. In August the members of the sixth Lambeth Conference assembled and there was much talk of reunion among them. It was the second time that Davidson had presided over such a gathering, and his chaplain worked laboriously to organize it. Beneath the flat in Morton's Tower where Bell and his new wife Henrietta lived, a conference office was opened, and, above them, a smoking and reading room (the bishops of the Anglican Church were found often to be pipe smokers). The first matter on the agenda was entitled 'Relation to and Reunion with other Churches'; the sixth addressed 'Christianity and International Relations, especially the League of Nations'.[9] But above all the conference devoted itself to an 'Appeal to all Christian People', a grand statement which invited Christians from every church to 'unite in a new and great endeavour to recover and to manifest to the world the unity of the Body of Christ for which He prayed'. At once this became famous throughout the church.[10]

In 1925 600 representatives from thirty-seven nations met at Stockholm for the first international conference of the Life and Work movement. In August 1927 the Faith and Order movement gathered at an equally impressive conference at Lausanne. By 1930 a new Lambeth Conference, chaired by Davidson's successor, Cosmo Lang, could observe with 'deep thanks to Almighty God ... the signs of a growing movement towards Christian Unity in all parts of the world'.[11] The Church of Scotland was 'now happily united'. A delegation from the Free Church Federal Council had attended one of the sessions of the conference. Cardinal Mercier, whose unofficial contacts with other churches had inspired brief hopes that the Roman Catholic Church might move more closely towards churches it had never before recognized, was praised for his 'courage and Christian charity'.[12] The conference looked eastwards, and found the Ecumenical Patriarch encouragingly ecumenical: there were even hopes of a joint doctrinal commission. The Old Catholic Church, and the archbishop of Utrecht, were moving towards closer relations with the Anglican communion, and it was believed that full intercommunion might be achieved with the Separated Eastern Churches. Bishop Lund had visited England on behalf of the Church of Sweden. A new commission would be appointed by the archbishop of Canterbury to explore relations with the Church of Finland. Those who sought church union in South India were making progress, and much was written of it. Promising developments were reported in Persia. In July 1930 the patriarch of Alexandria and others had met bishops of the Church of England at Lambeth and agreed to appoint a joint commission for the consideration of questions of doctrine. There had been negotiations with the Moravians. Well might the members of the seventh Lambeth conference feel that this last decade had brought perceptibly nearer the unity of all Christians in Europe and throughout the world.

9 For a complete description of the conference, its members and agenda, see *The Lambeth Conference 1920: encyclical letter from the bishops, with resolutions and reports* (London, 1920).
10 For a comprehensive discussion see Alan M.G. Stephenson, *Anglicanism and the Lambeth Conferences* (London, 1978), pp. 128–54.
11 *The Lambeth Conference 1930: encyclical letter from the bishops with resolutions and reports* (London, 1930), p. 48.
12 Ibid.

ENGLISH AND GERMAN PROTESTANTISM

The nature of the church and its relationship with the state

The Church of England was by law the established church of the nation. The Elizabethan settlement had ordained an Act of Uniformity which affirmed that the nation was Anglican and the Church English. This was never the reality. The protestant faith was to be found in many different traditions which in time lived amongst the parishes of the country without violence and with diminishing suspicion. But the establishment of one national Church brought to public life an image of unity in authority and simplicity in relationships. The monarch was the supreme governor of the Church, and was in turn, crowned by the archbishop of Canterbury. Bishops lived and worked at the heart of the political state, and sat in the upper house of parliament, the house of lords. The passage of time brought disruptions, but by the close of the eighteenth century the original, precise symmetry of church and state looked as if had lasted without doubt or confusion for a thousand years, and would continue to do so. Only in the nineteenth century was the connexion of church and state eroded by a perceptible weakening of loyalties and the steady integration into the political realm of men of other persuasions. In the twentieth century this was not a state church in the way that much of the Christian world understood that phrase. Its bishops were nominated by prime ministers, and their choices confirmed by monarchs, but these secular powers were advised by men who were eminent in the Church, or had its interests at heart. Rarely did the arrangement offend. If the Church was accountable to parliament, only occasionally did politicians intervene in its affairs: most of the time the Church governed itself with genuine freedom, and by the middle of the twentieth century it appeared to have all the bodies of self-administration and expression that an independent church could require. Since 1855 the two provinces of Canterbury and York had held convocations, and after 1867 Lambeth Conferences took place every ten years. In 1919 an Enabling Act created a Representative Church Assembly which afterwards met in London three times a year. National Church Congresses had once been more popular than now but they continued, sporadically. Meanwhile, every bishop chaired regular diocesan conferences. The Church of England taught that the state was divinely ordained and that Christians must be loyal to the state that ruled them justly. But most of its bishops viewed the Church not as a subordinate institution, and certainly not a department of the state, but as partner in authority – and in some senses the senior of the two. If politicians erred it was the duty of the Church to censure.

The historical ties that bound church, state and society together encouraged Christians to think politically and socially. By the middle years of the twentieth century they could recall the role evangelical Christians had played in the abolition of the slave trade. The Christian socialism of Frederick Denison Maurice had inspired his successors to face the challenge of industrial society. At the turn of the nineteenth century an impressive number of bishops had joined the Christian Social Union, a movement led by the likes of Brooke Foss Westcott, the bishop of Durham, who had settled a mining dispute, Charles Gore, the first bishop of Birmingham, and Henry Scott Holland at Oxford. Although their

Christian socialism was broadly defined, they were capable of framing progressive ideas and upsetting members of governments with their criticisms in the
house of lords. They argued that it was not enough to sponsor charitable works
when the state had the power to eradicate poverty at the root, and that an
economic system based upon competition and not co-operation must produce
exploitation and oppression. The social thought of William Temple inherited
these values and expanded them. This too was the Christian culture which Bell
imbibed as a young ordinand in Leeds and a student at Oxford. It affirmed that
the very credibility of the Church rested on its commitment to redeem a fallen
creation and work for the kingdom of God on earth. However strong this consensus of ideals, few Anglicans were sure how they might be given practical meaning. Controversial times could expose their doubts and divisions cruelly, and the
more one bishop might seek to develop his views the more he risked leaving
others behind. Most believed they could address the political world practically
and still transcend the partisanship of parties. In fact, conservatives were inclined
to think their allegiances lay to the left of the political spectrum and socialists
suspected that they were conservatives at heart.[13]

The effects of the Reformation in Germany were very much more complicated.
In the sixteenth century Germany was a collection of some 300 states. In 1555
the Treaty of Augsburg granted to the prince of each the right to determine
whether his should be a Catholic or a Lutheran state. In time the Reformed
Christianity of Calvin grew popular among the princes of the northern and
western states, and, accordingly, their churches adopted the Calvinist tradition.
The prince continued to govern the church; he was the *summus episcopus*,
with authority over its property, ecclesiastical jurisdiction and its doctrine. The
consistory of theologians and lawyers who managed its affairs performed their
tasks as state officials. In 1817 the king of Prussia, Frederick-Wilhelm III,
celebrated the 300th anniversary of the Reformation in Germany with the establishment of a union of the Lutheran and Reformed churches in Prussia. By 1822
a new service book had been adopted by most of them, in the face of criticism
that the king was overstepping the proper mark of his jurisdiction over the
churches by intervening in their liturgies and doctrines. As the nineteenth century
unfolded synodical bodies were increasingly a part of church life, and in 1848
some 500 protestant Christians came to Wittenberg for what would prove the
first of sixteen successive church congresses, the *Kirchentage*. In June 1852
the first Evangelical Church Conference met at Eisenach, gathering together
representatives from twenty-four *Landeskirchen*.[14] Thereafter, the conference was
held biennially, and it soon grew in authority, debating marriage laws, education
and ministry. The birth of the German Empire in 1870 wrought few changes.
When he sought to describe the Wilhelmine church in his study of 1938, the
dean of Chichester, A.S. Duncan-Jones, still found it 'dessicated'.[15] At the onset
of the twentieth century there existed fifty-five *Landeskirchen*. But on the 420th

13 For surveys of the Church of England and its response to politics and society see Donald Wagner,
   The Church of England and social reform since 1854 (New York, 1930); E.R. Norman, *Church
   and society in England 1770–1970. A historical study* (Oxford, 1976); P. d'A. Jones, *The
   Christian socialist revival 1877–1914* (Princeton, 1968); and John Kent, *William Temple.
   Church, state and society in Britain 1880–1950* (Cambridge, 1992).
14 The established provincial protestant churches of Germany.
15 A.S. Duncan-Jones, *The struggle for religious freedom in Germany* (London, 1938), p. 15.

anniversary of Luther's birth, in November 1903, a *Deutsche Evangelische Kirchenausschuss* met to serve as a standing committee for the evangelical Church Conferences, affirming a new coherence if not a search for unity.

The destruction of the *Kaiserreich* at the end of the Great War of 1914–18 brought fundamental change to the German churches. The prince of each state disappeared. Germany was now a republic, and while the churches continued to receive subsidies as public corporations, the new constitution offered no new alliance between the state and the protestant faith. Moreover, the post-war settlement revised Germany's boundaries. Now there were twenty-eight *Landeskirchen*, some of them reduced in size. Without invitation or guidance from the state, church leaders sought to adapt to new circumstances. By 1924 twenty-six of the churches had new constitutions; princes were replaced by committees, whose authority lay in the votes of provincial synods. Seven churches, among them the Lutheran churches of Hanover and Schleswig-Holstein, appointed bishops. In May 1922 a new German Evangelical Church Confederation, the *Deutsche Evangelische Kirchenbund*, was established with a *Kirchentag*, or assembly, of 210 representatives, a *Kirchenbundesrat*, or Church Confederation Council, and the *Kirchenausschuss*, an executive committee of thirty-six members drawn equally from the other two bodies.

In dangerous days Luther had survived because of the protection of sympathetic princes. In his treatise of 1523 on secular authority he had drawn a distinction between the province of the church and that of the law, inaugurating a tradition in which the 'two regiments' of religion and politics were decisively detached, in theory at least. The church trusted the 'Godly prince' with the order of society, and its own development, because he was himself Christian and sought to govern as such. It was the church of those in authority, and so it remained. The association so greatly defined the nature of German protestantism that it appeared remote from the popular doubts and disturbances which disfigured German society in the nineteenth century. There were few forays into the realm of 'Social Christianity', but even the celebrated social work of Johann Wichern was apparently motivated by a wish to sustain ruling powers in the face of discontent. In the young German Empire the 'Christian-Social' idea became firmly attached to nationalism and antisemitism in the work of Adolf Stöcker, a court chaplain to Wilhelm II, and Rudolf Todt. Like Wichern before him, Stöcker was also driven by a fear of communism. Bismarck, meanwhile, used Stöcker's Christian Socialist Workers' Party to weaken the Socialist Party. After 1918 the protestant churches regarded the new Weimar Republic with hostility, and continued to nurture Hohenzollern sympathies. Few sensed that the church had been granted its freedom. The men who were powerful in its synods looked back nostalgically to an intimate relationship with political authority, and wished to return to past realities. When Christians in Britain sought the redemption of society, German Christians were seeking the conversion of the individual. While preaching quietism many German protestants simultaneously espoused the cause of authoritarian conservatism. At elections they favoured the two authoritarian nationalist parties, the *Deutsche-nationale-Volkspartei* and the *Deutsche Volkspartei*.[16]

16 For discussion of German protestantism in these years see W.R. Ward, *Theology, sociology and politics: the German protestant conscience 1890–1933* (Berne, 1979); Kurt Nowak, *Evangelische Kirche und Weimarer Republik: Zum politischen weg des deutschen Protestantismus zwischen 1918 und 1932* (Göttingen, 1981); and J.R.C. Wright, *Above parties: the political attitudes of the German protestant church leadership 1918–1933* (Oxford, 1974).

The theology of the church

Headlam had argued that the Lambeth Quadrilateral of 1888 provided a framework for reunion. Others were not so sure. When, in 1921, the bishop of Durham, Herbert Hensley Henson, published a collection of lectures on Anglicanism which he had given in Sweden, he spoke more cautiously:

> These lectures were designed with the object of assisting Swedish students to understand the highly perplexing phenomenon which is called Anglicanism, of which the extraordinary character is rarely appreciated even by English Churchmen, and which must needs present an aspect of baffling perplexity to foreigners.[17]

Henson's recognition that Christians from other churches might well find Anglicanism mysterious struck a truer note. It was equally clear that English Christians might find the Christianity of other protestant cultures remote and even alienating. Before 1933 German protestantism appeared to English Anglicans a very distant and foreign spectacle. Its origins and traditions were, to all but a few, obscure; its faith and order different and questionable; its present realities difficult. The German churches were not named when ecumenical affairs were debated at Lambeth in 1920 or 1930. Even George Bell, who sought to bring English and German Christians together, was only weakly aware of the character of protestantism in Germany. The historian Gordon Rupp once commented, 'Of the intricate theological issues between Lutherans and Calvinists, of the four hundred years of Confessional divisions, of the complexities of dialectical theology, Bell knew as little as most Englishmen.'[18]

The figure of Martin Luther was not a part of English Christian culture. If Cranmer had admired him, his successors were less ardent and soon he was little regarded. 'The story of Luther in English dress is of a few intermittent bursts of translation. The rest is silence', observed Rupp.[19] Luther had inspired Bunyan and Wesley. In the nineteenth century Henry Cole had translated 'the kind of Luther who appealed to English Evangelicals',[20] and the works of Luther could be found in the libraries of intellectuals of various persuasions: Coleridge, Carlyle and Froude knew him, each in their way. The Cambridge scholar Julius Hare wrote of him with insight; Mandell Creighton, scholar, priest and later bishop, lectured on Luther thoughtfully, but with detachment. These writers were too isolated from each other to offer a genuine or continuous tradition of academic understanding. In the twentieth century Luther attracted little excitement in the divinity faculties of the universities. When a young student from Cambridge, Richard Gutteridge, studied at Tübingen in 1933 his tutor asked him: when English students read their Luther, did they do so in German or English? Gutteridge shocked him by replying that they read hardly a word of Luther in either. His tutor was baffled. How, then, might they be true protestants at all?[21]

If Luther retained a symbolic significance in England, he was still to some Evangelicals the prophet of the Reformation, the fearless critic of papal corrup-

17 Herbert Hensley Henson, *Anglicanism* (London, 1908), p. v.
18 Gordon Rupp, *I seek my brethren: Bishop George Bell and the German churches* (University of East Anglia Mackintosh Lecture, 1975), p. 9.
19 Gordon Rupp, *The righteousness of God* (London, 1953), p. 37.
20 Ibid.
21 Richard Gutteridge: conversation with the author.

tion, and the popularizer of the Bible. But when, in 1930, Archbishop Lang received an invitation to send representatives to a commemoration of the 400th anniversary of the Augsburg Confession in Germany he wrote to George Bell:

> Evidently from the terms of the invitation the German Lutherans regard their confession as having some importance outside their own communion. They describe it as being 'Ecumenical' and regard it as a rallying point for Evangelical Churches. This is giving it an importance which I cannot share and it would be very unfortunate if just before the Lambeth Conference I were in any way to seem to identify the Church of England with [the] Evangelical Church at home or on the Continent.[22]

While a number of secular English newspapers marked the 450th anniversary of Luther's birth in November 1933, the Anglican press did not.

It was sometimes observed that English theology owed many debts to the work of German theologians, and in the twentieth century connecting strands are not difficult to find. But German theology also aroused suspicions amongst the bishops. Headlam, typically robust, thought it 'a riot of theories, unproved and unprovable'. They were all, he wrote, continually indebted to the German scholars, 'not only for the material with which they supply us, but also for the mental stimulus which the examination of their ingenious errors and one-sided presentation provides, but we must candidly say that they seem to us most inadequate guides in our search for truth'.[23] Henson read these words in Durham, and wrote of the *formgeschichte*, or form criticism, of Martin Dibelius, 'So far as I can understand this latest German vagary, it is mainly nonsense'.[24] The German theologian seemed perversely inclined to make life difficult for the faithful Christian. Dibelius, remarked Headlam, did little to 'nourish the soul'.[25]

Now there was Karl Barth. Since 1921 Barth, who was Swiss by birth, had taught at Göttingen, Münster and Bonn. When Sir Edwyn Hoskyns translated Barth's *Epistle to the Romans* he offered the book to the Christian public with detectable caution. 'What Karl Barth has to say', he observed in his preface,

> lies embedded in a wealth of allusions which must be largely unfamiliar to the English reader. Indeed, the disturbing effect of his book among German-speaking people was due in no small degree to his extremely critical sensitiveness to movements of thought of which we in England may perhaps have heard, but which do not hang heavily in the air we breathe.[26]

Later he would write to Barth himself, 'We are separated by the very real barrier of a different language, a different political tradition, a different quality of piety and impiety, a different structure even of theological and untheological heritage.' But he added, 'your work has not been altogether misunderstood in England'.[27] Reviewing *The epistle to the Romans* in the journal *Theology* in December 1934, J.K. Mozley wrote:

22 Lambeth Palace Library (L.P.L.), Lang Papers, 99, fo. 10: Lang to Bell, 5 Mar. 1930. I am grateful to Ronald Feuerhahn for drawing my attention to this letter some years ago.
23 A.C. Headlam, *'Formgeschichte'*, Church Quarterly Review, CXIX (Jan. 1935), 293–4.
24 Dean and Chapter Cathedral Library, Durham, Journal of Bishop Henson, 61, p. 253: 16 Jan. 1935.
25 Headlam, *'Formgeschichte'*, p. 294.
26 Karl Barth, *The Epistle to the Romans*, transl. Edwyn Hoskyns (London, 1933), p. xi.
27 Edwyn Hoskyns, *Cambridge sermons* (London, 1938), pp. 218–19.

It is as a prophet of the transcendence of God pushed to its furthest extreme that Barth has come as the challenging note of interrogation to the Christian theology of our age. And when he speaks of it there is never the smallest trace of qualification or apology. Rather does he seem to delight in choosing words that will deeply shock those who claim and rejoice in a religious experience of the friendliness of God.[28]

Barth, he remarked, used a language which did not come easily to an English reader of Hooker and Butler. Though the academic world was eager with its gratitude to Hoskyns, not a few suspected that the translator must be tainted by his text. This was not true: Hoskyns declared that Barth was 'quite right about man, but quite wrong about God', which was hardly a superficial criticism.[29] Barth had his disciples, particularly among the young, but they were hard to find in the house of bishops. Headlam accused him of 'unreal, irrational soteriology'.[30] Henson thought his theology 'only a reaction which will pass'.[31] As for Temple, 'He was no Barthian' writes his biographer firmly, lest there be any doubt.[32] To them such theology appeared to offer little to celebrate. The congregationalist, Nathaniel Micklem, once encountered the New Testament scholar B.H. Streeter on a train to Cambridge. Christianity, Streeter told him, was 'in a bad way. Karl Barth has shown that we know nothing about God, and *Formgeschichte* that we know nothing about Jesus Christ. The residuum is not satisfactory.'[33]

In 1924 Bell left Lambeth Palace to become dean of Canterbury. Anxious that German theology was the expression of 'vanquished men',[34] and encouraged by the theologian Adolf Deissmann to think that the gulf between English and German thought was not unbridgeable, he now organized a series of conferences. In 1927 and 1928 a collection of eminent scholars from both countries assembled, first in Canterbury and then in Eisenach. The fruit of these gatherings was a single volume, *Mysterium Christi*, containing essays by Gerhard Kittel and Edwyn Hoskyns, J.K. Mozley and C.H. Dodd.[35] Bell reported that the German speakers were almost as likely to disagree among themselves as with their English friends. But he revealed too that differences between Anglicans and Lutherans − 'in some cases of a far-reaching kind' − arose upon the relations between the kingdom of God, their central theme, and the life of the Church itself.[36] The book caused some interest, but its exploration of language was not attractive to many English minds. Charles Raven found that it hardly alluded to man's experience of the natural world − and it was here that the differences between English and German theology were most profound.[37] In March 1931 a third gathering took place at Chichester, where Bell was now bishop. This

---

28 J.K. Mozley, Review of *The epistle to the Romans by Karl Barth*, *Theology*, XXIX (Dec. 1934), 368−9.
29 Edwyn Hoskyns and F.N. Davey, *Crucifixion: resurrection: the pattern of the theology and ethics of the New Testament*, ed. Gordon S. Wakefield (London 1981), p. 59.
30 Headlam, '*Formgeschichte*', p. 295.
31 Durham Cathedral Library, Henson Journal, 68, p. 174: 20 Dec. 1936.
32 Iremonger, *William Temple*, p. 608.
33 Nathaniel Micklem, *The box and the puppets 1888−1953* (London, 1957), p. 52.
34 Rupp, *I seek my brethren*, p. 6.
35 *Mysterium Christi*, ed. G.K.A. Bell and Adolf Deissmann (London, 1930).
36 See Jasper, *George Bell*, p. 66.
37 See F.W. Dillistone, *Charles Raven: naturalist, historian, theologian* (London, 1975), pp. 207−8.

time the chosen theme was corpus christi, and a number of contributions were afterwards published in *Theology*.[38]

1933: THE IMPACT OF NATIONAL SOCIALISM

As dean of Canterbury Bell worked to establish a new church council which would relieve the archbishop's office of the growing burden of ecumenical contacts, gather information and cultivate relations with churches abroad. There already existed an Eastern Churches Committee, an Anglo-Continental Society, and other assorted bodies, but now the creation of the Archbishop of Canterbury's Council on Foreign Relations would bring the ecumenical idea into the very heart of the Church's life. When the archbishop was reassured that such a body would not complicate his relations with other churches, and when the Church Assembly had voted for its establishment, the new Council began to meet. Its chairman was Bishop Headlam of Gloucester, whose experience as an ecumenical thinker and politician was incontestable, and its librarian the rector of St Dunstan-in-the-West, A.J. Macdonald. Forty members first met on 2 February 1933. Four sub-committees were convened, for the Roman Catholic Church, the Orthodox Church, the lesser Eastern churches, and continental churches. Links with other churches were provided by regular correspondents who were either Anglican chaplains at foreign embassies or members of other churches.

The arrival of the new Council on Foreign Relations virtually coincided with a dramatic change in the political life of Germany. Adolf Hitler became the chancellor of a coalition government on 30 January 1933. Many German protestants embraced his coming. The Roman Catholic Church viewed the new authorities with trepidation and made a quick peace with them. Abroad, meanwhile, most of those who led the English churches watched anxiously. They found themselves drawn to German affairs by their commitment to judge the political powers of the age, their ecumenical convictions, and by the belief that a nationalist government must undermine the internationalist vision they sought to promote. All of these strands were strongly present in the character of George Bell. He, and many others, soon found his attentions fixed on the persecution of Jews, the treatment of political prisoners in concentration camps, the fate of the Christian churches and the threat that now existed to the peace of Europe.

The hostility of Anglicans

Many English Christians saw the coming of Hitler as a judgment. By 1933 the Versailles Treaty looked like an unjust peace which robbed Germans of their patriotic dignity. The victorious powers of the Great War had subjected the defeated nation to reparations and excluded a reformed Germany from the international fold. Archbishop Lang now believed that Hitler had been given power by a country unfairly denied its 'just and rightful place of equality' in the family of nations. He could not but recognize the 'justice and force' of this new popular

38 *Theology*, XXII, 3 (1931), 301–46.

movement.[39] At Lambeth Palace his chaplain and secretary Alan Don wrote in his diary, 'however strongly one may condemn Hitler's insensate nationalism and all its brutal accompaniments, the fact remains that Germany has been driven to desperation by the unwillingness of her conquerors to fulfil their pledges'.[40] Until January 1933 little had been said of Germany, or of National Socialism, but now such views were often heard. The church press pondered the failure of democracy in Germany; in the first weeks of the new regime some observers remarked that the Germans were not suited to it. The Anglican weekly, *The Guardian*, pronounced: 'There is nobody like a German in his readiness to be ordered about, particularly if he is allowed to dress up in some kind of uniform.'[41] Hitler himself attracted much comment. The *Church Times* reported that in the beginning Hitler was a house decorator in Austria, and in the war a private in a Bavarian regiment.[42] The evangelical Anglican weekly, *The Record*, reported wonderingly that he was not yet forty-two.[43] Both papers agreed that he was here to stay. *The Guardian* suggested that he was 'imprisoned' by older and more moderate voices in his coalition.[44] The *Church Times* doubted that he was in a position to press the 'fantastic programme' which he had declared in earlier days. Perhaps he would learn the art of concession and moderation, and throw his extremes overboard in an attempt to keep himself up in the air?[45] When Hitler won a substantial, though not overall, majority in the elections of 5 March 1933 the tone grew darker. Bishop Henson wrote in his journal that Hitler owed this 'not very impressive majority' to violence and cynicism.[46] *The Guardian* concluded that the German people 'still acquiesce in being dragooned by "strong" men, and in voting as they are bidden'.[47] *The Record* remarked, 'there is no organised opposition to the Steel Helmets and the Brown Shirts, so that it looks as if Herr Hitler is now an absolute dictator'.[48] Some could not imagine that a people who had given to the world the writings of Goethe and Heine, and the music of Beethoven, should for long tolerate such a government. In the meantime, they watched the exodus of its victims – men like Albert Einstein and Bruno Walter – with incomprehension. That a modern European society could revive the vices of the medieval era by persecuting Jews seemed extraordinary and unaccountable. In June 1933 the *Church Times* declared that this new state would 'suppress a new Kant and exile a new Goethe'.[49]

Those who met German friends in 1933 were often assured that Hitler had saved society from communism. This did not strike a chord. English Christians were far less preoccupied by the spectre of communism than were churches abroad, and rarely did they fear that Europe was vulnerable to the lengthening shadow of eastern Bolshevism. In January 1933 few welcomed Hitler as a new

39 See the two speeches made by Lang on 27 June 1933 (reported in the *Times*, 28 June 1933, p. 16b) and 13 Oct. 1933 (reported in the *Times*, 14 Oct. 1933, p. 14b).
40 L.P.L., MS 2862, p. 72: Journal of Alan C. Don, 15 Oct. 1933.
41 *The Guardian*, 5 May 1933, p. 307a.
42 *Church Times*, 3 Feb. 1933, p. 127a.
43 *The Record*, 3 Feb. 1933, p. 61c.
44 *The Guardian*, 3 Feb. 1933, p. 67a.
45 *Church Times*, 3 Feb. 1933, p. 127a.
46 Durham Cathedral Library, Henson Journal, 57, p. 114: 7 Mar. 1933
47 *The Guardian*, 10 Mar. 1933, p. 159b.
48 *The Record*, 10 Mar. 1933, p. 125d.
49 *Church Times*, 30 June 1933, p. 227a.

bulwark against the tide. When the former dean of St Paul's Cathedral, Ralph Inge, met Adolf Deissmann in May 1933, he remarked in his diary, 'I found to my surprise that he really thinks that Hitler has saved Germany from the imminent danger of a Bolshevik revolution. I don't believe it, but it is very significant that so intelligent a man should hold this view.'[50] The new German state appeared to be a neurotic, fanatical nationalist state which demanded the unconditional loyalty of every citizen and sought to dominate every aspect of social life. Many soon described it as ideological and totalitarian. Commentators in the church press saw National Socialism, like communism, as a new political faith, but they struggled to identify its principles. Sidney Dark, in the *Church Times*, thought 'Nazi-ism' a 'confusion of ideas, some strange, some stupid, some sane'.[51] On 13 April a columnist in *The Guardian* dismissed Hitler's 'Twenty-five points' as 'a mass of contradictory proposals in which every class of voter was guaranteed exactly what it desired'.[52] *The Record* found the new chancellor's May Day speech 'high-sounding and obscure',[53] while the *Church Times* owned to 'serious doubts whether he himself knows what Hitlerism is, or whether he knows where he going'.[54] Hitler was a mystic demagogue, a prophet, but not an impressive example of the dictatorial species when placed alongside Stalin or Mussolini. From the beginning there were too many reports of persecution, of Jews, communists, socialists and pacifists, to inspire sympathy. To the *Church Times* Hitler's Germany resembled the France of the *ancien régime*, the Holy Roman Empire, the Geneva of Calvin: it was a 'pagan puritanism' (September 1933), in January 1934 a 'gross and vulgar tyranny', by May of that year a 'return to the tree-tops'.[55] The private words of many bishops were comparable, although their public statements strove to be responsible. When the German ambassador suggested to Lang that Hitler's revolution was a moral revolt, a purging of national life, Lang was not convinced. Nazism offended him. Within weeks he feared for its victims. Bell shared his anxieties. By the end of 1933 many bishops had protested against its concentration camps at public meetings.[56] In March 1934 Archbishop Temple confessed to Headlam an 'antipathy' that was 'intense'.[57] In the same month Woodward of Bristol spoke of 'a nation gone mad'.[58] At Durham Henson saw reason, morality and religion unseated. By February 1936 he could remark to himself, 'who would not applaud the German who, in the interest of elementary morals, killed Hitler? I should give them Christian burial without hesitation.'[59] Henson often took an unusually sharp view of matters, but it remains significant that an English bishop, whoever he was and wherever his words, could record such a judgment at such a time. It would be true to argue that the great majority of churchpeople who took care to learn of the political life of the continent

---

50 Magdalene College, Cambridge, Journal of W.R. Inge, 23 May 1933.
51 *Church Times*, 5 May 1933, p. 523a.
52 *The Guardian*, 13 Apr. 1933, p. 265d.
53 *The Record*, 5 May 1933, p. 241c.
54 *Church Times*, 5 May 1933, p. 523a.
55 *Church Times*, 1 Sept. 1933, p. 227a; 12 Jan. 1934, p. 31b; 11 May 1934, p. 559b.
56 See Andrew Chandler, 'The Church of England and Nazi Germany 1933–1945', Ph.D. dissertation, University of Cambridge, 1991, pp. 6–44.
57 L.P.L., MS 2643 (Headlam Papers), fo. 116: Temple to Headlam, 8 Mar. 1934.
58 *The Record*, 2 Mar. 1934, p. 139a.
59 Durham Cathedral Library, Henson Journal, 66, p. 117: 26 Feb. 1936.

found the new state of Hitler ugly and threatening. Even those who did not view Germany with great seriousness sensed danger. 'I can't take Hitler seriously', Dick Sheppard had written in March 1933. 'He's too like Charlie Chaplin with that moustache – but Heaven knows we may have to!'[60]

INFORMATION

This book is essentially about information and interpretation. A great deal of information about the crisis in the German churches was at once made public in Britain by the newspapers. In the middle years of the twentieth century journalists were aware of the public and moral significance of Christianity, and they sought to represent it. In the columns of the *Times* the convolutions of the church struggle were reported vividly at every turn. When the dean of Chichester, A.S. Duncan-Jones, visited Berlin in the summer of 1933 he promptly met the *Times* correspondent, Norman Ebbutt. Ebbutt, whose accounts had been particularly valuable, assured him that he would continue to send regular, comprehensive accounts of new developments to his editor. When Headlam criticized the newspaper at the Church Assembly in June 1937 Bell replied that the *Times* had always been 'singularly illuminating and continuous' in its reports, and praised its 'straightforward and clear account of the Church crisis'. The whole church, he declared, owed the newspaper 'a great debt for the way in which it had reported the affairs of the German Evangelical Church'.[61]

This much was common knowledge – or, at least, such information was available to those who had ears to hear. But more lay beneath the surface, in the private and confidential world of the responsible. In the twentieth century public life and political knowledge in Europe had become a matter for experts and departments. In a sense, the creation of the Council on Foreign Relations showed the Church of England to be responding to the issue of knowledge in the same way as other institutions. As its chairman Bishop Headlam received regular, thorough reports from the chaplain at the Berlin embassy, Roland Cragg, and also a steady succession of memoranda recording visits to Germany, or significant conversations with German churchpeople, often by members of the Council. These documents were marked 'confidential' and circulated only to selected names. Meanwhile, Archbishop Lang received a number of accounts of German affairs from his bishops and clergy, and from laity who had connexions or concerns there. Principal among these was Bishop Bell, with whom he often corresponded. To these he responded personally, or through his chaplain.

The quantity and the nature of available information also depended upon the Church's relationships with other public institutions. Here the establishment of the Church of England proved significant, for the formal and informal currents which attached church to state permitted a modest access to official sources and insights. Lang enjoyed sympathetic relations with members of the Baldwin and Chamberlain governments. Bell was a personal friend of Alan Leeper, a counsellor at the Foreign Office between 1933 and 1940. But too much should not be

60 *What can we believe? Letters exchanged between Dick Sheppard and L.H.*, ed. Laurence Housman (London, 1939), p. 210.
61 *Report of the proceedings of the Church Assembly* (London, 1937), XVII, 274–5 (22 June 1937).

made of these links. Lang did not receive information as a matter of course; he asked for it occasionally, when his concern on a particular issue was aroused, and he did so cautiously. Contacts provided by the ecumenical movements were more confident, and in this area Bell found himself at the heart of an international network of reports, accounts and views provided regularly by authoritative ecumenical authorities in France, Sweden and the United States. He was also in a position to cultivate valuable personal friendships; in particular, he learnt much from the Swedish chaplain in Berlin, Birger Forell, the Swiss ecumenist Alphons Koechlin, and the young theologian Dietrich Bonhoeffer when he was the pastor of the Lutheran congregation at Forest Hill between 1933 and 1935. After January 1933 German churchpeople were sensitive to the fact that telephones were tapped and letters opened in a police state, and they feared that any contact with a foreigner might be compromising, and even dangerous. But Bell's ecumenical work gave him reason enough to visit the country, to see how matters stood for himself, and to listen to what could be said in private conversations. Fear of exposure naturally produced an insistence on anonymity, and at times this makes difficulties for the historian. But most of the material circulated by the Council on Foreign Relations attached names to opinions with some freedom. It may be argued that while English Christians lacked a cultural understanding of German protestantism, they were soon familiar with the narrative details of the controversy which now almost consumed it.

THE GERMAN CHURCH STRUGGLE 1933–1939

The arrival of Hitler was to throw the German protestant churches into confusion. The first fact to confront them was the combination of popular appeal and political intimidation which the new state presented. But they were also receptive to the claims of the new government. They had feared Bolshevism: Hitler destroyed the threat. They had suspected democracy: democracy, suspended for three years before, was now abolished. They had harboured antisemitic prejudices: Hitler pronounced that the influence of the Jews in national life must be ended. Many Christians saw the future to lie in a choice between Bolshevism and Nazism, and Hitler offered them things they could value: a rebirth of national confidence after years of bitter despondency, a sense of responsibility to society, order, discipline and purpose where there had been self-indulgence and confusion, morality instead of vice, and the assurance of support for an undefined 'positive Christianity', which was no less than an article of the party programme.

Once the new regime found its feet its leaders pressed forward a process of *Gleichschaltung*, or 'co-ordination', to remove parties or interests that would not comply, refashion those which remained necessary in civil life, or remind others that they were not political entities at all, and that opposition must be improper. The National Socialist Party recognized the social significance of ideals like leadership and loyalty, and knew that most institutions and bodies could be converted if those who led them were persuaded or replaced. They also saw that the process of co-ordination was facilitated if the dynamics of institutional or corporate life were simplified, and different groups integrated into new, unified forms. The abolition of the free trades unions and the creation of a single German Labour Front under Robert Ley was, in this sense, a powerful example of such co-ordination. In six months the shape of political life had been transformed, and much of civil life too. It was inevitable that the churches should be a part of this process. In the concordat of 20 July 1933 the Roman Catholic Church attempted to secure its right to exist by renouncing all political influence. No such agreement appeared possible with the protestants, whose twenty-eight *Landeskirchen* defied a simple settlement. Hitler knew that the religious sentiments of the people presented him with sensitive ground, and looked to the dynamics unleashed by the national revolution to do much of the work of co-ordination for him. He supported a plan to create one, united *Reichskirche* for the nation, and a growing movement, the *Deutsche Christen*, set about the work of unifying it under a National Socialist leader.

The ensuing church struggle, or *Kirchenkampf*, was a protracted war of attrition between parties which unfolded within the design of a totalitarian state committed to the extinction of Christianity.[62] It led not to unity, but to new divisions and antipathies, and even to violence. Already by the late summer of 1933 processes of nomination and election had been corrupted, church leaders had been deposed and restored, and the life of the church had been filled by bitterness and recrimination. The developments of the next six years may be divided into three periods.

The Müller period

The strength of nationalism in twentieth-century German protestant culture made a convergence between National Socialism and protestantism unsurprising. In 1930 two new movements had come to life: the German Christian Movement (*Christlich-deutsche Bewegung*) and the German Christian Faith Movement (*Glaubens-bewegung Deutsche Christen*). These were small, but included powerful and eminent patrons; among the first were the theologians Paul Althaus and Emanuel Hirsch. Now that Hitler had come to power these groups sensed their moment had came. Their demand for the creation of a unified peoples' church (*Volkskirche*) found favour among many Christians who were sensitive to a new atmosphere of national unity and revival around them. In April 1933 Hermann Kapler, the president of the German Church Federation (the *Kirchenbund*), was invited to review the constitution of the church with Bishop Marahrens, the Lutheran bishop of Hanover, and Dr Hesse, of Elberfeld. On 20 May they issued the Manifesto of Loccum, calling for a unified church under a single *Reichsbischof* who would be supported by a Spiritual Ministry and a national synod. They appointed Friedrich von Bodelschwingh to lead the new church. Almost at once it was evident that the appointment of Bodelschwingh would be contested. Three days later Ludwig Müller, once an army chaplain and a friend

---

62 For surveys of the German church struggle the following studies may be consulted: Klaus Scholder, *Die Kirchen und das Dritte Reich* (2 vols., Franfurt, 1977), translated into English by John Bowden and published as *The churches and the Third Reich* (2 vols., 1987–8), and *A requiem for Hitler and other new perspectives on the German church struggle*, transl. John Bowden (London, 1989). The first covers the periods 1918–33 and 1934 in great depth; the second is a collection of articles. John S. Conway's book, *The Nazi persecution of the churches* (London, 1968), remains excellent. See too Ernst Helmreich, *The German churches under Hitler* (Detroit, 1979), and Victoria Barnett, *For the soul of the people: protestant protest against Hitler* (New York, 1992). Early, but still valuable, is A.S. Duncan-Jones, *The struggle for religious freedom in Germany* (London, 1938).

of Hitler himself, was made *Schirmherr* (protector) of the *Deutsche Christen* movement. On 26–7 May the choice of Kapler's committee was confirmed by large majorities of the church representatives on the council of the Church Federation. Immediately, the *Deutsche Christen* began to campaign for the appointment of Müller.

At this point the government intervened. The *Reichskultusminister*, Rust, appointed a new state commissioner for church affairs in Prussia. His name was August Jäger. Jäger, in turn, appointed sub-commissars to administer the Prussian church. Finding his authority undermined, Bodelschwingh retired from the office he had barely entered. Soon Jäger began to intimidate pastors in Prussia, and a number were removed from their parishes. A wave of indignation followed and forced an intervention by the German president, Paul von Hindenburg. Hitler dismissed the state commissars and placed the minister of the interior, Frick, in charge of church affairs. Müller now made himself chairman of the Church Federation; Jäger appointed the *Deutsche Christen* leader Joachim Hossenfelder vice-president of the Evangelical Church Council and then made Müller head of the church of the Old Prussian Union.

In July 1933 the campaign began for elections to the assembly which would endorse a new *Reichsbischof*. Bodelschwingh and his supporters found themselves overwhelmed by the intimidation of their *Deutsche Christen* opponents. Then, on the very eve of the vote, Hitler broadcast his support for Müller. On 23 July Müller won a formidable though dubious victory. On 5 September he was acclaimed first bishop (*Landesbischof*) of Prussia by the synod of the Evangelical Church there. Provincial synods were abolished; an 'Aryan Paragraph' would be enforced to exclude from the ministry pastors who were partly Jewish. A dissenting group, the 'Gospel and Church' party, walked out of the synod in protest. By the end of the month Müller had his victory confirmed at the first German national synod at Wittenberg. He now proceeded to appoint his Spiritual Ministry.

But the opposition to Müller was not defeated; instead, it was growing and organizing. The *Deutsche Christen* movement fractured after a triumphal rally at the *Sportpalast* in Berlin, when its main speaker, Dr Krause, declared that the Old Testament should be put aside and the New Testament revised. The national synod was in disarray, deciding now to suspend the acts of the provincial synods and the 'Aryan Paragraph' which it had passed in September. By November 1933 a Pastors' Emergency League, the *Pfarrernotbund*, had declared its determination to resist the new church government. Müller, meanwhile, defeated the leader of the Evangelical Youth organizations and assumed responsibility for them himself. At the end of the year they had been incorporated into the Hitler Youth movement. On 4 January 1934 Müller attempted to suppress dissent and factionalism with a new decree, soon named the 'muzzling order' by his critics. Pastors who preached controversial sermons or published their views on the struggle now faced the prospect of suspension and loss of earnings. It did not work. Three days later the Pastors' Emergency League protested from the pulpits. Hindenburg again intervened by meeting Hitler. On 25 January Hitler met representatives of the church groups in Berlin. During the conference the Prussian minister of the interior, Göring, intervened with a secret police report of a telephone conversation involving a leading member of the Emergency League, Martin Niemöller. Niemöller, it claimed, had remarked to a friend that Hitler was receiving 'severe unction' from the president. Hitler flew into a rage and declared that he would not tolerate an attempt to drive a wedge between him and the president. The Lutheran bishops who had been Niemöller's allies buckled under the pressure. Two days later they affirmed their loyalty to Müller.

Between January and April 1934 a succession of opposition synods took place across Germany, not only strengthening resistance to Müller, but beginning to establish a parallel structure of church government. This marked the emergence of a new Confessing church. Bishops Wurm and Meiser were soon drawn towards this movement. Müller conceded a little and revoked the 'muzzling order' of 4 January, but he also stepped up the campaign to incorporate the different provincial churches into the *Reichskirche*. After 19 April 1934 he signalled his determination to repress opposition by making the controversial Jäger legal member of his Spiritual Ministry. On 29–31 May the Confessing movement met at Barmen and appointed a Council of Brethren (*Bruderrat*). The two groups now faced each other in open confrontation, both claiming to be the single legitimate source of authority in the church. By mid-July, however, Müller and Jäger could inform Hitler that twenty-two of the twenty-eight churches were in their hands.

In August 1934 the second national synod of the *Reichskirche* took place in Berlin. It granted Müller full powers, and a new oath of loyalty to him was now framed and required of all pastors. On 23 September Müller was finally installed as primate of the German *Reichskirche* in a ceremony at the protestant cathedral in Berlin. All this time, however, a struggle for the incorporation of the churches of Württemberg and Bavaria was proving increasingly ugly, as bishops Wurm and Meiser resisted intimidation, dismissal and even house arrest in their defence of their churches. When Jäger himself turned up in Munich with a detachment of secret policemen crowds protested. This was too much for a number of *Deutsche Christen* too; Jäger responded by removing three of them from influence. But he had gone too far: on 26 October 1934 he was forced to resign. Two days later the coercive acts he had imposed on Bavaria were annulled. Müller also faced intense pressure, not least from those who had once supported him in the ranks of the *Deutsche Christen* party. On 22 November the Confessing Church established a Provisional Church Government. Hitler now sensed that Müller had failed to legitimize his authority and unify the churches, and in January 1935 he told the *Reichsbischof* that he must proceed without the assistance of a state commissioner. But this did not signal a decision to abstain from church affairs; those who would not swear loyalty to the *Reichsbischof* faced the threat of arrest. On 28 March the first pastor was interned in a concentration camp; as many as 700 others were detained in the same month. In Baden state grants to the church were suspended. Above all, the government was now seen as a powerful sponsor of the neo-pagan German Faith Movement. On 10 April the Provisional Church Government remonstrated with Hitler. The courts meanwhile vindicated the opposition of pastors who declared that Müller's regime had no legal foundation. It was clear that a change of policy was necessary if division and confusion were not to prevail.

The committees

On 19 July 1935 Hitler intervened again by appointing Hans Kerrl as the minister of a new Reich ministry for church affairs. Kerrl was a party man with little experience of the churches. It was his task to press ahead with the creation of a single state church, and he threatened 'swift and stern measures' against those who opposed him. The new instrument of co-ordination would be the committee. On 14 October Kerrl appointed a Reich's Church Committee representing all parties. It was chaired by Dr Zöllner, a Lutheran superintendent and an ecumenist who commanded respect. The first pronouncement by the new committee affirmed its belief in a national development founded on 'Race, Blood and Soil'. This did not reassure the pastors of the Confessing Church, who were represented on the new body, but not by men of their own choosing. The Confessing synod refused to recognize Zöllner's group, but Kerrl established a series of regional church committees to encourage support for his policies, and they took root. Meanwhile the state stiffened its censorship of church publications. On 28 November the trust funds of the Confessing Church were confiscated. By the beginning of December 1935 Kerrl had assumed dictatorial powers. Niemöller was banned from public speaking. Confessing pastors who opposed the provincial administrations set up by the ministry were threatened with charges of high treason. The bishop of Hanover, Marahrens, now affirmed his support for Kerrl.

Kerrl's striking success was to divide the Provisional Church Government of the Confessing movement. After the national synod of the Confessing Church met at Oeynhausen in February 1936, the churches of Bavaria, Württemberg and Hanover were no longer represented on the Council of Brethren and the Executive Committee. They now established a Lutheran Church of Germany with Saxony and Mecklenburg. On 28 May 1936 the second Provisional Church Government and the Council of the German Evangelical Church sent a memorandum to Hitler which included articles criticizing the state for its persecution of the Jews. This was leaked to the foreign press in July and, while opinion abroad welcomed the stand it made, its authors moved with embarrassment to find the culprits. One of them, Friedrich Weissler, later died in police custody. The hostility of the government to Christianity was becoming increasingly obvious. In August the Confessing Church made another pulpit protest against paganism, and in December Kerrl's own church ministry voiced the same criticisms. Hitler sought to placate them in a public statement in December 1936, but the state still forced its own officials to renounce the church and excluded supporters of the Confessing Church from the universities. In December Kerrl decreed that the Council of Brethren of the Provisional Church Government had no legal authority. He appointed Friedrich Werner to be solely responsible under him for the administration of the whole Evangelical church. On 9 January 1937 nine pastors were arrested in Lübeck. The Reich's Church Committee protested, and when Zöllner tried to visit the pastors he was prevented from doing so. On 13 February his committee resigned.

State intimidation and confiscation

In February 1937 Hitler ordered elections in the church, pronouncing that the state would have no part in them. The division which had opened between the Lutheran bishops and the Provisional Church Government of the Confessing Church was at once ended. Interim administrations were duly appointed. But the state continued to intervene in the months that followed. Martin Niemöller and the general superintendent of Berlin, Otto Dibelius, had their passports confiscated and the German Evangelical Church went unrepresented at the international conference on 'Church, Community and State' at Oxford in June. Hermann Muhs was appointed the new secretary of state in the Ministry of Church Affairs, and he moved to assert his authority over the church, while the minister of the interior, Frick, who had been appointed by Hitler to oversee the elections, intervened in the financial affairs of the Confessing Church. On 25 June Kerrl assumed responsibility for the finances of all the protestant churches of Germany. A week later Martin Niemöller was arrested. On 17 October the Prussian supreme court pronounced that the Confessing Church was not legally a part of the German Evangelical Church. The very existence of the Confessing Church was now dangerously threatened.

In February 1938 Niemöller was tried for abuse of the pulpit in the court of Alt-Moabit prison in Berlin. On 2 March 1938 he was acquitted of attacking the state and the National Socialist Party, but immediately escorted to a concentration camp. Discussions as to whether pastors should consent to take a civil servants' oath dragged on through the summer while the international situation darkened around them. When the Confessing Church issued a prayer for peace during the Sudeten crisis in September Kerrl accused them of treason. The Lutheran bishops, Wurm, Meiser and Marahrens, agreed to sign a statement condemning the prayer, and once again left the leaders of the Confessing Church weakened and defensive. Financial restrictions were tightened; the salaries of Confessing pastors were blocked. In February 1939 Werner issued four decrees further centralizing power in the church, permitting the forcible transfer of pastors from their parishes, and abolishing the right of parishes to choose their ministers. By the outbreak of war in September 1939 the Confessing Church was under siege from a state which no longer saw reason to disguise its true values or purposes.

THE CHURCH STRUGGLE THROUGH ENGLISH EYES

In an ecumenical age English church leaders were quick to argue that the well-being of German Christianity was their proper concern. This at once confronted a powerful political orthodoxy which affirmed that the internal affairs of sovereign nations were a concern only to themselves, but the bishops of the Church of England were insistent that the life of the universal church could not defer to this secular view. In December 1933 George Bell wrote to a remonstrating correspondent that the condition of German Christianity 'raises the question of the principles of the Christian Church as such'.[63] At all events, the ecumenical movements had to judge which elements in the German churches should be recognized by their councils and represented on them. In January 1934, Archbishop Lang observed to convocation that this was a 'matter of profound interest to the whole of Christendom',[64] and again, in June 1934, 'the issues here go far beyond the mere confines of the German nation'.[65] Preaching in the English Church in Cologne Bishop Batty declared in May 1936:

It is not for us to interfere with internal regulations framed by the State for the better management of national institutions, but, although a branch

63 L.P.L., Bell Papers, 5, fo. 80: Bell to Walpole, 30 Dec. 1933.
64 *Chronicle of convocation* (London, 1934), p. 4 (24 Jan. 1934).
65 Ibid., p. 283 (7 June 1934).

of the Church may be national, the Christian Faith is international, and we feel bound to utter our protest against any attempt to impose upon the Faith of the Church as expressed in the Creeds any doctrines of human rather than divine origin.[66]

But if that mandate appeared clear, English observers still found that the personalities, institutions and arguments of the German drama were rarely easy to understand. What was the struggle about? It was precipitated by a campaign to unify the German churches. The value of unity was clear to all ecumenical Christians; they found little to criticize in the notion that there should be a single protestant church for Germany. But to English minds this was fundamentally a political crisis; a conflict of church and state. It was a struggle to preserve the integrity of Christianity against the new political values of race and nation, which were pressed by a militant state and its creatures. It signalled the determination of a totalitarian state to suppress any independent beliefs in a society it wished to make entirely its own. They could not think that an alliance of Christianity and National Socialism could be credible because they perceived a church must be at odds with this ideological state. In what they called the 'Confessional' Church they found the prophetic courage of true Christian faith.[67]

This was not a theological understanding of the crisis. Before 1933 English Christians knew little of the culture of German Christianity and probably little sensed how profoundly different it was from their own. Now they interpreted the church struggle in ways that were quite different from the views of the participants. Many German Christians at the heart of the conflict saw it not as a contest between church and state, but a dispute between forces working within both church and state. The English bishops who read the Barmen Declaration made sense of its paragraphs by translating them into views which would have mortified its authors. The dean of Chichester, Duncan-Jones, found the very title of his book *The struggle for religious freedom in Germany* criticized by Julius Rieger, a German pastor who spend much of the period in England. This, said Rieger, was a struggle not for freedom but faith.[68] The remark would have baffled English Christians. Certainly they did not see the *Deutsche Christen* movement as evidence of the bankruptcy of natural theology. They understood it as the corrupt Christian expression of a political power. Theirs was a political interpretation of the crisis, and an appreciation of German theology was hardly necessary to sustain it. Because such an understanding of the church struggle began with the political facts of German life, and interpreted the ecclesiastical crisis in the terms it established, the nature of the Anglican response was defined in those same terms. When Archbishop Lang protested against the oppression of pastors he appealed to Hitler. In 1933 he described the chancellor as 'all-powerful'; even if he was not the principal author of the oppressions they deplored, he had the authority to restrain, and evidently did so when he

---

66 *The Record*, 8 May 1936, p. 291a.
67 The adoption of the term 'Confessional Church' by English commentators is noteworthy. In Germany itself the 'Confessing Church' (*Bekennende Kirche*) was the church of Niemöller, the Christian movement which defined its views at the Barmen synod in May 1934. The phrase 'Confessional Church' (*Bekenntnis Kirche*) defined a much broader commitment to the confessions of the Reformation.
68 Daphne Hampson, 'The British response to the German church struggle 1933–1939', D.Phil. dissertation, University of Oxford, 1973, p. 247.

chose.[69] In March 1934 the German ecumenist Hans Schönfeld urged Bell to direct his criticisms not against the German government but the Church administration of *Reichsbischof* Müller. But Bell replied firmly, 'It is because the present Church government is both tyrannical and owes its existence to the tyrannical weapons placed in its hands by the State, that we are bound to oppose it.'[70]

Against the grain of this consensus one bishop pressed a different view of the controversy, and he was to be heard most clearly in the Council on Foreign Relations itself. Bishop Headlam argued that those who criticized the German state were bringing the church into perilous political waters. He also perceived that most parties in the dispute had some measure of justice on their side. He did not care for the theology of the Confessing pastors which he thought obscure and remote, and he thought them obtuse. He did not believe that a faith which exalted race over God could be accepted by Christians, but he suggested that in every society the duty of the church was to preach the Christian faith in a language that was attractive and meaningful. This is what he believed many of the *Deutsche Christen* represented. He found many of them theologically orthodox. He also discovered that most German pastors belonged neither to the Confessing nor the *Deutsche Christen* party, but continued to work quietly and devoutly in their parishes. This was what the church should be about. To his own mind he spoke as the voice of cautious and detached balance in the midst of a confrontation between Bell, Duncan-Jones and their supporters on the one hand, and the librarian of the Council on Foreign Relations, A.J. Macdonald, on the other. But few agreed and gave him their support. Whereas Bell's views made him a centre of attention and a source of authority, Headlam's arguments brought him withering criticism, isolation and censure. When he sought advice Lang turned not to the chairman of his Council on Foreign Relations, but to the bishop of Chichester. He also received a number of reports from Basil Staunton Batty, bishop of Fulham, who was responsible for the chaplaincies in North and Central Europe, and whose duties led to frequent and even extraordinary expeditions across the face of the continent. Batty was convinced that they must support the Confessing Church. Many judged that Headlam had become an apologist for the Nazi state and its allies. What he failed to recognize was that his sense of balance was achieved by granting the German state and the *Deutsche Christen* a credibility which their critics denied.

Much of this dispute was conducted in private. The Council on Foreign Relations submitted its reports to the Church Assembly, and here, at first, the protagonists sought to suppress their differences and avoid public embarrassment. On 22 June 1934, when the second report of the Council on Foreign Relations was discussed at the assembly, Headlam criticized 'the tendency in some quarters to be too anxious to interfere in the internal troubles of another Church', and stressed that the Council was 'not directly concerned with the correction and improvements of other Churches'. Its purpose, he stressed, was to gather and disseminate information, and to cultivate understanding and friendship. It should avoid controversy, and not move to judge too quickly.[71] A year later, on 20 November 1935, the fourth report of the Council on Foreign Relations was

69 *The Times*, 28 June 1933, p. 16b.
70 L.P.L., Bell Papers, 5, fo. 306: Bell to Schönfeld, 23 Mar. 1934.
71 *Proceedings of the Church Assembly* (London, 1934), XV, 368–9 (22 June 1934).

submitted to the Church Assembly, and this time it contained a survey on German affairs by A.J. Macdonald. Headlam suggested that members of the assembly should draw their own conclusions from the report. Archbishop Lang observed that he was glad to find Macdonald's report prefaced by a note disclaiming any official status for what followed, and he added, 'The conflict was not merely constitutional or doctrinal, but went to the very roots of Christian faith.'[72] The fourth report was overshadowed by the debate on the persecution of the Jews in Germany later that day, when Bell moved a motion of sympathy for the victims and Bishop Henson intervened against his critics with an explosive indictment of the antisemitism of the National Socialist state.[73]

But two years later the strain of disagreement made itself felt. On 22 June 1937 the seventh report on the affairs of the continental churches was brought to the Church Assembly. It contained a second survey by Macdonald which appeared to many, and even to Headlam himself, over-sympathetic to the German government and those who were its allies in the churches. Because he feared criticism Headlam himself had written a preface, wishing to strike a balancing note. It did not; his own views were too provocative, and his language too robust. By the time the assembly gathered he complained that he had been subjected to 'very violent criticism', and again accused his critics of partisanship. He restated his case that the 'Confessional' Church did not alone represent Christian ortho-doxy in Germany, and that it was a small minority when placed within the large body of 'moderate' protestant Christians there. He thought its dissociation from the new Zöllner committees 'unreasonable', and observed the sincerity of many German Christians who believed that National Socialism was a force sympathetic to Christianity, citing the work of Fabricius, the author of *Positive Christianity in the Third Reich*. Fabricius had said that neo-pagan movements lacked official sponsoring, and Headlam himself thought their importance exaggerated. There was, he declared, no persecution of religion in Germany. They would intervene in the controversy more effectively if they desisted from criticisms. This time Headlam did not escape his critics. Bell responded at once that he was 'very sorry' that the bishop of Gloucester had written his preface; he found it 'most misleading and calculated to cause harm'. He dismissed Fabricius and turned instead to the words of Hitler, Rosenberg and Goebbels. Hitler had interfered in the church elections of 1933. All three had encouraged the 'systematic secession' of Christians from the church. No doubt some 'German Christians' were moderate, but 'the real trend of the German Christian temper was revealed in their enthusiasm for the race and for nationality'. Bell spoke of 'the intensity of the persecution' of Christians, and said that because of their sufferings the pastors of the 'Confessional' church saw 'the principles at the heart of the conflict much more clearly than any others'. He spoke of the dynamics of a revolution, and how they must prove irreconcilable with moderation. He noted the attacks made against the church in the German press, and the wave of arrests over the last fortnight. If he could, he would appeal to Hitler that his 'all-powerful might' should not oppress.

A prominent laymember of the assembly, Sir Raymond Beazley supported Headlam, but Archbishop Temple declared that he could not but think the logic

72 Ibid. (1935), XVI, 454–8 (20 Nov. 1935).
73 Ibid., pp. 466–79.

of totalitarianism hostile to religion. The honorary general secretary of the Council on Foreign Relations, Canon John Douglas declared that the bishop of Gloucester had merely 'exercised his faculty of seeing both sides'. Headlam returned to accuse Confessional pastors of being tactless and irritating. Lang concluded again that an acceptance of the report by the assembly did not express its agreement, but briefly noted his own sympathies by observing that Hitler had never used his power to beneficial effect in the controversy.[74]

The period of the committees excited far less public attention in Britain, and interest waned. Even Bell at first hoped that Kerrl would bring peace to the churches. But by 1938 Kerrl was discredited, Zöllner, who had long seemed ineffectual, had departed, and Niemöller had been imprisoned. The trial of Niemöller presented to the world the heartening spectacle of Nazism defied; the splendid image of a Christian conscience unbowed before a cruel and soulless tyranny. Headlam did not care for Niemöller, and said so. This was too much for Lang, who feared that Headlam was embarrassing the Church of England itself. He and Bell exchanged public letters to emphasize that Headlam's views were his own alone, and not those of his church.[75] Only narrowly did the bishop of Gloucester survive a conspiracy to remove him from the chair of the Council on Foreign Relations. A new committee was established to disseminate information on the situation in the German churches, but it met only a few times and achieved little. By the end of the year, however, the international situation was deteriorating rapidly and minds were turned towards the prospect of war. By the next summer the bishops of the church were busy with practical preparations in their dioceses. For most, the fate of German protestantism had receded into the background.

RESPONSES

That the bishops of the Church of England watched events in Germany with dislike or hostility is clear. But how, if at all, should such views be articulated? Their response to the German church struggle was shaped by a number of forces. The first was their commitment to those who were the victims of oppression. This provided a powerful imperative, and a morality to fortify. Ecumenism added weight to it, affirming, and seeking to represent and make effective, the solidarity of Christians in the face of the powers of the age, and hoping to sustain a universal church of integrity. But the ecumenical vision still respected the right of churches to order their own affairs, and this gave reason to pause. The third offered some discouragement. It was the thorny question of the relationship between the church and politics. The establishment of the Church of England encouraged a public role and, it was believed, did something to make it effective and authoritative. But the Church was a national church, and this was a foreign controversy. Within these frameworks, each with its own incentives and reasons for hesitation, the question of response was further defined by a set of pragmatic considerations. Would intervention improve matters by encouraging those who deserved Christian sympathy, or aggravate them by provoking the dangerous

74 Ibid. (1937), XVIII, 270–92 (22, 23 June 1937).
75 *The Times*, 26 July 1938, p. 17f.

forces which they confronted? This dilemma sharpened the senses of careful and responsible men, who were already conscious of standing on difficult ground. It did much to determine the decision to respond, the form of response adopted, the moment chosen, and the language.

It would be wrong to argue that the bishops, clergy and laity of the Church of England were all roused to respond to the spectacle of National Socialism. The private feelings of an individual were not always translated into the public and responsible views of a bishop or a clergyman. Those who spoke on the subject were often moved by clear ecumenical or international commitments. Others, less certain of themselves, were careful to desist from addressing political affairs which might not be seen as their proper concern. In October 1935 Edward Woods, bishop of Lichfield, wrote in his diocesan magazine, 'We have no right to quarrel with "nationalist socialism" '.[76] Others were cautious, lest they moved into a region with which they were too little acquainted. When the prominent writer and laymember of the Church, Dorothy Buxton, drafted and sought signatures for a letter to the *Times* protesting against the plight of German Christians, many bishops wrote to Bell for advice (the fact that they wrote to the bishop of Chichester, and not the bishop of Gloucester, is suggestive). The ongoing convolutions of the church struggle, never easy to understand, surely lost many of those who were not personally drawn to them, and left them reluctant to jump into such deep and cloudy waters. When the issues seemed to clarify – for example, at the trial of Martin Niemöller – the response of churchpeople across the country was far stronger. Some were absorbed by diocesan concerns. Canon Ronald Lunt once recalled to the present author that his father, bishop of Ripon, was more devoted to the pastoral demands of a difficult diocese than the issues of the world beyond: 'it would not have occurred to him to commit himself to public utterance on the rise of Nazism'.[77] The bishop of Birmingham, Barnes, admitted to a correspondent that he little concerned himself with the state of German protestantism because he so disliked its theology.

Prayer, recognition, dissociation

The Christian church has been for almost 2000 years a continuing community of prayer, and the historian who busily searches for recorded statements or official acts must first make a space for this. The prayers of Christians, made in public intercessions or weekly services, lie at the heart of the Christian response to the world. The ongoing intercessions of the church are an integral part of its life, and rarely recorded. But there are many indications that members of the Church of England affirmed their anxiety for their fellow Christians in Germany in church services throughout the 1933–9 period. The most recorded occasion took place on 17 July 1938, when Jewish and Christian congregations in England prayed on the same day for the persecuted of Germany.[78]

The very fact that church leaders in Britain took care to learn about the situation in the German churches, and to declare that knowledge in the public

---

76 *Lichfield Diocesan Magazine*, Bishop's letter, Oct. 1935.
77 Canon Ronald Lunt, letter to the author, 11 Jan. 1989.
78 See Andrew Chandler, 'Lambeth Palace, the Church of England and the Jews of Germany and Austria in 1938', *Leo Baeck Institute Yearbook*, XL (1995), 231–4.

sphere, was in itself a significant form of response. Hitler believed that the protestant churches were hopelessly divided and isolated from foreign interest. He soon discovered, and to his surprise, that what occurred in the churches provoked concern abroad. Meanwhile, recognition was allied with a determination to dissociate the Church of England from the policies of controversial authorities in the church struggle. This demonstrated a wide awareness of the stature of the church, and the way in which formal or even personal contacts may be used by the *Deutsche Christen* to legitimize their views and actions. (Conversely, Bell and others were acutely conscious that the Confessing movement sought sympathy, and were sustained by the recognition accorded to them by leading church figures abroad.) In 1933 the prospect of a ceremonial installation of Ludwig Müller as the new *Reichsbishof* demanded a reply from the Church of England, whose representation at the ceremony was invited. Archbishop Lang was disinclined to accept the invitation, and found his view confirmed by Bell and Batty. The theologian Edwyn Hoskyns encouraged him to attend, or at least be represented. Lang did not agree, and the new Müller era began unsanctioned. Bishop Burroughs of Ripon found himself dodging the *Reichsbischof* while on holiday on the continent. When Müller wrote to Lang to commend Hossenfelder, who had been invited to England by Frank Buchman, the archbishop merely returned an acknowledgement of his letter. Other, different episodes illustrate the determination of bishops to steer clear of other compromising meetings. The bishop of Winchester, Cyril Forster Garbett, was once encouraged by Lord Brocket to meet Ribbentrop at a reception at his country house. Garbett replied that he would attend only if he was free to protest against the persecution of Christians and Jews in Germany. He was not invited.[79] Bishop Henson found himself in a similar situation in 1936, when Lord Londonderry invited Ribbentrop to his inauguration as mayor of Durham.[80] These were perhaps little more than occasional moments or personal gestures. But when Henson publicly demanded that British universities decline invitations to the 650th anniversary celebrations of Heidelberg University and the bicentennial of Göttingen University because he saw that their representation must grant those universities an international acceptance that they could not deserve, he brought the act of dissociation into the correspondence columns of the *Times*, and pressed his case powerfully.[81] At large, however, the wish to register disapproval by dissociation did not grow into a broader argument of boycotting German goods or business, as happened in the United States. When Archbishop Temple arrived in America for a lecture tour in 1938 he was surprised to find himself criticized there for crossing the Atlantic on a boat that was owned by a German company widely boycotted by American Christians and Jews.

Letters, declarations, motions and resolutions

It was often quipped that a bishop in the Church of England could be sure that his letters to the *Times* would be published. Both Bell and Lang recognized the

---

79 York Minster Library, MS Memoirs of Archbishop Garbett, Part IV, p. 59.
80 The near misses of Henson and Ribbentrop are recounted in Owen Chadwick, *Hensley Henson. A study in the friction between church and state* (Oxford, 1983), pp. 260–1.
81 Ibid., pp. 258–62.

status of the newspaper, and knew that it presented them with a forum for the expression of views. The correspondence columns of the *Times* became one of Bell's principal platforms during the years of the church struggle. A number of his letters to Müller were made public and printed there. On 7 January 1934 he protested against the 'muzzling order' of 4 January.[82] When, in February 1934, misleading reports of his meeting in London with Bishop Heckel appeared in the press he again wrote to the *Times* to put the record straight and make his views known.[83] On 3 June 1935 the *Times* printed a further protest deploring the 'internal war ... which the leaders of the National Socialist State are waging against freedom and against Christianity'.[84] A letter published on 2 January 1937 sought to show a recognition of recent developments and to demonstrate his sympathy for the Confessing pastors.[85] On 24 March 1937 Bell wrote to challenge the German state to refrain from interference in the new elections which it had proposed.[86] Lang also resorted to the correspondence columns of the *Times*, but not on behalf of the Evangelical Church in Germany. His two letters of May 1934 and November 1938 were forceful condemnations of the persecution of German Jews.[87]

Because of its establishment, the Church of England enjoyed a presence in the house of lords. But this did not afford an opportunity for motions and speeches about the plight of German Christians because the issue did not concern national policy. The platforms that were available to church leaders were offered by the councils and assemblies of the Church itself, principally, the houses of convocation, the Church Assembly and the diocesan conferences which each bishop led. These were reported thoroughly in the *Times*, and accordingly they reached Germany itself. The published word showed the Church's status as a public force, and it became a principal weapon in the campaign to exert pressure.

On 31 May 1933 Lang addressed the upper house of convocation with thoughts about the disarmament conference at Geneva and the new political state in Germany, voicing in particular his anxieties for the persecuted German Jews.[88] On 24 January 1934 he declared his anxiety that the search for a united church might be at the cost of 'spiritual freedom', admired the courage of those who sought to 'render to God the things that are God's' and hoped they would be free 'to give their own unhindered witness and influence to the national life'.[89] On 7 June 1934 two motions expressing concern for the German Evangelical Church were brought before convocation. Bishop Bell moved that the upper house was 'convinced that the present struggle in the German Evangelical Church is a struggle which, in its essence, is concerned not merely with organisation but with the actual substance of Christian faith in which all Christians have an interest'; and 'that the situation was one which must cause most anxious concern to the whole Church of Christ throughout the world'. In Germany he saw the forces of Christianity engaged in a struggle with the forces of paganism for the

---

82 *The Times*, 7 Jan. 1934, p. 8c.
83 Ibid., 20 Mar. 1934, p. 10b.
84 Ibid., 3 June 1935, p. 15e.
85 Ibid., 2 Jan. 1937, p. 6a.
86 Ibid., 27 Mar. 1937, p. 13e.
87 Ibid., 16 May 1934, p. 17e; 12 Nov. 1938, p. 13e.
88 *Chronicle of convocation* (1933), pp. 220–1 (31 May 1933).
89 Ibid. (1934), p. 4 (24 Jan. 1934).

soul of the country. The root of the matter 'sprang in part from the overwhelming importance attached to the Aryan race, in part from the doctrines of the totalitarian state, and from the introduction of a new Nordic or Germanic religion, exalting the race and exalting the State'. The bishop of Oxford, Thomas Strong, observed that German religion was 'in really serious peril'. A theologian, he acknowledged how much English theology owed to German scholarship. He condemned antisemitism and said that what was happening in Germany represented 'a resuscitation of pure paganism, and this will ultimately lead to serious disturbance throughout the whole of European Christendom'. Bishop Pollock of Norwich made clear his unease at the theology of the conferences at Barmen and Ulm, and Barnes of Birmingham remarked glumly that 'the theological armour of the opposition was largely derived from the teaching of Karl Barth'. But they both deferred to Bell's knowledge and experience, and supported him.[90]

Meanwhile, in the lower house Duncan-Jones moved a motion to 'draw attention' to the 'serious situation' that had arisen, and to 'express concern at the possibility that doctrines of race and nation may be imposed on the Evangelical Church in Germany in such a way that the substance of Christianity would be impaired and the sympathy of other Christian Communions'. A laymember, Dr Relton, attempted to rule the motion out of order: 'It had been sprung upon them at a moment's notice, asking for an expression of opinion on the internal domestic affairs of another body of Christians without having been called upon to do any such thing in an authoritative capacity.' The prolocutor, Canon Kidd, said that the upper house was discussing a similar motion, and both motions were framed and proposed with the consent of the archbishop. Canon Douglas pressed Relton's criticism. Duncan-Jones appealed to broad principles: 'he was sure the House of Convocation regarded its Christianity as something wider than England'. But he was defensive, insisting that his motion affirmed no political opposition to National Socialism and adding that their German friends must know of their interest and sympathy for their age-long struggle for unity. He spoke of the supremacy of Jesus Christ that was affirmed in the Barmen declaration, and sought to return to the heart of the issue, pronounced by his motion. This did not reassure. The debate became entangled in a succession of amendments, none of which questioned what Duncan-Jones saw to be fundamentally important. The archdeacon of Kingston, G.H. Martin, observed the genuine importance of English opinion in Germany, and the need to exploit the right of free speech which they enjoyed, but which was denied to their German friends. The archdeacon of Dudley, Dr Shepherd, thought that they should express 'abhorrence' of the persecution of the Jews and political propaganda. They might be more sympathetic to the German churches if those churches had themselves been less sympathetic to a state which did such things. The provost of Birmingham, Arthur Hamilton Baynes, affirmed their right to show sympathy to fellow Christians and to Jews in Germany. By now three amendments had been proposed. A fourth appeared, and was seconded. Duncan-Jones remarked that he did not mind very much about the words; 'it was the sense that mattered to him'. One speaker wondered what form of words had been adopted by the upper house. The prolocutor did not know. Duncan-Jones had the text of the proposed motion with him, but Kidd replied that it did not concern them. He aimed for unanimity,

90 Ibid., pp. 283–96 (7 June 1934).

saying that whatever was passed would be of 'world-wide importance'. It was achieved with the words: 'That the Lower House observes the serious religious situation that has arisen in Germany, and expresses its concern at the possibility that doctrines of race and nation may be imposed in such a way as to impair the substance of Christianity'.[91]

In his presidential address to the upper house of convocation on 5 June 1935 Lang once again returned to the plight of the German churches, in the knowledge that the Confessing movement was at that time holding a synod at Augsburg. Now he spoke words of 'apprehension and warning': 'We cannot shut our eyes to what seems to be the attitude of the German State to the Christian Church both Lutheran and Reformed.' The authorities seemed to him 'actively engaged in a propaganda of religion', of 'harassing interference', on behalf of a racial religion which 'certainly travesties, if it does not deny, the fundamental faith which all Christians hold'. If new intimidation took place, 'this could not be regarded as a matter which concerned Germany alone ... it could only be regarded as a menace to the Christianity which is the only ultimate security for those principles on which alone the peace of the world can be built and stand'. Lang wanted the state to release pastors from the concentration camps and restrain the new racial religion instead of encouraging it: 'this would bring the most welcome relief to all who wish well to Germany'. Lang hoped that his appeal would reach Hitler himself or his advisers.[92]

But by 19 January 1938 the archbishop could still observe 'the continued oppression of the Roman Catholic and Protestant Churches in Germany, and the interference by the State with the proper activities of any Church'. He declared that he had 'repeatedly' asked the authorities in Germany why they should 'alienate' those who so wished for friendship abroad in this matter. He feared those who identified the German race 'as embodied in the State, with God himself'.[93] Bell moved a motion expressly disavowing 'all political motives' but voicing 'deep sympathy with their fellow Christians in Germany, both Catholic and Evangelical, in the persecutions they are now suffering at the hands of the German State'. He invited convocation to 'rejoice at the steadfastness of the priests and pastors, laymen and laywomen, who have chosen rather to suffer affliction and imprisonment than to fail in their witness to the freedom of the Gospel'.[94] Headlam, who thought this political, resisted, but Lang promptly silenced him and his criticism was not seconded. Bell's motion was passed without contradiction.

On 9 February 1939 a laymember of the Church Assembly, Arthur Loveday of Peterborough, moved a motion observing the 'intense persecution' of Christians in Russia, Spain, Mexico and Germany. Lang supported the motion and spoke of Germany, drawing a distinction between 'a persecution of Christianity itself' and 'a persecution of Christians because of their adherence to the independence of the faith of the Church'. But he pronounced that the reality of the persecution there was 'quite undoubted'.[95]

91 Ibid., pp. 321–35.
92 Ibid., pp. 234–6 (5 June 1935).
93 Ibid., pp. 2–4 (19 Jan. 1938).
94 Ibid., pp. 110–12 (20 Jan. 1938).
95 *Proceedings of the Church Assembly* (1939), XX, 142–6 (9 Feb. 1739).

Engagement with a view to influence

As chairman of the Continuing Committee of Life and Work in 1933, and as a leading light in the movement thereafter, Bell was deeply immersed in the intricacies of ecumenical diplomacy. In this capacity he sought to participate personally in the church struggle, and to assist the causes he favoured. Between 1933 and 1939 he exerted a genuine influence in the controversy by maintaining his connexions with German churchpeople, and visiting the country himself.

In the early years of the Third Reich Lang and Bell found themselves able to work to some effect with the staff at the German embassy in London. Leopold von Hoesch, the ambassador there until 1936, was very much a diplomat of the old order. He and his colleagues were out of temper with the new regime and prepared to listen to the protests of English church leaders. They also represented these views with some force in their reports to Berlin. Bell's wish to cultivate personal and private relationships with Joachim von Ribbentrop and Rudolf Hess indicated his belief that the German state was the crucial force in the drama. Equally, when Lang saw Ribbentrop – and he often did, when Ribbentrop visited as Hitler's personal envoy and, after 1936, when he replaced Hoesch as ambassador – he did so because he judged that he was 'in the confidence of Hitler himself'.[96] But this was a disappointing relationship. Ribbentrop was obviously only dimly aware of the issues that concerned churchpeople, and when Hitler's foreign policy moved away from friendship and towards confrontation he had little reason to listen to the remonstrations of intervening bishops.

Intervention

Between 1933 and 1936 the concern of the German embassy was that Britain and Germany should enjoy peaceful relations. Lang and Bell stressed that the German church crisis provoked concern in Britain and threatened to complicate that peace. In 1933 and 1934 Bell was able to exploit a sympathetic embassy and the wish of the Berlin government to maintain in these early months a working relationship with Britain. At critical junctures, between 1933 and 1939, Lang, Bell and Headlam sought to intervene directly in the church struggle. These efforts were private, but threatened to move into the public sphere and to embarrass the German government by throwing the collective weight of foreign church opinion against it. In 1933 the vehemence of the *Deutsche Christen* campaign against Bodelschwingh caused Lang to write to the foreign secretary, Sir John Simon, enquiring if his anxiety could be made known through the embassy in Berlin. He found politicians and diplomats reluctant to interfere. Later that summer the dismissal of leading clerics and the forcible suppression of dissent in the protestant churches dismayed Bell. He and Lang worked with the leaders of the Free Churches to frame a statement of protest to be conveyed to the German government, threatening to make their disapprobation clear to the world. This was suspended after German churchmen intimated that the declaration would be best left unsent, and then President Hindenburg intervened. In October 1934 Bell met Otto Christian von Bismarck at the London embassy and found Bismarck so receptive that he was even asked to formulate his precise

96 L.P.L., Bell Papers, 6, fo. 407: Lang to Bell, 7 Nov. 1934.

demands for change.[97] Lang wrote again to Sir John Simon that he suspected that a new intervention in the affairs of the churches might take place in the wake of the Saar plebiscite. He asked if his concern could be conveyed to Hitler or 'other proper authorities' in Berlin, and threatened 'the sternest possible protest' in Britain, the United States and elsewhere if his fears were realized.[98] This letter was passed on to the British ambassador in Berlin, Sir Eric Phipps. At Hitler's new year reception in 1935 Phipps met the German foreign secretary, Neurath: 'I pointed out how certain it was that any attempt at coercion would cause a strong expression of public opinion in the United Kingdom and how unfortunate this would be in the interests of the good relations of our two countries.' Neurath responded 'in very good part', and asked Phipps to reassure the archbishop. Phipps was encouraged by Neurath's good sense and apparent moderation. Of Hitler he was far less sure.[99] In 1938 another attempt to threaten the German government with a joint public protest by the churches arose when Martin Niemöller was imprisoned. Lang summoned Ribbentrop to Lambeth Palace and made his disapprobation clear. But by then such diplomacy had lost its power.[100]

SIGNIFICANCES

A significance for these strands of commitment, understanding and response may be claimed. Historians have observed the decline of Christianity in twentieth-century Europe, and, certainly, the religious life of society has been pushed to the fringe of the dominant historiographical arguments. Now it may astonish a student of history to find that so much attention, concern and indignation was provoked in Britain by the persecution of German Christians between 1933 and 1939. A broad, but often inarticulate, recognition of the Church, and a cultural commitment to Christian ideals, could still make itself felt. The importance of the Church was still declared by the columns of the newspapers, where the words of bishops were frequently reported at length. Martin Niemöller became a symbol of moral courage in the face of political injustice not only among clergy and congregations, but in secular culture more widely. The subject may also encourage us to measure the political significance of the Church more clearly. The establishment of the Church of England provided a number of connexions and relationships which were clearly advantageous to its bishops and leaders. But they did not represent anything like an identifiable structure of association with political authority. The value of the establishment lay in the fact that when the archbishop of Canterbury wrote to the foreign secretary he received a sympathetic reply. But the foreign secretary did not write to the archbishop of Canterbury for a view or for guidance. Political power was defined and organized by political departments and professional advisers. The nature of power in the twentieth century left archbishops and bishops on the fringe of the

97 L.P.L., Bell Papers, 6, fos. 233–6: Bell to Lang, 13 Oct. 1934.
98 L.P.L., Lang Papers, 319, fos. 75–6: Lang to Simon, 18 Dec. 1936.
99 Ibid., fos. 85–6: Phipps to Lang, 2 Jan. 1935.
100 Daphne Hampson's doctoral thesis, 'The British response to the German church struggle' offers a most valuable analysis of these interventions, making use of both British and German archives.

argument, and if they moved to the centre it was because they were drawn by personal ideals not institutional logic. More important was the significance of the Church of England in the eyes of German diplomats and politicians, who perceived that a national church of prince bishops represented a source of authority and a representation of public sentiment.

On 5 September Bell wrote to a number of German churchpeople:

Be sure that your friends here are your firm friends as ever, and that we understand a little of the suffering you endure, and of your love for your own homeland . . .

We are brethren in adversity. The trouble draws us closer together than before. May God reconcile the nations now at war; may He assuage the suffering which will be so heavy on both sides, and may He give us peace![101]

Those who had sought understanding and unity among Christians had found little of either. Christian values were diverse and they were fashioned by profound traditions and cultural loyalties. The political values of churches in one country remained a confusion to churches abroad. In 1939 it seemed extraordinary to English Christians that Bishop Marahrens should assure the National Socialist regime that the German protestant church had always supported the arms of Germany with the prayers of the church. It was still more alarming to find that Martin Niemöller, whose courage they had so applauded, had offered to sail another U-boat for the government that had imprisoned him. The last exchange of letters in this volume is between George Bell and Karl Barth. After six years of copious reports, conversations, visits and discussions, Bell found himself confronted with the awful truth that a fellow Christian like Niemöller, whom he had sustained so faithfully, could respond to the outbreak of war in a way that was utterly incomprehensible. 'Niemöller', Barth replied, was 'a good – a too good – *German*', and 'a very good – a too good – *Lutheran*'. But he added:

There is a little minority of men and women, who – also since the outbreak of the war – see [what there] is to see, who suffer and hope and (secretly) fight with us. They need our deep sympathy. They need our prayers. A day is coming when they will be visible and audible.[102]

101 L.P.L., Bell Papers, 9, fo. 355: Bell to various German friends, 5 Sept. 1939.
102 Ibid., 74, fo. 4–5: Barth to Bell, 8 Dec. 1939.

THE TEXT

With two exceptions the sources in this volume have been selected from the collected papers of Bishop Bell and Archbishop Lang, both at Lambeth Palace Library in London. The complete Bell archive offers the historian a formidable series of no less than 368 volumes, many of them comprising material relating to German affairs during the National Socialist era. Meanwhile, the Lang Papers present four volumes of material concerning Germany in the same period, two of them catalogued when the series was first assembled, and two later discovered in the Council on Foreign Relations archive in the ecumenical affairs department at Lambeth Palace.

My selection of documents from this accumulation of letters, memoranda and reports has been guided by a number of broad principles, and it is important to present them to the reader. The purpose of this volume is to show how the leaders of the Church of England perceived and interpreted the crisis in the German protestant churches in the period 1933–9, and how they viewed that affair when visiting the country themselves, or meeting those who had done so. The business of selecting material has not always been a straightforward one, and even a confident editor must expect to regret later the omission of certain letters or episodes. First, I have left to one side documents describing the efforts made by the leaders of the Church of England to respond to the German church struggle by protesting through a number of channels or intervening directly in the dispute. To do this aspect of the story justice would require a much larger volume, and one which included a range of documents from a number of other archives, ecumenical and political. I have been fortified in this decision by the knowledge that Daphne Hampson's excellent doctoral thesis, 'The British response to the German church struggle 1933–9' (University of Oxford, 1973), offers a comprehensive account of these matters. Second, it is obvious that Bell was a leading light in the ecumenical world, and often he addressed German affairs not primarily as a bishop of the Church of England, but as a powerful force in the Life and Work movement. I have chosen not to include documents relating entirely to this aspect of his work, and, although such a detachment must raise proper suspicions, it still appears to me tenable and necessary. The debate about the representation of German churchmen in the Life and Work and Faith and Order movements presents a different, though relevant, narrative. Third, English churchpeople did not always visit Germany in this period in search of information about the church struggle itself. For example, Dorothy Buxton, a prominent laywoman who knew a good deal about German affairs, visited the country in March 1935 to urge protestant and Roman Catholic church leaders there to take up the cause of the concentration camps. Others went as members of study groups committed to the discussion of a variety of issues. I have chosen to concentrate singly on the crisis in the protestant churches. I am sure that the present book works more effectively by pursuing one thread and sustaining a clear narrative than by spreading its load. In the introduction and in the chronologies I have sought to place the chosen issues and themes within the broader political and ecumenical picture.

This book emphasizes the role of Bishop Bell of Chichester, but it also seeks to place his relationship with German protestantism in the National Socialist era in the context of the wider debate on the subject which arose in the Church of England between 1933 and 1939. Certainly, the distinct significance of Bell's views can only be clear when they are measured alongside those of others. The present work seeks to identify the important connexion that existed between Bell and Archbishop Lang, and to show the nature of Lang's own contribution to the affair. Bishop Headlam, furthermore, is to be found striving for balance between the judgments of Bell and his allies on the one hand, and the views of the librarian of the Council on Foreign Relations, A.J. Macdonald, on the other. It was Headlam's belief that he alone occupied the middle ground of the debate on the German church. It may not have appeared a persuasive argument at the time - nor might it now - but the material in this collection does something to make it comprehensible. The public dispute which took place over the German church struggle could be characterized by more repetition than development, and I have chosen private or confidential documents which seem most effectively to make the important points. For much of this period the bishop of Gloucester received regular reports from the Anglican chaplain in Berlin, Roland Cragg. These noted developments in the church struggle faithfully at every turn, but generally contain more information than interpretation. A particularly vivid example is presented here to establish Cragg's contribution to the debate. The complete set would require a separate volume.

My concern to present a certain kind of material has sometimes produced surprising consequences. George Bell is barely represented in the first year of 1933, even though his authority on these issues within his own church was widely recognized by the summer of that year. Because the bishop of Durham, Herbert Hensley Henson, did not visit Germany or record personal encounters with German churchpeople, his own important contribution to the public debate on National Socialism does not appear here. Meanwhile, the private role of Basil Staunton Batty, the bishop of Fulham, is strongly present. In each year the quantity of material varies. The catalogue of the Bell Papers at Lambeth Palace Library makes the point that in 1933 and 1934 much was written and received. By 1935 less was being said and done, and afterwards the narrative in Germany appeared to slacken.

I hope that this volume will encourage a study of personal experiences and impressions, offer an insight into the confidential world of church authority, and provide a record of the difficulties which citizens of one nation face when they seek to understand the affairs of another.

A NOTE ON EDITORIAL PRINCIPLES

After consideration and discussion I have chosen to correct inadvertent misspellings of names in the texts. All capitals and italics have been retained, except when they have been adopted idiosyncratically or irregularly by the authors. The original punctuation has been retained throughout, although I have occasionally introduced changes or additions for reasons of clarity.

Rather than presenting a great number of footnotes with biographical details, I have chosen to write a biographical section at the end of the book describing the most important characters to appear in the preceding texts. Other individuals, appearing only briefly in the volume, are mostly described at least adequately in the texts themselves. Personalities referred to in passing receive brief footnotes.

LIST OF LETTERS

1933

1. H.N. Bate to C.G. Lang, 27 Apr. 1933, Lambeth Palace Library, Lang Papers, 37, fos. 1–2.
2. C.G. Lang to Bate, 30 Apr. 1933, L.P.L., Lang Papers, 37, fo. 3.
3. 'Conditions in Germany', memorandum of a conversation with Dr Adolf Deissmann, 25 May 1933, L.P.L., Lang Papers, 37, fos. 15–16.
4. 'Germany and the Jews', memorandum of a conversation with Dr J.R. Mott, 31 May 1933, L.P.L., Lang Papers, 37, fo. 17.
5. A.S. Duncan-Jones to Caroline Duncan-Jones, n.d., from the private collection of Mrs E.E. Duncan-Jones, Cambridge.
6. Report from Berlin by R.H. Cragg, 5 July 1933, L.P.L., Lang Papers, 37, fos. 77–9.
7. A.C. Headlam to G.K.A. Bell, 6 July 1933, L.P.L., Bell Papers, 4, fo. 162.
8. A.C. Headlam to A.C. Don, 10 July 1933, L.P.L., Lang Papers, 37, fo. 88.
9. From the diary of A.C. Don, 11 July 1933, L.P.L., MS 2862, p. 40.
10. H.N. Bate to C.G. Lang, 24 July 1933, L.P.L., Lang Papers, 37, fo. 95.
11. A.C. Don to H.N. Bate, 26 July 1933, L.P.L., Lang Papers, 37, fo. 96.
12. Memorandum by A.S. Duncan-Jones on his visit to Germany, 26 July 1933, L.P.L., Bell Papers, 11, fos. 75–88.
13. Memorandum by A.J. Macdonald on his visit to Germany, 6 Sept. 1933, L.P.L., Bell Papers, 11, fos. 86–8.
14. Memorandum by H.W. Fox, 'The "Gospel and Church" Group in Germany', Sept. 1933, L.P.L., Bell Papers, 11, fos. 73–4.
15. Memorandum by Ruth Rouse on her visit to Germany, 31 Oct. 1933, L.P.L., Bell Papers, 11, fos. 107–17.
16. Memorandum by C.G. Lang of a conversation with Ruth Rouse, 31 Oct. 1933, L.P.L., Lang Papers, 37, fo. 149.

1934

1. B.S. Batty to C.G. Lang, 6 Jan. 1934, L.P.L., Lang Papers, 37, fo. 185.
2. Memorandum by B.S. Batty on the situation in the German Church, Dec. 1933, L.P.L., Lang Papers, 37, fos. 187–92.
3. C.G. Lang to B.S. Batty, 9 Jan. 1934, L.P.L., Lang Papers, 27, fo. 194.
4. Memorandum, 'The German Crisis', by B.S. Batty, Feb. 1934, L.P.L., Bell Papers, 11, fos. 142–5.
5. Memorandum by G.K.A. Bell, 'German Evangelical Church', 9 Feb. 1934, L.P.L., Bell Papers, 5, fos. 155–62.
6. B.S. Batty to G.K.A. Bell, 16 Feb. 1934, L.P.L., Bell Papers, 5, fo. 191.

7. Memorandum by C.G. Lang, 'German Evangelical Church', 1 May 1934, L.P.L., Lang Papers, 37, fo. 226
8. H.N. Bate to G.K.A. Bell, 4 June 1934, L.P.L., Bell Papers, 6, fo. 15.
9. Memorandum by H.N. Bate, 'Report on a Visit to Germany, 21–26 May 1934', L.P.L., Bell Papers, 6, fos. 16–26.
10. B.S. Batty to C.G. Lang, 4 Aug. 1934, L.P.L., Lang Papers, 37, fo. 250.
11. B.S. Batty to G.K.A. Bell, 15 Aug. 1934, L.P.L., Bell Papers, 6, fo. 123.
12. Memorandum by G.K.A. Bell, 'Interview with Joachim von Ribbentrop', 6 Nov. 1934, L.P.L., Bell Papers, 6, fos. 393–8.
13. C.G. Lang to G.K.A. Bell, 7 Nov. 1934, L.P.L., Bell Papers, 6, fo. 407.
14. Memorandum by C.G. Lang, 'German Church Conflict', 7 Nov. 1934, L.P.L., Bell Papers, 6, fos. 408–9.

1935

1. Memorandum by G.K.A. Bell, 'Interview with Rudolf Hess', 20 Sept. 1935, L.P.L., Bell Papers, 7, fos. 361–3.
2. Memorandum by G.K.A. Bell, 'Interview with Reichsminister Kerrl', 28 Sept. 1935, L.P.L., Bell Papers, 13, fos. 412–13.
3. Memorandum by G.K.A. Bell, 'Interview with Bishop Marahrens', 23 Sept. 1935, L.P.L., Bell Papers, 13, fos. 418–20.
4. B.S. Batty to C.G. Lang, 2 Nov. 1935, L.P.L., Lang Papers, 319, fo. 184.
5. Memorandum by B.S. Batty, Oct. 1935, L.P.L., Lang Papers, 319, fos. 185–6.
6. B.S. Batty to G.K.A. Bell, 27 Nov. 1935, L.P.L., Bell Papers, 7, fos. 159–60.

1936

1. B.S. Batty to C.G. Lang, 26 Nov. 1936, L.P.L., Lang Papers, 319, fos. 275–6.
2. Memorandum by A.J. Macdonald, 'German Evangelical Church Discussions', Dec. 1936, (written 23 Mar. 1937), L.P.L., Bell Papers, 11, fos. 322–47.

1937

1. Memorandum by G.K.A. Bell, 'Visit to Berlin, January 28-February 1, 1937', n.d., L.P.L., Bell Papers, 11, fos. 42–62.
2. A.C. Headlam to J. von Ribbentrop, 5 Feb. 1937, L.P.L., Lang Papers, 320, fos. 199–203.
3. G.K.A. Bell to C.G. Lang, 12 Feb. 1937, L.P.L., Bell Papers, 8, fos. 337–8.
4. Memorandum by G.K.A. Bell, 'Non-Aryan Christians', interview with Dr Spiero and Fraulein Friedenthal at the Paulusbunde, 31 Jan. 1937, L.P.L., Bell Papers, 8, fos. 3–7.
5. C.G. Lang to G.K.A Bell, 19 Feb. 1937, L.P.L., Bell Papers, 8, fo. 8.
6. A.C Headlam to C.G. Lang, 16 Apr. 1937, L.P.L., Lang Papers, 320, fos. 19–20.

7.   A.C. Headlam to C.G. Lang, 22 Apr. 1937, L.P.L., Lang Papers, 320, fo. 25.

1938

1.   Memorandum by G.K.A. Bell, 'A Visit to Berlin and Hanover, April 20–22 1938', L.P.L., Bell Papers, 11, fos. 69–72.
2.   A.C. Headlam to C.G. Lang, 11 July 1938, L.P.L., Lang Papers, 320, fos. 163–71.

1939

1.   G.K.A. Bell to K. Barth, 15 Nov. 1939, L.P.L., Bell Papers, 74, fos. 2–3.
2.   K. Barth to G.K.A. Bell, 8 Dec. 1939, L.P.L., Bell Papers, 74, fos. 4–5.

1933

CHRONOLOGY

28 January:	The government of Schleicher resigns.
30 January:	Adolf Hitler appointed chancellor of a coalition government. Papen is vice-chancellor.
1 February:	The *Reichstag* is dissolved.
2 February:	The first meeting of the Archbishop of Canterbury's Council on Foreign Relations takes place.
3–4 February:	The administrative committee of Life and Work meets in Berlin. Bell discusses the situation in the German churches with German church leaders.
4 February:	A new presidential 'Decree for the Protection of the German People' restricts the freedom of the press and freedom of assembly.
6 February:	Archbishop Lang announces the appointment of the new Council on Foreign Relations under the chairmanship of the bishop of Gloucester at the spring session of the Church Assembly.
8 February:	The Church Assembly approves the representation of the church at the second international conference of the Faith and Order movement in 1937.
27 February:	The *Reichstag* fire. Civil liberties are suspended and many communists are arrested.
28 February:	Hitler is granted emergency powers by presidential decree.
March:	The ecumenical study conference for Life and Work meets at Rengsdorf and attempts to define the 'basic theological principles' which may determine the character of the churches' social vision.
5 March:	Elections to the *Reichstag* take place across Germany. The Nazi Party wins 288 seats, but falls short of an overall majority in the *Reichstag*.
5–7 March:	The state governments of Hamburg, Hesse, Lübeck, Bremen, Baden, Saxony and Württemberg are 'co-ordinated'.

8 March:	Minister of the Interior Frick announces the establishment of concentration camps.
13 March:	The establishment of the ministry for popular enlightenment and propaganda under Josef Goebbels.
21 March:	Dibelius preaches to a congregation including Hindenberg and Göring in Potsdam at the opening of the new parliament.
21 March:	The 'Malicious Practices Law' prohibits criticism of the new regime. Special courts are created.
23 March:	The *Reichstag* passes the Enabling Law by 444 votes to 94 votes, creating the legal justification for dictatorship for a four year period.
30 March:	Archbishop Lang declares his concern for the Jews of Germany in light of the imminent official boycott of Jewish businesses there in the house of lords.
31 March:	The First Law for the Co-ordination of the Federal States is passed in Germany.
1–3 April:	The national boycott of Jewish businesses in Germany.
3–5 April:	Congress of *Deutsche Christen* in Berlin calls for a unified *Reichskirche*, organized on the Führer principle and adopting the Aryan Paragraph.
7 April:	The Law for the Restoration of the Professional Civil Service and the Second Law for the Co-ordination of the Federal States are passed.
23 April:	The president of the German Church Federation, Hermann Kapler, is authorized to arrange a new constitution for the church. He is to work with the Lutheran bishop of Hanover, Marahrens, and the Reformed pastor of Elberfeld, Dr Hesse.
25 April:	The Law against Overcrowding of German Schools and Universities is passed, limiting places for Jews to 1.5 per cent.
25 April:	Hitler appoints Ludwig Müller as his 'representative with full powers' to 'promote all efforts directed towards the creation of our Evangelical German National Church'.
2 May:	The free trades unions are abolished in Germany.
5–6 May:	The administrative committee of Life and Work meets at London. Affairs in Germany are again discussed. Bell expresses his concern in a letter to Kapler, the president of the German Church Federation.
6 May:	The creation of the German Labour Front under Robert Ley.
10 May:	Book-burning takes place in a number of university towns.

20 May:	Kapler's committee issues its 'Manifesto of Loccum'.
23 May:	Müller is appointed 'Protector' of the German Christian movement. He stands for election as *Reichsbischof* of the new unified church.
27 May:	Kapler's manifesto is approved by the Church Federation. It nominates Friedrich von Bodelschwingh as its candidate. The candidate of the *Deutsche Christen*, Ludwig Müller, opposes this. The *Deutsche Christen* begin their campaign to make him *Reichsbischof*.
31 May:	Archbishop Lang registers his anxiety for the Jews of Germany in convocation.
June:	A public declaration of protest against attacks on the 'religious liberty and constitutional rights of the Church' in Germany is secretly prepared by Lang, Bell and other English church leaders.
14 June:	The *Times* publishes Bishop Bell's letter calling attention to the crisis in the German church.
24 June:	The *Reichskultusminister*, Rust, appoints Jäger as state commissar for church affairs in Prussia. Jäger appoints his subcommissars, depriving the church of administrative authority and assuming full administrative powers for himself. Bodelschwingh retires. The church in Prussia is now supervised by the police. Pastors accused of hostility to the government are dismissed. Hindenburg intervenes and meets Hitler. Hitler passes responsibility for the church to the minister of the interior, Frick. The state commissars are removed.
28 June:	Müller appoints himself chairman of the German Church Federation.
1 July:	The dean of Chichester, A.S. Duncan-Jones, flies to Berlin to see how matters stand in the German church.
2 July:	Appointed by the general superintendent of the Prussian church as a Day of Penitence and Prayer. The leader of the *Deutsche Christen*, Joachim Hossenfelder, declares it a Day of Praise and Thanksgiving, marking the intervention of the state.
4 July:	The public declaration by the leaders of the Church of England is suspended after advice from German sources.
5 July:	The Catholic Centre Party officially disbands.
6 July:	Hitler announces the end of the 'national revolution'.
7 July:	Jäger appoints Müller head of the church of the Old Prussian Union.

8 July:	The concordat with Rome is signed.
11 July:	The election campaign begins for the election of representatives who will appoint members of a synod to 'acclaim' a new *Reichsbischof*. The two candidates are Bodelschwingh and Müller.
14 July:	The suppression of all political parties and the establishment of a one party state is announced.
14 July:	The new constitution of the German Evangelical Church is published.
20 July:	The concordat is ratified.
22 July:	Hitler speaks a day before the elections and declares his support for Müller.
23 July:	The *Deutsche Christen* party wins the election, gaining 75 per cent of the seats in the new synod. There is much criticism and many claims that the process has been corrupted.
29–30 July:	Members of the German Faith Movement gather at Eisenach and ask for legal recognition of the movement.
August:	Müller is appointed *Landesbischof* of Prussia by the senate of the Prussian church. Elections take place for the synods of the evangelical state churches' representatives to the general synod.
25 August:	Müller declares his view of the national church.
September:	Bishop Hossenfelder and Professor Fezer visit England at the invitation of Frank Buchman of the Oxford Groups movement.
5 September:	Synod of the Evangelical Church of Prussia meets. Müller is acclaimed as first bishop of Prussia. Future synods are abolished; the *Führer prinzip* is adopted. An Aryan Paragraph is to be adopted for the pastors of the church. Pastors held to be critical of the state are to be dismissed. A dissenting group, the 'Gospel and Church group' protests and walks out. A church senate is granted the powers previously enjoyed by the general synod, including the power to revise the constitution of the church.
9–12 September:	Life and Work conference at Novi Sad, Yugoslavia. The German churches are represented by a delegation of four, led by the 'ecumenical bishop' Theodor Heckel. Heckel provokes controversy by questioning the principles of the movement, declared at Stockholm in 1925. The movement confronts the threat of a split. Bell resolves the crisis, suggesting that the anxiety of delegates about antisemitism and the suppression of freedoms in Germany, and their

discussion of ecclesiastical events there, be recorded. He will write to Müller and other German church leaders of the council's concern. Heckel abstains from this motion.

21 September: The first German national synod takes place at Wittenberg. The new Pastors' Emergency League registers its opposition to the Aryan Paragraph, supported by the theological faculty at Marburg University and other academics.

22 September: The Reich Chamber of Culture is created.

27 September: Müller is adopted by the national synod as *Reichsbischof*. He appoints a Spiritual Ministry to re-codify the church law.

14 October: Germany leaves the League of Nations and the Disarmament Conference at Geneva. At his diocesan conference Archbishop Lang expresses his anxiety.

24 October: Bishop Headlam publishes a letter, 'In German eyes', in the *Times*.

12 November: Elections to the *Reichstag* and a referendum take place across Germany.

13 November: Assembly of the *Deutsche Christen* movement to celebrate the 450th anniversary of Luther's birth at the Sportpalast in Berlin. Hossenfelder chairs the meeting. Krause makes a controversial speech advocating the discarding of the Old Testament and the revision of the New Testament. A resolution demanding the dismissal of pastors opposing state religious policy is passed. A storm of criticism follows. Müller dismisses Krause, but the meeting marks the end of the triumphalist phase of the *Deutsche Christen* movement. Now it begins to fracture. The opposition now solidifies into the *Pfarrernotbund*, the Pastors' Emergency League.

13 November: Bell's letter to Müller is published in the press, drawing attention to the Aryan Paragraph and coercion in the German church.

16 November: The national synod suspends acts by the provincial synods, and so suspends the application of the Aryan Paragraph.

19 November: Members of the *Pfarrernotbund* read from their pulpits a protest against the church government.

30 November: The *Gestapo* is created.

1 December: The law to ensure the unity of party and state is passed.

4 December: Müller forbids pastors to belong to any ecclesiastical groups.

8 December: Müller announces that the Aryan Paragraph has been suspended, and that efforts to create a unified German church will continue.

12 December: Bell writes to Müller requesting information on the state of
                    the Christian Youth Movement.

15 December: Heckel writes to reassure Bell that the Sportpalast meeting
                    did not represent the majority of views in the *Deutsche
                    Christen* movement.

19 December: Müller passes authority over the Evangelical Youth Move-
                    ment to Baldur von Schirach, leader of the Hitler Youth.
                    Bishops Wurm and Meiser of Bavaria and Württemberg
                    deliver an ultimatum that the acts of the Spiritual Ministry
                    are illegal because it lacks a theological member stipulated
                    by the constitution.

1 H.N. BATE, DEAN OF YORK, TO ARCHBISHOP LANG, 27 APRIL 1933

My dear Archbishop,

I hope I may venture, in view of the existence of the Council of Foreign Relations, just to report to your Grace a fact which has just come to my knowledge.

Two years ago a Pastor (Lutheran) from Breslau was recommended to me, and he and his wife stayed at Hadleigh. He was making a survey of the work of English religious bodies upon social problems, and their relation to the working classes: an excellent man in all ways.

I have now had a most pitiful letter from him. It appears that his mother was of Jewish descent: and this fact alone will cost him the loss of his work and livelihood, and deprive him of all hope of continuing to function as a Lutheran pastor. He is in such grave fear of trouble that he does not even sign his letter to me.

The poor man in his desperation even asks whether he could come over here and serve our Church. I have sent word through a neutral channel to warn him against building on that kind of hope.

This is the first case of this kind which has come to my knowledge: & it seemed to me that as we now find this anti-Jewish fever attacking Christians of even distantly Jewish antecedents, this new development might well be reported to your Grace.

Believe me
Yours most faithfully
H.N. Bate

2 ARCHBISHOP LANG TO DEAN BATE, 30 APRIL 1933

My dear Dean,

I thank you for your letter of the 27th. I am distressed and indignant by your account of this good Lutheran pastor at Breslau. I do not know whether I am more indignant at the whole attitude of the new revolutionary Government in Germany to the Jews or with the Lutheran Church for submitting, as it seems to have done in such a case as this, to dictation as to the qualifications for its Ministry. But no doubt it is difficult for us in this country to understand the ferment which is now agitating Germany. I fear it would be useless for him to think of coming to this country and think of being ordained in it. I can only hope that when the first excitement is over in Germany and a time of quiet and reflection comes he, and such as he may find a place for themselves in their own country. It is good for me to know of such an instance as you have given me.

Yours very sincerely
Cosmo Cantuar

3   MEMORANDUM BY ARCHBISHOP LANG OF A CONVERSATION WITH ADOLF DEISSMANN, 25 MAY 1933

Conditions in Germany

I had a long talk with Dr. Deissmann of the University of Berlin at Lambeth on May 25th 1933. He gave me a most interesting account, much of which is quite unknown in this country, of recent Ecclesiastical developments in Germany. I give a summary of what he said.

Part of the general Revolution of Youth at the present time has been a movement among younger Hitlerites for the formation of a party of what they call German Christians, and as everything now depends upon individual leaders the leader chosen for this movement, with Hitler's knowledge and consent, is a certain Pastor Hossenfelder who appears to be a person of very little theological knowledge or ecclesiastical experience but of the form of enthusiasm common in Germany to-day. Their desire is to have one great German National Protestant Church. Meanwhile the same impulse has of course been going on for many years, and there has been a Federation of the different Evangelical churches. But the general movement in Germany has led quite recently to the formation of a Triumvirate of three able men, headed by (?) Kapler I think, to take steps to bring all these churches together under some one flexible constitution in which Bishops, or even Archbishops, will have a place. Hitler, though nominally a Roman Catholic, is apparently very much interested in these Evangelical Churches, and he has appointed as his representative a certain Müller, who is a trained theologian and good Christian and an intimate friend of himself, to keep in communication with this Triumvirate. Also the faculties of theology in the universities met in Deissmann's house and appointed again, following the new practice, one man a certain professor at Tübingen by name Fezer, whom Deissmann described as a combination of Karl Barth and Hitler, to be in touch with Herr Müller and the Triumvirate. The result was that only last week Fezer and Müller, invited by Hitler, have framed a new ecclesiastical programme for the Nazis. It is Christian. It accepts the main Credal Confessions such as the Nicene Creed, the Augsburg Confession, etc. It professes to have no racial distinctions and is eager about Missions and urges the necessity of one German Church with Bishops at its head.

As to the Jews, Deissmann confirmed everything that I had heard from the German Ambassador about the reasons why the Jews have become so intensely disliked in Nationalist Germany.[1] He did not defend much that has happened but I could see that he was in a good deal of sympathy with this dislike of the Jews. When I asked why it was that the Evangelical Churches had made no kind of remonstrance he pointed out − (1) that anything of this kind is not allowed to appear in the Press in Germany; (2) that what is done has to be done very quietly; (3) that the stoppage of the Jewish boycott on trade was largely due to the representations of Church leaders. Deissmann was rather pathetic in his plea

---

1 Lang met Hoesch in London on 16 May 1933. The meeting was recorded by Lang's chaplain and secretary, Alan Don. See Lambeth Palace Library, MS 2862, p. 14: Journal of Alan C. Don, 16 May 1933.

that I should try to help people here to understand things from the point of view of the German people themselves.

C.C.

4 MEMORANDUM OF A CONVERSATION WITH DR J.R. MOTT, 31 MAY 1933. BY ARCHBISHOP LANG

I saw Dr. J.R. Mott at Lambeth on May 31st 1933. He had just returned after spending some days in Germany where he had had prolonged conversations with many leaders of the protestant Churches, including Dr. Kapler one of the Triumvirate.[2] He gave me his impression that all the younger pastors and people were eager Hitlerites, that they were sweeping the middle-aged with them, and that older people (however troubled) did not dare raise any objection or offer any criticisms. He said that the man who was most influential over the youth of the Protestant Churches was a certain Herr Lilje, who is I gather also very prominent in International Y.M.C.A.[3] work.

As to the Jews, he confirmed impressions already received and said that even the most spiritually-minded of the Protestant Churches, while anxious to do what was possible in a charitable way with individual Jews, did not seem disposed to make any kind of public protest which he thought would be unavailing and provocative, and he was bound to admit that he could not but have at least some understanding of the reason that had made the Jews so unpopular to this new Nationalist generation in Germany.

C.C.

5 A.S. DUNCAN-JONES, DEAN OF CHICHESTER, TO CAROLINE DUNCAN-JONES, N.D. [2/3 JULY 1933]

Sunday
Grand Hotel
am Knie

Dearest

I don't know when you will get this. I was tempted to telegraph when I arrived, but became economical. I cannot possibly describe the last 24 crowded hours even if it was wise to do so, which it is not. I have a feeling that my arrival is already known. I thoroughly enjoyed the journey, except the noise. I, of course, made friends with a lady on the voyage, a Mrs. Richard Guinness, a oner. She introduced me to Hanfstängel on arrival, who is intimate with *Der Führer*, and I hope I may see him to-morrow. He is the famous picture reproduction firm. On arrival at am Knie I started at once. Saw the *Times* and the *M[orning] Post*. Immense telephoning and tension followed. It is difficult and almost dangerous to get into touch with people. But I saw 2 eminent persons, one in a distant suburb, which occupied me till 10.30. – no food since Amsterdam! I got back to the hotel changed into a blue suit and joined *Times* and *M. Post*

---

2 'The Triumvirate' was the group of three churchmen, appointed by the Church Federation to draft a constitution for a new church. It was chaired by Kapler, and included the bishop of Hanover, Marahens (Lutheran), and Hesse of Elberfeld (Reformed).

3 Y.M.C.A.: Young Men's Christian Association.

at a Tavani, when at last I had some food. These were also there the *Hamburger Nachrichten* young John Walter, who had stayed with the Villiers at Schloss Stumm, a fellow of Newnham,[4] of great erudition, a young Graf Schulenberg, – & others, all at a *stammtisch*. When I did get home I slept! Up at 8 after breakfast, I went to Kaiser Friedrich Gedächtniskirche and heard the head of the German Xtians, Hossenfelder. I am not surprised that the General Superintendent would not have him. Church crowded – Nun Danket, Ein Feste Burg, Hallelujah Chorus, and all that. Lots of Nazis. Well, well! Had a talk with Pfarrer Hauk. Lunched at Hardenburg Strasse, and am now enjoying a cigar and a glass of Mosel till I go to see the Times. Tomorrow I try to see to Cultus Minister if the Embassy can arrange it. I have to see somebody who lives in the suburbs at 9 a.m.! tomorrow. Shall fly back on Tuesday. I feel as though I have been in an Anthony Hope, Phillips Oppenheim, Edgar Wallace story![5] Hope the dinner went well & all the other things.

VVL[6] Arthur

Oh how German are the Germans, & Luther the worst of all!

6   REPORT FROM BERLIN, BY THE CHAPLAIN, ROLAND CRAGG, SENT TO BISHOP HEADLAM, 5 JULY 1933

Events are moving so fast that what one writes today is out of date tomorrow, and the information obtained yesterday is no longer correct today.

The nervous tension under which everyone lives in Berlin today makes the obtaining of first hand information very difficult and the newspapers are so entirely one-sided as to be useful only for bare facts and of little or no value as the reflection of public opinion.

You will probably have access to the despatches on Church matters which go home from the embassy and will accordingly get much information therefrom. There are, however, points which are not raised in these despatches which may interest you in getting a view of the whole situation. One of the main questions if not the main question is 'What is the dispute about?' Why has the government stepped in, in the unification of the Church? One answer and that the most obvious, is, that the dispute is as to the method and form of the union of the 28 'Landeskirchen' and the bringing of them under one head. Should that be done by the church itself or should the state have the final and most powerful voice in the decision? It is probably true that the debates and discussions on the unification of the Church were not proceeding fast enough for the government, which had acquired the habit of giving orders and having them executed at once. It is also urged that in the councils of the church were many who were more concerned with the legal and canonical side of the question of union than with the practical side of arranging a speedy union, so that the church might be ready to help the government in the general unification of the nation. It may be urged that it was for these reasons that the government stepped in. Their effect in the first place to work through a 'Reichsbischof' had failed, in that the man elected,

---

4 Newnham College, Cambridge.
5 Anthony Hope, Philips Oppenheim and Edgar Wallace were English writers of popular adventure stories, characterized by headlong narratives and fantastical settings.
6 A family code: all is said.

Pastor Bodelschwingh, would not consent to work at the dictation of the government. They accordingly appointed a 'Commissar' for the church, Dr. Jaeger, a layman who in assuming control stated that 'the relation between the various "Landeskirchen" of the Old Prussian Union, and between them and the government will take place through *my* person', and who further proceeded to dismiss Dr. Dibelius the General Superintendent of the Kurmark (a diocese in the neighbourhood of Berlin). (Dr. Dibelius had preached the sermon in Potsdam on the occasion when Hitler had assumed office.) The causes of the dispute may have been these, but my own feeling is that the cause is deeper far. Dibelius, Kapler, General Superintendent of Berlin and President of the 'Kirchenausschuss' (Synod), both of whom have been dismissed, Karow, General Superintendent of Mark Brandenburg, men such as these and Dr. Deissmann, all men of foresight and learning, realised the tendency of the new movement the 'Deutsche Christen'. They could foresee that if the Church came completely into the hand of the State, was dictated to by the State, there was grave likelihood of interference with the Creeds of the Church. They must have known and probably protested against what has subsequently been made public. The throwing over of the Old Testament as a Jewish book, the only guarded acceptance of the New Testament. They would have realized the danger now foreseen on all sides by devout church-folk that the person of Our Lord would be the next attack. His birth in Palestine, His origin in the flesh, His use of the O[ld] T[estament] are already being excused and He is said to have used the O[ld] T[estament] because He did not know any better! This I see as the real question, the main danger. The 'Deutsche Christen' are keen, enthusiastic, have a desire to bring the church into touch with the people truly, but the danger is that in doing so they throw over the Creed of the church and produce some kind of modernistic Paganism.

Freedom of the Church

A question was put to Pfarrer Müller who is the nominee of Hitler and the leader of the church appointed by the government. It was. How far will this movement leave the church free? The answer was that the church was to be entirely free in all things but that it must conform to the arrangements and orders of the 'Deutsche Christen'. In other words not to be free at all. The orders published by Herr Jaeger are illuminating in this point:
'1. Our thanks are due to God and to His instrument Adolf Hitler for having prevented Bolshevist chaos. A church cannot exist if the nation does not exist.
2. The newly nominated commissars of the Protestant Church provinces and National Churches met here today and have been authorized to form anew the representative councils of the churches with a view to establishing a German Protestant Church. I have given these officials full power over councils chosen by the elected representative bodies of the churches. In cases of doubt the decision rests with my commissioner.
3. I herewith suspend Dr. Dibelius, General Superintendent of the Kurmark from office.'
The President protested in the following letter to Hitler:
'The schisms in the Protestant Church and the disputes which have arisen between the government of the Prussian State and the administration of the National Churches in Prussia have been to me both as a Protestant Christian

and Head of the State a source of great anxiety. The numerous telegrams and letters I have received clearly prove that the German Protestant Christians are greatly troubled because of these disputes and are filled with forebodingas to the inner liberty of the Church. Should the present situation continue, or even become more critical, the result would be catastrophic for people and country alike and the unity of the nation would also suffer. Before God and my conscience I feel it my bounden duty to do everything in my power to prevent such irreparable harm.

After my conversation with you yesterday regarding these questions, I know that you fully understand my great anxiety and are prepared to help me bridge over these difficulties. I feel assured that you, as a far-sighted statesman, will be successful in dealing with the representatives of the Prussian National Churches and the deputies of the Prussian state so that peace may once more reign in the Protestant Church, and that on this basis the desired unification of the various national churches may become an accomplished fact.

With friendly greetings,

v. Hindenburg.'

Pfarrer Hossenfelder speaking at the specially ordered thanksgiving service at the Kaiser Wilhelm Church said: 'If your conscience conflicts with the State, your conscience is wrong'!

This is a freedom which is better called slavery. The situation is undoubtedly fraught with grave danger both as concerning the Evangelical Church and the very large number of earnest church-folk who are being driven out by this movement and as regards Rome which will not tolerate dictation.

7   BISHOP HEADLAM TO BISHOP BELL, 6 JULY 1933

My dear Bishop,

Many thanks for sending your Dean in such an adventurous way. I'm sure it was a good thing to do under all circumstances. You shall have the £25 in due course when we get our finances into order. There is money. I was sorry he could not be back and tell us his experiences yesterday,[7] but having got to Berlin it was much better that he should stay there if there was anything for him to do or anything for him to see.

We spent more than an hour over Germany yesterday. Keller gave us information, but not really very much. But altogether we collected a good deal. The Bishop of Fulham of course knew a great deal, and so did Fox. My own feeling is that the best thing is to wait at present and not be too anxious to do anything. If the Church of England makes any protest, Hitler and his friends will reply that there are no grounds for our speaking, that all that they want is that they should have the same control over the Church in Germany as the State has in England — namely that they should appoint the Bishops. I don't think we have any answer to that.

Yours ever

A.C. Gloucester

7 The committee of the Council on Foreign Relations met in London on 5 July 1933.

8   BISHOP HEADLAM TO ALAN DON,[8] 10 JULY 1933

Dear Dr. Don,

I do not think at the moment that it is desirable that we should do anything with regard to the ecclesiastical affairs in Germany. I think we must just see how things are going on. But it has been pointed out to me that the wisest way in which the Church of England could intervene would not be by any public memorial but by a private letter addressed to responsible authorities in Germany, which might be sent through the British Embassy. That was done in the case of the Jews by a number of people at Cambridge and was, I believe, quite effective. What we ought to emphasise when we do anything is:

1. That we widely sympathise with the desire for National Church Union.

2. That we hope that our aspirations for the spiritual autonomy of the German Church are shared by those in authority, and

3. That we should welcome anything which brought us into closer religious sympathy with the Church in Germany.
Yours very sincerely
A.C. Gloucester

9   FROM THE DIARY OF ALAN DON, LAMBETH PALACE, TUESDAY, 11 JULY 1933

The Dean of Chichester came for the night, to tell C.C.[9] of his visit to Berlin last weekend. He flew to Berlin on Saturday July 1 and was there for four days – he had a most thrilling time, seeing many of the Church leaders, both 'German Christian' & otherwise – Müller, Deismann, Dibelius etc – he actually had an interview with Hitler himself! Hitler, he says, is 'volcanic' – a consuming fire burns within him. The impression he got was that Hitler was sorry that he has got mixed up with the Church dispute – but forces have been too strong for him. The atmosphere is electric – a revolution is afoot and no-one can tell what will happen tomorrow. Duncan-Jones was welcomed by these Germans, coming as he did in an 'official' capacity as Chairman of the Committee of the Council of Foreign Relations that has to do with Germany – thus his presence was not resented.

10   H.N. BATE TO ARCHBISHOP LANG, 24 JULY 1933

My dear Lord Archbishop,

I wrote sometime ago about a German pastor who has been reduced to total unemployment thro' the Hitlerite 'Judenheze'.[10] This man, as a 'Nichtarier'[11] i.e. the son of a Christian mother who was a Jewess by birth, has now been forced into exile, and is now (alone) in Czecho-slovakia. I wonder whether it would be possible and wise to attempt the collection of any funds from sympathizers

8 Archbishop's secretary and chaplain at Lambeth Palace.
9 Cosmo Cantuar.
10 Literally 'Jew-hatred'.
11 Literally 'non-Aryan'.

in this country which could be used for assisting such cases? No doubt this problem has been already presented to your Grace's mind, & perhaps a decision upon it has been made. I can see the great difficulty of taking any action, and the many obstacles which would hamper the distribution of any fund. Yet I venture to ask whether, for instance, the Bishop of Fulham has reported in any way which bears upon this aspect of the German situation.

At present I have only been able to send more words of sympathy: only if action on a large scale is felt to be unwise, I might just try what I can do, with the help of personal friends, to meet the particular case which I have in mind.
Believe me, Your Grace
Yours faithfully
H.N. Bate

11   ALAN DON TO DEAN BATE, 26 JULY 1933

My dear Dean,
The Archbishop has received your letter of July 24th. He has the greatest possible sympathy with people like your friend the German pastor who find themselves in a state of destitution owing to the persecution of the Jews in Germany. He thinks that you might well try and help him privately but he knows of no public fund in this country which has been formed for the purpose of helping cases of that kind. His Grace, suggests, however, that you should get in touch with Professor Adolf Keller whom you no doubt know. His Geneva address is [   ]

Professor Keller came to see the Archbishop the other day and explained to him the work which he was trying to organise from Geneva for the purpose of helping, among others, Protestant ministers of one sort and another who have suffered through the revolution in Germany. It is possible that Professor Keller may still be in this country, but of that I am not sure.
Yours sincerely,
A.C.D.

12   MEMORANDUM BY A.S. DUNCAN-JONES, 26 JULY 1933

ABSOLUTELY PRIVATE AND CONFIDENTIAL

THE CHURCH OF ENGLAND
COUNCIL ON FOREIGN RELATIONS.

———

Memorandum by
THE DEAN OF CHICHESTER
on
His Visit to Germany.

———

On June 30th I received a request from the Bishop of Gloucester to go to Germany at once, to find out as much as possible about the situation of the German Evangelical Church. Accordingly, on July 1st, I flew to Berlin. I arrived at Berlin at 4.30 and immediately got into contact with representative people in the Church, especially those who were interested in defending the independence of the Church and the preservation of its Faith and Order.

I think it is better not to mention names because the situation is so critical for many of the people concerned. But I may say that I saw at once a representative of the Professoriat[12] and a representative of the General Superintendents. The critical nature of the situation was immediately brought home to me by the fact that the first person I visited said to me: 'It is very dangerous for me to see you, but as you have come here on this special mission representing the Council on Foreign Relations of the Church of England, I will see you and give you all the information I can.'

It would be difficult to exaggerate the sense of living under great anxiety which I experienced on contact with these men. They urged that the situation was very critical for the future of the Church in Germany. On the one hand there were those who since the War had come to value the independence of the Church and the rediscovery of the basis of its life in the Christian Creed. There was amongst them a strong sense of the necessity of asserting what they called the old Lutheran view, by which I understood them really to mean the Apostle's Creed, the dominance of the Incarnation and the Atonement, of Grace.

It should be understood, of course, that when I arrived the ecclesiastical position was this. In response to an invitation from the Chancellor, the Church authorities had proceeded to the election of a Reichsbischof, Dr. Von Bodelsch-wingh, but after that election the State had intervened and appointed Herr Wehrk-reispfarrer Ludwig Müller as the President of the Kirchen-bundesrat with full powers to act on behalf of the Chancellor. Also Herr Pfarrer Hossenfelder, the leader of the German Christians had been put in command of the Church in Prussia in co-operation with the Commissar, Dr. Werner.

This act of aggression on the part of the State, as it seemed to the General Superintendents, was strongly resisted by a number of them. On the 26th June a number of the General Superintendents of Prussia had written a letter to their communities, calling attention to the fact that the life of the Church was at stake.

They also stated that it was against their conscience to recognise such a personality as Herr Hossenfelder as suitable to occupy the highest spiritual office of the Church. The consequence was that a number of the General Superintendents were suspended from office.

The position of every pastor in Prussia was made exceedingly difficult, as the Sunday immediately after I arrived had been ordered to be observed as a Day of Prayer and Penitence by Dr. Von Bodelschwingh, while Herr Hossenfelder had issued orders that it should be a Day of Thanksgiving. Therefore, every pastor had to make up his mind which he was to obey. I asked one of the persons I interviewed on the Saturday night what would be the attitude of the pastors. He said: 'Some will give thanks, some certainly will not, and some will conduct an egg-dance in between.'

My first impressions were of a pessimistic kind. Indeed, one whom I interviewed said that it was the end of the Lutheran Church in Germany. 'Church History shows' he said 'that the more the Church becomes under the control of

---

12 This is an unusual phrase, and it is difficult to be quite sure what Duncan-Jones means by it. Very possibly he is referring to the elders of the church council, or he may simply mean the protestant professors of Berlin, Breslau, Greifswald and Marburg.

the State, the more superficial becomes its teaching. But' he said 'it will not be
the end of the evangelical religion. In ten or twenty years' time you will find it
springing up here and there, in groups, in towns and districts, people who will
demand a real deep religion and piety. That has happened in Germany before
and it will happen again.'

On the Sunday I went to hear sermons delivered from two opposite points of
view. In the morning I attended the Kaiser Wilhelm Gedächtniskirche where
Herr Hossenfelder was to preach. The Church was a very large one with big
galleries and was completely crowded. The service was one of thanksgiving –
the Hallelujah Chorus, Ein feste Burg, and all that kind of thing. The Nazis were
much in evidence with their flags. The sermon was on the identity of Church
and State where you have a Christian Government. Germans should welcome
and rejoice in 'The Third Empire.' Where the Government is Christian, its orders
are the will of God, and if your conscience tells you that it is not so, it is your
conscience that is wrong. I did not feel, however, that there was real spiritual
unity, or a hearty spirit of thanksgiving in the Church. Germans are undemonstra-
tive, but it seemed to me that there were signs of perplexity and bewilderment,
and the preacher, who possessed no magic, merely shouted, and did not seem
to me to grip his audience. That, of course, is only a personal impression.

When the service was over I waited behind and had an interview with the
pastor of the Church, and I asked him: What was really being aimed at? He said
that what was aimed at was the restoration of order and faith in which the Church
must co-operate.

I then asked 'How exactly is it that many men of importance who are entirely
in favour of the new regime have yet been removed from their offices?' He said
'Many of the old leaders of the Church, General Superintendents and the like,
have been too closely connected with the Nationalist Party, and it was important
that there should be no centres through which it could be restored.'

In the evening I heard in the same Church Herr Gerhard Jacobi, one of the
most impressive and spiritual preachers in Berlin, who it seemed had been
preaching a course of sermons in this church. The whole of the floor of the
church was full, and the atmosphere was a totally different one from that of the
morning. There was now complete unity of feeling, so far as one could judge.
Those who were there had come to pray. There were many men amongst them
of all ages. Herr Jacobi's sermon was on the theme of Prayer, of the Lordship
of Christ and the Power of Grace. He said that if you study Church History you
will see that there are two streams. One, the powers of the world have constantly
thought that they could step in and make the Church do what they liked, and
for a time they have seemed to be very successful. But there has always been
the little flock that had nothing, no force – only prayer and faith. And over and
over again they have come up and the powers of the world have passed away.

At the end of his sermon he made a very important announcement. He
described how Herr Grossmann at Dahlem in the morning had refused to put
flags in his church or to read a letter from Herr Hossenfelder ordering a Day of
Thanksgiving. He had denied the charge made by Herr Rust (the Minister of
Worship) against the Church, that the Church had not done anything against
godlessness during the last few years. He had said that such a statement rested
on false information or was a lie. Immediately after the service, Herr Grossmann
had been arrested by the Nazis. This announcement was, I gathered, part of a

plan that had been made by a number of the pastors to announce to their congregation any attack on any of their number.

In point of fact, after Herr Grossmann's arrest many of the pastors telegraphed to President Hindenburg, who sent a telegram to say that Herr Grossman must be released and I think he was. I know that Herr Jacobi himself was removed from office on the Monday.

On Monday I went to pay a call on Herr Wehrkreispfarrer Müller. With him was Admiral Meisel,[13] who was acting as his assistant. I was warmly welcomed by them and they were glad to give any information in their power. They were now engaged in drawing up a new constitution for the Reichskirche and in that work they would co-operate with all parties, with the Neue Reformatische Bewegung[14] (which represented the more churchly party) and also the German Christians. They wanted as soon as possible to produce unity and order, which was desired by them, by the President and by the Chancellor. I might add at this point that Dr. Von Bodelschwingh, Dr. Marahrens, the Bishop of Hanover and others, who represented the churchly party, were engaged in the work of preparing the new constitution. I was unable to get into contact with Dr. Von Bodelschwingh – although he was staying in my hotel – because he felt that it would be unwise of him to have any communication at this stage with any foreigner. But I had some conversation with other members of the group.

To return to Dr. Müller and Admiral Meisel. Their point of view seemed to be this. There were numbers outside the Church. The Church should give moral force to the Nation and everything must be done to bring into the Church those who were outside. Why were they outside? They were outside because of the emphasis on the old dogmas which were unintelligible to them. We must give up the old language in which God is spoken of as being a kind of Sultan in Heaven, and we must find Him and appeal to Him in the hearts of the good, German people.

They were certain that this would bring in many people and especially the younger men. A religion which got rid of dogma and appealed to generous minds would be adequate for the purpose. One of the younger members of their staff said to me: 'We are now going to have a more manly religion, with less emphasis on sin and on grace.'

I thought that it would be useful at this stage to get into contact with members of the Government. I suggested to the Embassy that I should be glad if I could have an interview with Minister Frick, Minister of the Interior, or with Minister Rust, or, best of all, with the Chancellor. I was informed that an interview with the Chancellor was entirely impossible as many people had waited for weeks without seeing him. I then proceeded through private connections to arrange for an interview with the Chancellor, which was made for the next day at one o'clock. I gathered that there had been considerable difficulty in obtaining this interview, and when I went in to see him I felt that the atmosphere was somewhat strained. But when he discovered that I could talk German, even badly, he spoke freely in giving me his point of view.

13 Admiral Wilhlem Meisel, later chief of naval staff under Dönitz in 1943.
14 'New Reformation Movement'. This group met at the home of Gerhard Jacobi in Berlin and its leading lights included Hanns Lilje, who edited the group's journal, *Junge Kirche*, Walter Künneth and Dietrich Bonhoeffer.

The Chancellor gave me the opportunity of speaking first, a somewhat embarrassing one. I pointed out to him what indeed I said all the time to everybody, that I had not come there to interfere, but merely to find out the facts as a representative of the Church of England, which was naturally interested in anything profoundly affecting the German Church. I told him that I came as a representative of the Council of the Church of England on Foreign Relations.

I asked him whether he wanted the Church to be free to fashion its own faith and worship and its own organisation, particularly stressing the last point. He said emphatically 'Yes. I do not want to interfere.' On my remarking that he had intervened, he said 'Yes. I did so merely because there was a crisis, and there were quarrels and controversies, and it was necessary to get something settled.' But he now wished the Church to have complete freedom, to create its own constitution for the one Church for the German *Reich*.

He said 'I am a Catholic. I have no position in the Protestant Church and I do not want to be mixed up in its affairs, and there is only one thing that I ask – that is, that there should be one Protestant Church for Germany as there is one Catholic Church, so that when I have to conduct negotiations with them I may receive a firm answer from a representative body representing all German Protestants.'

I gather that he wanted the support of the forces of religion in the conflict against materialism and Communism and he thought that he had a right to demand that support in a contest of that kind. After that he spoke of other matters.

In an interview that I had with the Foreign Office afterwards I was assured that it really was the Chancellor's wish to stand aloof from ecclesiastical controversy. Subsequent events seem to have supported this view.

The next day I had an interview with a very important lay member of the Catholic Church, who said to me 'Germany is once more hungry for Religion as she was immediately after the War. Unfortunately, immediately after the War the Protestant Church, which had been too much connected with the State was unable to give the Message which met the demand. But since the War a deeper feeling of religion has sprung up, and now you will find that wherever there is an earnest preacher there you will find the people.' He said the German people need grace, power that is from above, and they need a definite symbol, they need something which calls out the spirit of worship, something which can claim their allegiance in the highest sense, and what they are being given in the Nazi movement is *ersatz religion* – a substitute for religion.

I had also arranged an interview with Minister Frick through the German Foreign Office, but unfortunately when I saw him for a few moments he was so busy that he was unable to give me an interview.

Before leaving, I also saw Herr Stange, who is closely connected with the Life and Work Movement, and with him were the representatives of the Y.M.C.A. in Germany. Their chief concern was to justify the forbidding of any criticism of the Government.

While I was waiting to see Minister Frick I fell into conversation with a Roman Catholic priest, who was also going to see him on ecclesiastical matters. When I told him my mission and who I was, he appeared to be greatly interested. He said 'This is the situation. Minister Rust put it rightly when he said the other day "What is the Protestant Church? Is it the People, or is it half a dozen

General Superintendents?"' And also he said 'I say (with all respect to their Eminences) "What is the Catholic Church? Is it the People or is it half a dozen Bishops?"' Upon my remarking that this was a somewhat dangerous discussion from the point of view of a Catholic, he said 'Oh, no. That is what a great many of us feel.' He was obviously anxious to talk with me because I was an Anglican, and we tried to make arrangements to meet again, but were unfortunately unsuccessful.

I had a number of other interviews. Practically the whole of my time was spent either in taxis or interviews, but it would be useless to go into them all in detail. I flew back on July 5th.

I will now try to sum up the impressions I received.

First. Is the regime likely to last? I asked one of those who was suffering under the regime whether the Chancellor would not before long have made himself so many enemies that there would come a reaction. To which he replied 'Certainly not, for the simple reason that the only alternative is Bolshevism, and therefore many of us, who dislike many things in the present regime and are intending to do everything we can for the spiritual independence of the Church, are yet whole-hearted supporters of the Chancellor.'

Further information along these lines was given to me by the report of the meeting of 1,000 students in the University of Berlin, which was addressed by Herr Müller in which he exhorted them to uphold Herr Hitler because he had brought back order and faith into Germany, and then went on to appeal to them to support the German Christians' point of view in regard to the Church. Whereupon the vast majority of the students left the room and conducted a meeting in the street outside, in which they declared their devotion to the Chancellor and their determination to uphold the faith of the Church.

There were many other signs that many pastors and others who are enthusiastic for the independence of the Church are also entirely for Herr Hitler. I found no voice raised in criticism of the proposal to have one *Reichskirche*.

Secondly. What evidence is there that those who are in favour of the spiritual independence of the Church will succeed?

Here, of course, prophesies are dangerous, but it is plain that there is amongst a number of the younger pastors and lay people a profound feeling that what is at stake is not only the Church as an organisation, but its faith and mission, and because of this they are preparing to join themselves together to suffer whatever may be necessary, whether it means the creation of a schism or being sent to prison. It is obvious that [from] the point of view of the Government, a reorganisation of the Church, which introduced greater disunity of a more profound character, would be exactly the opposite of what they want.

Thirdly. What exactly is the danger which the more churchly people feel? The teaching of the German Christians is a curious compound, so far as I can judge, of three things. The Liberalism or Modernism of the stamp of Harnack's 'What is Christianity?' together with a passionate belief that immanent in the German people there is a divine power which they connect with Christ. But for them Christ is regarded rather as a leader in a battle against Communism, than as a Saviour from sin. Thirdly, they have their apocalyptic element, without which the other two elements would not have very great force. They really believe, many of them, that Hitler is sent by God, and that the success of his movement after such small beginnings and after 10 years of struggle, is plain evidence that God has worked a miracle. It is for this reason that they regard opposition to Herr Hitler or even to the regime, or any criticism of the force which brought about that regime as in the nature of blasphemy.

Fourthly. It is significant that both sides appeal confidently to Luther. One side says 'We hold the old Christian faith which Luther taught, the faith of the Creeds.' The other says 'We are really Lutherans because Luther, when he did away with the power of the Pope, handed over to the godly prince the position of *Summus Episcopus*.' Both of course are right. The German Christians say that since the War they have had no *Summus Episcopus*, because they have not had a Christian Government. Now that they have a Christian Government that Government steps into the place of the *Summus Episcopus*. And so they rebut the charge that what has been happening is the interference of the State with the Church. They say it is the Church dealing with the Church.

Fifthly, the visit revealed to me in an unexpected way, what a high regard there is in Germany for the Church of England, and incidentally what are the potentialities of our Committee. It was quite clear that doors were opened to me which are not usually opened, simply because I came quite frankly as a representative of this Committee and semi-officially as the representative of the Church of England, and also because I came not to interfere but to obtain information.

Sixthly. What more can we do? Any public expression of sympathy with those who are undergoing oppression and persecution would by the agreement of all responsible persons to whom I spoke, be absolutely disastrous. Equally, it was very fortunate that the arrangements for my visit were not made through the Embassy or the Foreign Office. If they had been they could hardly have failed to have a political complexion. What can be done is to assure those who are being persecuted of our prayers and of our profound sympathy. But this must be done in my view through personal and private channels. It is very important that all the contacts which have been established before and in this time of stress, should be maintained as consecutively as possible.

I would like to add a word of gratitude to the very admirable correspondents of the *Times* and the *Morning Post*, Mr. Ebbutt and Mr. Gillie, who were of the greatest possible assistance to me, and who indeed, may be said to have been the ultimate cause of our taking any action in the matter. They are deeply interested in the Church question and have endeavoured to arouse interest in their papers in this, an historic struggle of the first importance.
26th July 1933.

13   MEMORANDUM BY A.J. MACDONALD, 6 SEPTEMBER 1933

STRICTLY CONFIDENTIAL.
THE CHURCH OF ENGLAND COUNCIL ON FOREIGN RELATIONS

Memorandum by
The Rev. Dr. A.J. Macdonald
on
A RECENT VISIT TO GERMANY

Between August 2nd and August 29th of this year I stayed at Freiburg im Breisgau with a retired High School Professor of Languages. During this period I had the opportunity of observing the effect of the Hitlerite regime on the town and neighbourhood, and of discussing the Hitlerite Movement with people of different character and status.

I received the impression that Herr Hitler's Government has supplied the German people with an effective lead, which is very obvious even in a distant province like Baden. Whether in obedience to orders from Berlin, or as the result of confidence in the existing Government, steps are being taken to organise work both of a public and industrial character. Great attention is being paid to young people of both sexes. Encouragement for the various kinds of outdoor exercise and sport, which have been widely developed in Germany since the War – football fields exist even in country villages – is a leading feature of Hitler's rule. Of more importance is the effort being made to prevent young unemployed people from falling into fixed habits of idleness. A system of 'Labour-Service' (*Arbeitdienst*) has been introduced, and bands of young men, thirty or forty in number, march out to do work of public utility, sometimes walking as far as 20 miles. They receive, at present, no more than their food and uniform. After next October all young men between the ages of 18 and 25 will be enrolled for this service for a maximum period of six months, which may be served by instalments. They will receive in addition to maintenance and uniform about twopence (two pfennige) a day. More impressive than the organisation of this work is the spirit of glad and willing service in which it is performed. The young men march along the roads singing national songs, and blithely greet the passing traveller on the way.

From my talks with people of all ages, belonging to the more stable and conservative elements of the urban class, and from observing the places where the swastika is displayed, I gathered that a majority of the working people, and the middle class almost to a man, are supporters of Hitler's movement in the Grand Duchy of Baden. This is the more remarkable since Baden has been less subject to political disturbance, and is more conservative in political temper than some other parts of Germany.

Conversation with some of the more observing and discreet elements of the people made clear some of the reasons for this widely-spread and deeply-rooted support of the Chancellor. It is the conviction of the German people that Hitler, and he alone, has saved the country from being over-whelmed by a Bolshevik revolution. They regard him as sent by God for this purpose. Secondly he has succeeded in uniting once again the German people into a single whole. A young medical doctor remarked to me that English Parliamentary government had taken some seven hundred years since Magna Carta, in which to secure its great achievements. The only result, he said, of the Weimar Constitution of 1918 in Germany had been to produce over thirty parties, each fighting for its own hand, regardless of the interests of Germany or of other sections of the German people. Hitler had not only checked all this, but had united the nation in spirit as well as political outlook. I said to him: 'It seems to me, as a mere superficial observer, that Hitler has created a resurrection for the German people.' 'Yes!' he replied 'that is indeed the truth.'

Everywhere I found disappointment and some resentment at the tone of the English Press. It was suggested that if the English newspapers did not understand German conditions, they should be silent, and leave Germany to work out its own internal destiny. Nowhere did I hear any desire for war, or for military training expressed.

I was not in touch with the German Protestant Ministers, but it was interesting to note that in many places in Baden, Lutherans and Calvinists have been united in single congregations for many years. It would be worthwhile if our Committee could ascertain how far this union movement existed in other parts of Germany before Hitler's ecclesiastical proposals were made. I observed the same feature in Strasbourg.

The impression received from my visit was that while no doubt the present Hitlerite programme and practice can be criticised on some points – perhaps on many – justice demands that it should be allowed a fair trial without hostile criticism from external sources. Its success so far, in uniting Germany and in supplying a people who had lost hope with a new faith in the future, indicates that it may yet justify Hitler's action and policy. Criticism is resented not by a single political party (Hitlerite) but by the majority of the German people.

6 September 1933

14 NOTES OF CONVERSATIONS BETWEEN H.W. FOX AND PASTOR X, SEPTEMBER 1933

PRIVATE AND CONFIDENTIAL

THE CHURCH OF ENGLAND
COUNCIL ON FOREIGN RELATIONS

Committee in Reference to The Affairs of the Continental Churches.

THE 'GOSPEL AND CHURCH' GROUP IN GERMANY.

Notes of Conversations between
The Rev. H.W. Fox and Pastor X,
September 1933

Herr X. is a young German, recently ordained, belonging to the 'Gospel and Church' group of the Westphalian Church, which up till now has been an autonomous province of the Old Prussian Evangelical Church.[15]

1. The Church of this Province is the only German Church in which a majority of 'Gospel and Church' members were elected to the Synod at the August Elections; fifty being returned out of a total of eighty-nine. It was these members who formed the opposition at the meeting of the Synod of the Old Prussian Church. Although there is this 'Gospel and Church'majority in Westphalia a 'German Christian' bishop will be appointed to this Province, since any autonomy which it formerly possessed will disappear in the new constitution of the Church. The Bishop will have the power to appoint and dismiss pastors without reference to the Synod or the congregations.

2. It is unlikely that pastors will be directly dismissed on account of their membership of the 'Gospel and Church' group. Other reasons will be found if necessary (such as irregularities in the performance of their functions) for their

15 The Gospel and Church group was a leading movement opposing the *Deutsche Christen*. Pastor 'X' is difficult to identify.

dismissal. The resignation of pastors (in contrast to dismissal) may be secured by direct or indirect pressure. Thus three General-Superintendents have resigned: Rendtorf (Mecklenburg); Dibelius (Kurmark, in the Old Prussian Church) and Schien (Breslau, Old Prussian Church).

Very few other pastors have resigned up to the present. Pastors who resign will probably receive a small pension. In the Old Prussian Church there are at least 100–120 pastors of Jewish origin who will no longer be able to hold any official position in the Church. Pastor X. could not tell me whether they would receive any pension.

3. The 'Gospel and Church' group has its largest membership in Westphalia and its centres are especially in Dortmund, Bielefeld and Tecklenburg. It is co-operating with a group in East Prussia, and there are a few members in Baden and Württemberg. The theology of this group is fundamentally Lutheran and has no modernist leanings; it lays emphasis on sin, the atonement and Christ as the Redeemer, in contrast to the German Christians who seem to minimise the fact of sin and the need of the atonement and who regard Christ as the victorious Hero and Leader. The group is receiving support from the Dutch Church, (not I think officially), and seven Dutch theologians recently met members of the group in conference in Westphalia. The group is carrying on propaganda among pastors, so far as its small financial resources will allow, in defence of the liberty of thought and preaching. This propaganda does not denounce the German Christians but issues alternative declarations, e.g. on the position of the Christian Jews in the Church. The group has no intention of leaving the German Protestant Church and forming a dissenting body, believing that it can exercise an increasing influence within the Church. Pastor X told me that the leaders of the 'Gospel and Church' group were most grateful for the sympathy of English Christians which had been conveyed to them and fully understood the absence of any public protest by English Churches. No protest of this kind will be advisable at the present moment, although the time might come when an affirmative declaration would be of use.

H.W. Fox.

15   REPORT BY RUTH ROUSE, 31 OCTOBER 1933

STRICTLY CONFIDENTIAL
THE CHURCH OF ENGLAND COUNCIL ON FOREIGN RELATIONS

——————

Report by
MISS RUTH ROUSE
on
Her Visit to Germany.

——————

I went to Germany to learn the truth, as far as was possible in an eight days visit to Berlin, about conditions in Church and State. I stayed at the Young Women's Christian Association Headquarters, the Burckhardthaus, in Berlin. With the help of German friends and a kind and most useful letter of introduction from the Bishop of Gloucester, I had talks with about forty-five different people. These included Reichsbischof Müller; Bischof Schöffel and Herr Weber (two of the five members of the Church Cabinet): other leaders in the new Church: leaders of the other party, pfarrers both D.C.* and otherwise, from many parts of Germany: young members of the Nazi Party (P.Gs) and of the S.A. (Storm Division): Under Secretaries of the Home and Foreign Offices: members, men and women, of the German delegation to the Disarmament Conference: Jews and Christian Jews: leaders of the Y.W.C.A. and the Student Christian Movement and of the German Missionary Societies: foreign clergy – English, Swedish and American.

I had a day with the General Committee of the German Student Christian Movement – (thirty-five men from different universities, many of them in S.A. uniform).

A general knowledge of the events which have led up to the present situation is assumed:

(a) The rise of the Deutsche Christen party within the year.

(b) The setting aside of the nomination of Pastor Bodelschwingh as the Reichsbischof.

(c) The Church elections in July, in which the German Christian party obtained a majority of 75% and Bishop Müller was elected as Reichsbischof.

N.B. The Deutsche Christen now claim 'Gleichschaltung', bringing into line every parish church council and other church organisations, i.e. that 75% of the members of all such must be D.C.

(d) The holding of the Prussian Synod early in September – freely referred to by the other side as a 'robber synod.' It adopted in the constitution of the Prussian Church the 'Aryan Clause' for all pastors and church officers, and a clause permitting the forcible retirement of any pastor or church officer, if it is in the interests of the Church, even if he is perfectly capable of fulfilling his duties.

(e) The holding of the National Synod at Wittenberg at the end of September. This was a more dignified affair. It adopted the constitution in the form the Council on Foreign Relations has seen it. It did not adopt or even consider the 'Aryan Clause.' It confirmed the election of Bishop Müller.

The New Church has lost a priceless and unique opportunity.
There was need for unity. The Church as it existed was divided into regional churches, some Lutheran, some Reformed, some United or Evangelical. The Hitler regime called for a united Protestant Church, and made the desirable easy.

There was need for reform. Much was stiff and traditional, conservative and dull. The average age of the Prussian Synod was sixty-five.

There was a wonderful opportunity for evangelism. The people, united nationally, and with their marvellous sense of a new life in a united nation, might have been ready for a strong spiritual lead from a united Church. Instead the 'German Christian' party seems to put loyalty to the Third Empire before loyalty to Christ, and to be so convinced that the Hitler regime is for Germany the Will of God and the revelation of God that they identify loyalty to National Socialism with loyalty to God. This they preach and demand that others should preach it.

* D.C. = Deutsche Christen – German Christians.

2. *The Deutsche Christen majority was obtained by fraud and force.*
A pfarrer, not a D.C., who announced an address to the parish electors on the coming elections, was warned by S.A. men, that if he persisted in giving the address they would break up the meeting, was abducted by some of them on his way to the meeting, and was kept out of the way till the meeting had been addressed by a D.C. and had dispersed. But one instance amongst many of the use of the S.A. men by the Church leaders.

A young man, a member of the N.S. party, and an S.A. man, a welfare worker by profession, and a keen intelligent fellow, told me that the D.Cs, without consulting him, put his name on their list of those to be elected on to the Gemeinderat (Pa[r]ochial Church Council) in his parish. He was quite willing as he saw that the 'Aryan Clause' and support of the N.S. regime were part of their programme, and he thought a young Nazi might do some good. He would certainly have been elected, but when he found he was required to swear on the Bible, he withdrew on the ground that he could not do that as he was not a Christian. But there were many candidates and voters not so scrupulous.

A Gemeinderat elected on such lines can make life a hell to a conscientious pfarrer who is not a D.C.

On the eve of the Church elections, Hitler recommended voting for the Deutsche Christen and heavily weighted the scales. Many Christian people who are Nazis but not D.C. consider this was one of the very few mistakes Hitler has made.

3. *The Axe has begun to fall.*
Only three pastors, so far as I could hear, have actually been forced to leave their charges, (one admittedly an impossible person), but many have been 'given leave of absence'; seven General Superintendents, including Herr Dibelius, were pensioned off; several theological professors have been dismissed or pensioned; the General-Secretary of the great Innere Mission[16] has been dismissed and well-known D.Cs nominated from above, as Chairman and Secretary.

The 75 per cent D.C. Gemeinderats will probably be left to deal with recalcitrant pfarrers. The dismissals are so far taking place rather from posts in societies than from pastoral charges, e.g. pastors in charge of local Y.W.C.A. work are being told that another man has been appointed in their stead.

4. *The New Church is a Revolt of Youth.*
Bishop Müller must be over 50, but Bishop Hossenfelder, head of the Church in Prussia is 34. Herr Weber, member of the Cabinet is 31, the lay member, Herr Werner, a young lawyer, is 26, and he presides over the National Synod: there is a Bishop of 29, who only passed his theological examinations last year.

The Church needed young leaders, but these are not only young but inexperienced; queer as it is, in Germany they care only for the practical: intellectual attainments count for nothing. Bishop Müller, an army chaplain, covered with military medals, told an American that in the last ten years he had only once opened a theological book, and had then thrown it into a corner. Gone is the German reverence for Professors.

16 Home or domestic missions.

5. *Under the New Church the very existence of Christian Youth Organisations is imperilled.*

I shall talk especially of the Y.W.C.A. but the position of the Y.M.C.A. is much the same.

The Y.W.C.A. in Germany is a powerful organisation with 280,000 members, closely connected with the Church and with a branch in practically every parish, besides large city organisations, a Training School for Women Church Workers, a large publishing business, etc. They see themselves confronted with two dangers:

(1) That on the 'principle of leadership', i.e. nomination to all offices from above, the existing leaders will be dismissed and D.C.s appointed in their stead. This has already happened locally in certain places.

(2) That the whole organisation will be brought under the Hitler Jugend, the Hitler Youth Organisation, which is the junior branch of the S.A. dealing with boys and girls up to eighteen. The theory of the State is that in a 'Unified State' there must be a 'Unified Youth Movement' and as far as possible a 'Unified Church'. A 'Unified Church', including both Roman Catholics and Protestants has not been considered impossible by Hitler idealists.

The new Church, unlike the Roman Catholic Church, has sold the pass, and has agreed to some form, not yet determined on, of affiliation of its Youth Organisations to the Hitler Jugend. The view of the Y.W.C.A. is that this will mean their practical disappearance. The Hitler Jugend already takes three evenings a week and most of the weekend of its members' time and even if the Y.W.C.A. were allowed one or two evenings a week, for its distinctive work, its members could not add this to their obligations to the Hitler Jugend. Reichsbischof Müller, when in East Prussia, actually handed over the whole of the Y.W.C.A. in Danzig to the Hitler Jugend unconditionally.

Bishop Müller in talking to me laid emphasis on the fact, (and hoped I would make it known in England) that no leaders of Youth Organisations were likely to lose their posts, and referred to his declaration (see below 6[(1)]). But he qualified his statement by 'unless they are impossible in their relationships with other people.' – a phrase which can cover a multitude of dismissals. He told me that some relationship with the Hitler Jugend there would have to be, but assured me that the Y.W.C.A. could pursue its own distinctive work, not perhaps without modification, but certainly, freely.

N.B. The five members of the Church Cabinet are each responsible for some special department, and will have an Advisory Council; and Bishop Hossenfelder unfortunately is responsible for Youth Work and Youth Organisations.

6. *The outlook is dark in and for the Church, but there are certain signs of hope.*

1. Bishop Müller and the other leaders are in some ways modifying their position. Bishop Müller has made the most unqualified public pronouncement that 'the era of politics in the Church is over'; that there is no possible danger that a pastor in the Church will find himself at a disadvantage because he belongs, or does not belong, to any particular party; and that the one object of the Church is to preach the gospel to the German people.

Many think that the Government perceived that the Church was going too far and that pressure was put on by the State to modify the action of the extremists.

Again it seems probable that Bishop Müller himself and some of the other leaders truly wish to preach what they conceive to be a pure gospel to the German people. A great Volksmission – Mission to the People – is to be initiated this week. But whether what we should understand as 'the pure gospel' will be preached or whether the main emphasis will be on 'a German gospel preached to the German people in a German way by Germans', the phrase used by Bishop Müller from the steps of the altar at the National Synod, it can hardly escape suspicion of political and anti-Semitic implications.

The general view appeared to be that he had been so anxious to be made Reichs-bischof that he had promised Bishop Hossenfelder and the extremists to put through their policy and is now unable to escape from what he probably suspects to be un-Christian. There are other men in the D.C. party in the same dilemma.

2. There are signs of withdrawal from the D.C. party. In Württemburg all the pfarrers, except about thirty, have withdrawn from the D.C. party. It is easier for them because their Bishop is a strong man and is not a D.C. A number of individuals who are enthusiastic Nazis and good Christians, are withdrawing from the D.C. party, because, although they believe in force in the State, they do not believe in force in the Church: and are appalled at what they see of it.

3. There is courageous expression of opinion from the opposition.

(a) 2500 pfarrers and pastors signed a memorandum which they wished to present at the Wittenberg Synod. Though they were prevented from doing so, it has nevertheless been published in the religious Press and in other ways. In it they take a firm stand against the 'Aryan Clause' as utterly un-Christian and condemn the lack of freedom in the Church elections and in the election of Bishop Müller. The number of signatures would have been much greater had it not been that they had to be collected within two weeks before the Synod. In any case, 2500 is 14 per cent of the entire clergy of the new Church.

(b) The Marburg Theological Faculty has unitedly issued a strong protest against German Christian action in the new Church, especially against the 'Aryan Clause'.

(c) A large number of the New Testament professors in theological faculties and Universities have signed a carefully thought out protest against the 'Aryan Clause'.

(d) There is a group within the Church called the *Junge Reformatorische Bewegung* – The Young Reform Party – which is keen on the new United Church and on Church reform and is mostly led by young men. This has an organ – Die Junge Kirche – in which appear articles about all sorts of movements in the Church and exact information about constitutions and regulations. This has so far been in no way interfered with and to read it is by far the best way to find out what is going on.

4) The crystallisation of various parties who wish for a really German religion into what is now spoken of as the Third Confession (as over against Roman Catholics and Protestants) is in some ways favourable to the opponents of the German Christians within the Church, the so-called *Evangelium und Kirche* – Gospel and Church party. The Third Confession calls itself *Deutsche Glaubensbewegung* – the German Faith Movement. The German Christians call themselves Glaubensbewegung der Deutsche Christen- The Faith Movement of the German Christians. It is hardly to be wondered at that our papers have at times confused the two.

This third Confession wishes to substitute the old German Myths for the Old Testament and in other ways to return to a primitive German faith.

Their existence has had a two-fold good effect within the Church.

(a) It has forced the German Christian party to take its stand formally on the Scriptures and the Historic Creeds:

(b) Because liberty is given to the Third Confession to express its opinions, it secures more liberty of expression for the opponents of the German Christians within the Church.

What can the Christian forces of other countries, and especially the Church of England, do to help the cause of righteousness and truth in the German Church?

The answers given me by German friends to this question may be summed up as follows:

1. *Take every possible occasion to make known to the German Church leaders what Christian opinion in other lands about German conditions both in Church and State actually is*

(a) Respect for opinion abroad appears to be the only thing holding the leaders back from certain excesses: the leader of a certain Christian youth organisation was definitely told recently by Church leaders, 'You'd have been dissolved long ago if it had not been for opinion in other lands.'

(b) They attach great importance to what the authorities in the Church of England say and thin[k]. They were 'much disturbed' at the Archbishop's presentation of the German situation at the Canterbury Diocesan Conference, as reported in the '*Times*', but have wisely decided not to get too excited till they can secure the full text of what His Grace actually said. I was asked again and again whether the Archbishop had or had not (i) invited to England (ii) received Bishop Hossenfelder during his recent visit: speculation was rife as to the Archbishop's action in either case.

(c) The Church leaders attach much importance to the Council on Foreign Relations, as an official organ of the Church of England.

(d) Much depends on *how* foreign opinion is made known. Several prominent non-D.Cs told me that they thought the Bishop of Gloucester's letter was on the right lines and calculated to do good: the Bishop of Chichester's action and attitude at Novi-Sad, they also welcomed, as contrasted with the public condemnation for which Pastor Wilfrid Monod asked. The general attitude was, 'Don't seem to interfere. Don't make public pronouncements. But let them know clearly and firmly what you think. You can say what we can't.'

(e) The Church leaders have an innocent idea that the worst is not known, and condemn as 'traitors to their country', those whom they think have given them away. At the Prussian Synod, a prominent non-D.C. who had merely said 'We must consider what they would say abroad' was greeted with shouts of 'To the Concentration Camp!' 'Out with him!' 'Traitor!'

It is important, therefore, to let them know casually and incidentally, of course, how accurate on the whole and how detailed are the reports of German Church affairs in our secular and religious Press, and not to give them the impression that some one non-D.C. has supplied you personally with undesirable information. They were always trying to find out *who* had told me this or that. In most cases I could truthfully say that I had 'read it somewhere' before coming into Germany. The 'Times' German Church information is almost always trust-worthy and exact, so I was told.

(f) The Home and Foreign Offices seem alive to the importance of Church opinion about Church matters, and the Under Secretary in the Home Office, showed me a file of clippings from English papers on German Church matters.

2. *Don't judge or make pronouncements hastily.* One grew weary of hearing that 'we are in the middle of a revolution,' and that 'it is impossible to tell you definitely yet how certain problems will be settled.' But there is a lot of truth in it. They scarcely know yet who is responsible for what. Their Church House was obviously in a state of confusion; a crisis had occurred one morning I was there. Bishop Müller summoned the Cabinet: messengers scurried to and fro: Bishops hung about hoping to see him: As one man said 'Fire breaks out now here, now there: constant calls for the extinguisher.'

3. *Keep communications open as widely as possible.* Unofficial visits of friendly investigation from the leaders of Christian organisations seem welcome, and are said to be 'very important.' 'But it is not the time for public meetings.'

4. *Tell your Church authorities not to take some people too seriously.* There was a certain uneasiness lest the kind reception given to Bishop Hossenfelder in England should 'increase his already badly swollen head.' It is difficult, of course, to steer a clear course between this Scylla and the Charybdis of losing, through over plain speech, the chance of influence.[17]

5. One man, whose opinion I should trust, laid great stress on the need for the heads of the Churches in other lands, e.g. the Church of England and the Swedish Church, to take counsel together about the attitude which it is wise to take towards the German Church on certain questions.
31st October, 1933.

16 MEMORANDUM BY ARCHBISHOP LANG, 31 OCTOBER 1933

I saw Miss Ruth Rouse at Lambeth on October 31st 1933. She gave me a great deal of interesting information about the position of the Church and of many types of Christian people in Germany at the present time. She described in great detail the character and record of the new so-called Bishops. She also assured me that more of what is being said in England by me and other persons is better known in Germany than I had supposed, and that many educated people continually read what was said in such English newspapers as are not banned. – E.G. She told me particularly that a great deal of notice had been taken of my remarks at the diocesan conference on the attitude of Germany to disarmament. She also told me (which is important) that on the authority of the Swedish Pastor in Berlin,[18] who seems to know all that is going on with the Scandinavian Churches (Sweden, etc.), they are very anxious not to be formally invited to Müller's installation or consecration as they would find very great difficulty in being represented at this present time.
C.C.

---

17 The Charybdis is the whirlpool in the straits of Messina, opposite Scylla, which almost sank Odysseus's fleet. Scylla, meanwhile, was a nymph who was turned into a sea monster by Amphitrite.
18 Birger Forell.

1934

CHRONOLOGY

4 January:	Müller imposes the Aryan Paragraph on the church in Prussia and forbids references to the church conflict in sermons, books or pamphlets. Those who resist face suspension and the withholding of one-third of their income.
7 January:	A protest by the Pastors' Emergency League is read out from pulpits.
13 January:	Minister Rust extends Müller's 'muzzling order' of 4 January to the universities.
18 January:	Bell writes again to Müller criticizing the new measures. A copy of the letter is also sent to Hindenburg.
24 January:	Archbishop Lang declares his anxiety about the state of the German church in convocation.
25 January:	Church representatives of all parties meet Hitler. Göring reports on a telephone conversation by Niemöller. The bishops are dismayed by this.
27 January:	The bishops declare their support for Müller and their opposition to the Pastors' Emergency League.
29 January:	The administrative committee of Life and Work meets at Chichester and endorses Bell's letter of 18 January.
30 January:	The Law for the Reconstruction of the Reich is passed.
1 February:	Bell's letter of 18 January is published by the press and supplemented by a resolution by the administrative committee.
8 February:	Bell meets Heckel, Krummacher and Wahl at the Athenaeum Club in London.
19 February:	Synod in the Rhineland adopts the Barmen declaration.
March:	Bishops Wurm and Meiser meet Hitler. They revoke the declaration made by the bishops on 27 January.
March:	Synod of Berlin-Brandenburg.
5 April:	Synod at Dortmund claims to establish the constitutional church of Westphalia, a 'Confessional Church' led by Praeses Koch.

13 April:	Müller annuls orders of 4 January.
19 April:	Jäger is appointed legal member of the Spiritual Ministry and head of the church chancery. Müller now makes efforts to incorporate more churches into the *Reichskirche*.
20 April:	Himmler is appointed inspector of the *Gestapo*.
22 April:	Ulm conference. Leaders of the Confessing Church declare themselves to represent the constitutional 'Evangelical Church of Germany'.
May:	Bishop Bell and J.H. Oldham prepare a new public protest at developments in the German church with the support of Archbishop Lang.
10 May:	Bell issues an Ascension Day message to the churches declaring his concern for the Evangelical church in Germany.
16 May:	The *Times* publishes a letter by Archbishop Lang protesting against the defamation of the Jewish people by the National Socialist paper *Der Stürmer*.
29–31 May:	Synod of the Confessing Church at Barmen, attended by representatives of nineteen provincial churches. The creation of the 'Council of Brethren'.
7 June:	The upper and lower houses of convocation debate the crisis in the German protestant churches and pass motions prepared by Bishop Bell and his dean, Duncan-Jones.
17 June:	Former Chancellor Franz von Papen criticizes the Hitler government in a public speech at Marburg.
22 June:	The second report of the Council on Foreign Relations is submitted to the Church Assembly.
30 June:	The S.A. is purged in the 'Night of the long knives'.
18 July:	Jäger and Müller meet Hitler. 22 out of 28 churches are now a part of the new *Reichskirche*.
1 August:	The offices of president and chancellor of Germany are combined.
2 August:	President Hindenburg dies. The *Reichswehr* swears loyalty to Hitler.
9 August:	The second national synod in Berlin. Müller assumes greater powers from the synod and orders a new oath of allegiance to the German Evangelical Church for pastors and church officials. The churches of Hanover, Württemberg and Bavaria are incorporated into the new *Reichskirche*.
19 August:	Hitler proclaims himself Führer and Reich chancellor.

24 August:	The situation in Germany is discussed by the conference of the Council of Life and Work at Fanö. At a private session Heckel is cross-examined on the coercive measures taken against Confessing pastors. News is leaked to the *New York Times*. Heckel is replaced by a new representative, Birnbaum. The conference passes a number of resolutions on German affairs, one of them expressing 'grave anxiety' that 'vital principles of Christian liberty should be endangered or compromised at the present time in the life of the German Evangelical Church'. The conference concludes Bell's chairmanship of the Council.
September:	Müller orders the dismissal of Aryan pastors who are married to non-Aryan women.
2 September:	Müller refutes the declarations made by the council of the Life and Work movement at Fanö.
September:	Bishops Wurm and Meiser resist incorporation and receive strong popular support.
19 September:	Müller addresses a gathering at Hanover and affirms Hitler's wish to preserve the rights of the church.
22–23 September:	The national synod meets. Müller is installed as *Reichsbischof*.
October:	Bell and Oldham continue to build international support for their new plan of protest. It will now become a co-ordinated, public *demarchement* by the heads of the protestant churches of England, Sweden, Norway, Denmark, Finland, France, Switzerland and Holland.
20 October:	Confessing synod at Dahlem. The Council of Brethren is formed to lead the church, and an executive inner council.
26 October:	Jäger resigns. Müller appoints a council of bishops to replace him.
28 October:	Jäger's acts in Bavaria are ruled illegal by the court.
30 October:	The bishops meet Hitler who declares that he washes his hands of the dispute.
6–7 November:	Minister of the Interior Frick prohibits discussion of church questions in the press or other literature.
8 November:	The Confessing Church demonstrates against Müller in Berlin.
18 November:	Müller refuses to stand down.
20 November:	Müller repeals his own law of enforcement.
22 November:	Leaders of the Confessing Church form a 'Provisional Church Council'.

25 November:	Müller rescinds all orders given since January.
26 November:	Karl Barth is suspended from his chair at Bonn for refusing to take the oath of loyalty.
December:	Archbishop Lang and Bishop Bell make their concern for the German church clear through the London and Berlin embassies.
21 December:	Barth is dismissed by a disciplinary court.
December:	Frick reissues his decrees of November.

1934

1 BISHOP BATTY TO ARCHBISHOP LANG, 6 JANUARY 1934

My dear Archbishop,

Pray excuse the delay in sending you a report of my recent visit to Germany. I was anxious that our ambassador[1] should see it before I sent it to you in order that he might correct any inaccuracy.

I am confident that the Pastors who wish to preserve the liberty and faith of the Lutheran Church will win the day.

Yours very sincerely and dutifully

Staunton Fulham

2 REPORT ON A VISIT TO GERMANY, BY BISHOP BATTY, DECEMBER 1933

Since writing this report the Emergency League have shown a desire to get rid of Reichs Bishop Müller owing no doubt to his inability to form a strong 'ministerium'.

S.F.

Report on the situation in the German Church
for the use of His Grace the Archbishop of Canterbury only.

When I arrived in Berlin I was informed that the enthronement of Reichs Bishop Müller fixed for Sunday, Dec. 3rd had been postponed. This was no doubt due to the controversy which had arisen after the Sports Palast meeting. Some months ago I warned the Council on Foreign Relations that the extreme section of German Christian party was demanding the elimination of the Old Testament and was attacking the Jewish ancestry of Our Lord, their aim being a national religion based on Teutonic mythology. Dr. Krause in a fiery speech at the meeting revealed the policy of this section. Bishop Hossenfelder was present at this meeting but it is stated that he left before Dr. Krause spoke. The Emergency League immediately demanded the resignation of Bishop Hossenfelder. This request was met by the dissolution of the 'ministerium', a council of four appointed by the Reichs Bishop to advise him on all matters and the report that reached us in November that Bishop Hossenfelder had resigned was not quite accurate. He ceased to be a member of the 'ministerium' on its dissolution as did the other members but he retained the bishopric of Brandenburg and the Presidency of the Prussian Church Union. Since my return to England it is reported that he has resigned these positions. I believe this to be for the good of the German Church. I formed an unfavourable opinion of him when we met in London and there is little doubt but that he supported the policy of the extreme

---

1 The British ambassador was Sir Eric Phipps. He had succeeded Sir Horace Rumbold in 1933.

section of the German Christians. I had a long conversation with Dr. Niemöller the organising director of the Emergency League. This League is strong spiritually and intellectually and I believe will save the German Church. As a result of the Sports Palast meeting most university professors have left the German Christians and have joined the League. There is also definite spirituality in its aims and as far as I could judge it is the only organisation in the conflict possessing spiritual and intellectual capacity. The ultimate victory seems assured.

I also had a long conversation with Dr. Karow, bishop of Berlin, a convinced Nazi and a German Christian, but not a sympathizer with the extreme section. He assured me that the majority of German Christians would remain faithful to the Augsburg Confession.[2] As regards the membership of the Church the Aryan clause was practically dead, but on my pressing him he admitted that it would be enforced by the German Christians with regard to the ministry.

There would be no law passed to this effect but the regulations would be framed to preclude non-Aryans on the ground that they could not take the university courses demanded by the church as necessary. I asked him his attitude towards the League, and his reply was:- 'We shall fight them.' He summed up his policy as 'Unity in the Church for the sake of Unity in the Nation.' I saw others in Berlin, including Dr. Deissmann, and on leaving Berlin I met interesting men in Southern Germany. All they told me strengthened my view that the Emergency League will win the day.

The Aryan Clause appeared to be in suspense after it had been applied with severity earlier in the year. I believe this to be due to the representations made from outside Germany, and especially the letter from the Bishop of Gloucester to Reichs Bishop Müller. The latter is in a difficult position as he is being urged forward by the German Christians and evidently has an intelligent appreciation of the power behind the Emergency League. Under the circumstances it was perhaps politic for him not to see me. He had accepted an invitation to dine at the embassy during my visit and postponed an important meeting of bishops in order to do so but in the meantime events proceeded very rapidly. His enthronement on Dec. 3rd was postponed and his position generally was insecure. On the day he was to meet me he sent a message to the embassy that urgent matters demanded his attention in Dresden and that he could not return until midnight. On his return I offered to see him the following morning but the reply was that he was in bed with a fever. I have since received a very cordial letter from him expressing his great regret and the hope that we may soon meet. I do not think he could have added to my information as the moment was a very delicate one.

I enquired into the relations between Reichs Bishop Müller and the Emergency League. Dr. Niemöller told me and others confirm this, that the time was inopportune for another election. The league would not therefore object to Dr. Müller provided he had a strong ministerium or cabinet to advise him. Such a combination might bring some peace. I went closely into the reports which had reached

2 The great statement of faith of the German Reformation, the Augsburg Confession of 1530 defines in twenty-one articles the fundamental doctrines of the Lutheran church. Philip Melanchthon was its principal author, while Luther himself approved it and submitted the document to the Emperor Charles V at Augsburg on 25 June 1530.

us of German Pastors being sent to Concentration Camps on religious grounds. I could not find any confirmation of these reports. Some cases had occurred of disciplinary action of rather a mild character against Pastors who had publicly protested against the presence of German Christian leaders at the Sports Palast Meeting but the sentences were quite trivial – such as one day's suspension. The one definite case I produced appeared to be more of a political than ecclesiastical nature. There is little doubt that Pastors have been removed from their posts by their Church Councils and much hardship has been inflicted in this way. This appears to have been done by Church Councils dominated by German Christians who had little care for the spiritual life of the respective parishes and wished the pulpits to be used for Nazi propaganda.

To sum the matter up I believe the Emergency League containing as it does the best elements in the Lutheran Church to-day will ultimately win a victory and symptoms we deplore will disappear. I do not think the Church of England can usefully take any official action at the moment. It is well known that we are anxiously watching the situation and are prepared to offer any encouragement we can to those who are striving to preserve Orthodox Christian Belief.

I do not think it advisable to go further than this. I was struck by the number of societies with high-sounding titles and imposing lists of patrons, etc. who apparently are sending resolutions, not always wisely worded, to the authorities of the German Church. It is conceivable that foreigners might attribute an official character to such communications. I think it important that some intimation should be given that official communications which have Your Grace's approval should go only through well-defined channels. Possibly I might be allowed to amplify this if Your Grace can spare the time for a short interview. I wish to recommend also that as this crisis in the German Church has a definite political aspect we should keep in close touch with the Foreign Office and our Embassy. I wish to acknowledge the kindness of our ambassador, who made it easy for me to gain much useful information. I also wish to record my satisfaction with the work done by the Rev. R. Cragg, our chaplain in Berlin. We are fortunate in being represented at Berlin by a chaplain of such sound judgement and discretion, upon whose reports we can place reliance.

Staunton Fulham
December 1933

3   ARCHBISHOP LANG TO BISHOP BATTY, 9 JANUARY 1934

My dear Bishop,

Let me send you a word of very cordial thanks for the report of your recent visit to Germany which you have sent to me. I have read it with the greatest interest. Of course since it was written a great deal has happened in the ever changing circumstances of the German Church. But your comments and reports of your interviews with many important persons enable one to realise very clearly the main issues which are at stake. It is quite clear to me that things have not reached any such stage in this conflict as to make any official relations between myself and the Church of England and the Church in Germany possible. We must await events. I would much like to have some talk with you on the matter and as soon as some of my heavy engagements are more clear. I will write and suggest a time. Meanwhile will you kindly let me know, if only on a post-card, how long you are likely to be in England?

Yours very sincerely

Cosmo Cantuar

4 MEMORANDUM BY BISHOP BATTY, FEBRUARY 1934

STRICTLY CONFIDENTIAL
THE CHURCH OF ENGLAND
COUNCIL ON FOREIGN RELATIONS.

————

THE GERMAN CRISIS.
By the Bishop of Fulham.

————

Before Christmas 1933. Issued Feb 1934 [Note by Bishop Bell]

The necessity for reporting on the crisis in the German Church has been obviated by the accurate accounts issued almost daily in the '*Times*'. I had an interview with the '*Times*' Correspondent in Berlin and found him well in touch with the situation. I have also seen Mr. Geoffrey Dawson who tells me that he has sent out an excellent assistant correspondent and we can rely upon the '*Times*' to keep us fully and accurately informed.

During my visit to Germany in December I had long interviews with Dr. Niemöller, Dr. Karow the German Christian Bishop of Berlin, Dr. Deissmann and many others. I also interviewed bishops and university professors of theology in other parts of Germany. Dr. Müller accepted an invitation to dine at the Embassy to meet me, but on the day was summoned to Dresden.

The German Christian leaders appeared anxious to assure me that they were faithful to the Augsburg Confession and repudiated the kind of teaching fore-shadowed at the Sports Palast Meeting. The Emergency League, on the other hand, looked upon the Sports Palast Meeting as a definite declaration of German Christian hopes and aspirations.

When I left Germany just before Christmas, the Emergency League, very ably led by Dr. Niemöller, was gaining ground, but since then a remarkable change has taken place. General Goering has apparently persuaded the Chancellor that the 6000 pastors and others who compose the Emergency League are a menace to the State and strong action has been taken against them, including a threat to confiscate their stipends. Dr. Niemöller was arrested but was released on his promise to report to the police daily.

The German Christians are therefore in power at the moment but I cannot believe that they will retain their position. They rely upon such force as the State can exact whilst the others are supported by spirituality and intellectual power. The struggle may be a long one but I have no doubt as to the ultimate issue.

In the meantime, taking advantage of the confusion in the Lutheran Church, a movement called the 'German Faith Movement' 'Deutsche Glaubens-bewegung' is gaining some ground under the leadership of Count Revent-low. It makes a facile appeal to the ethical idea and comes at a time when many are tired of the disputes within the Church. It is a movement which should be watched. The following extracts from a press report of a speech

by Count Reventlow will give some indication of the aims of the Movement:-
The lecturer said that he had often been asked why the movement called
itself a Faith movement. The answer is that it contains a religious element.
It is belief as opposed to criticism. The longing to know, he said, is very
strong in Germany to-day. The longing to believe is equally strong. The
movement is a longing for Faith itself. It contrasts with Nietzsche and the
materialists.

The great masses alienated from the Church say 'only what we see is real'.
The movement on the other hand believes that there is something real behind
everything.

The religious element is to be found in each individual. The movement
seeks to cultivate a feeling of responsibility each for himself.

On the question of REDEMPTION.
'On the teaching of redemption we differ from the Christian teaching in that
we are unable to accept the idea of inherited sin and the Sacrifice of Christ.'

'We do not say we redeem ourselves, that too is impossible. We strive to
attain the highest. Redemption in the Christian sense is not possible to imagine
or even to wish for. Conscience or that feeling of responsibility, or that
longing for higher things joins us to THE GREAT UNKNOWN.

WHY CALLED GERMANIC FAITH MOVEMENT.
It is absurd to think that we wish to revive the worship of the pagan
deities. It is equally absurd though that history should be misread as Cardinal
Faulhaber misreads. (A sermon attacking the movement preached for the New
Year). He (the Cardinal) misreads his Tacitus when he says that the ancient
Germanic peoples had no culture.[3] He should note this passage: 'Their conception of deities does allow them to enclose them within walls and make images
of them with human features but woods and groves are their temples where
they implore the unknown power by the names of their gods, which power
reveals himself to them in worship alone.'[4] This passage, said the lecturer,
is the germ of the whole. Real religion has no form.

IDEA OF SIN.
When we read the Christian confessions we cannot see what sin is. The
Bible says that sin is an offence against God (Jahwe). The Church has taken
over the Hebrew idea of sin. This is quite alien to the movement. Our German
forefathers had the feeling of "Schuld" "Guilt" which had to be made good.

THE MOVEMENT AND A CONFESSION OF FAITH.
Germans dislike dogma in their hearts. Fewer and fewer Germans can
accept the forms laid down by the Church for religion. They are not to blame,
the fault lies in the form which is foreign to German character. The movement

3 In Dec. 1933 Cardinal Faulhaber preached a series of sermons on the Old Testament at St Michael's
Church in Munich. In the last sermon, on new year's eve, he used the Roman historian Tacitus
to show how Christianity had civilized what had hitherto been a base German culture.
4 See Tacitus, *Germania*, trans. H. Mattingly and S.A. Handford (London, 1970), part IX, pp.
108–9.

would never dissuade a Christian from belief. It would use no pressure, as do Jews and Christians. The movement will not draw up a Confession but will give an explanation to the State. The movement is not materialistic. It fights materialism. It makes no use of propaganda. It will have no clerical class. The dislike of pastors is growing in Germany (loud applause).

THE MOVEMENT AND THE CHURCH.

There is bitter opposition on the part of the Church. The Church ought to welcome the movement as a Faith movement. Our opponents say we do not believe in God. What we call GOD is too high for us to conceive and beyond our comprehension. We cannot give him human attributes. The movement has never nor will ever attack Christian Confession. The opponents also declare that the movement looks upon 'RACE AND BLOOD' as God. This is absurd. Race and Blood are not God but God given forms for the true development of man. All that goes back to nature and is therefore real is soil for the development of man.

The Lecture was crowded and to judge from the *Reichswart* the official organ of the movement, it is spreading rapidly. Branches have been formed at Göttingen and Hanover.

5   MEMORANDUM BY BISHOP BELL, 9 FEBRUARY 1934

GERMAN EVANGELICAL CHURCH

(Dr. Heckel
Interview with (Dr. Krummacher
(Dr. Wahl
February 9th, 1934.

They came first to the Athenaeum[5] at 10 o' clock and we talked for nearly two hours. There was then an adjournment and we met again at 5.30 at the Church House[6] and had another two hours.

They gave me a general resume of the situation starting with the Meeting at the Sport-Palace, Berlin, November 13th, 1933. Immediately after that Meeting, Bishop Müller made a statement denouncing what had been said against the Bible etc., and Dr. Krause was deprived of his post. It was not clear what was the attitude of some of the German Christian Bishops, Heckel said — whether they were present, or if present approved. Bishop Hossenfelder's position was very delicate. The delay in dismissing him was due to Hossenfelder's political relations, as he had done much for the National Socialist Party. He was however dismissed by Christmas.

After the Sport-Palace Meeting, negotiations took place with the Pastors' Emergency League. Bishop Müller tried to form a Cabinet. Niemöller was offered a post but refused on the ground that he did not want his opposition to be regarded as giving him prizes in the Church. This refusal of Niemöller was,

5 The *Athenaeum* was, and remains, a gentleman's club, situated in Pall Mall, London.
6 Church House, Westminster. This was, and remains, the administrative heart of the Church of England. It is situated beside Westminster Abbey.

Heckel said, a great blunder in statesmanship. His description of Niemöller was interesting – that he was a good mariner but had not the qualifications for an admiral. He also said that the Pastors' Emergency League and the opposition generally showed little signs of statesmanship. When one opposes one ought to have a view as to the kind of Church or Government one wants, and Heckel thought that the opposition had not got any clear programme about this. Another good man refused to join the Cabinet, viz. Künneth, on the ground that he could not get the support of the South German Bishops. But by these two refusals the decisive chance for influencing the whole future of the Church was given away. The German Christians were then dissolving. The Sport-Palace Meeting had given a great shock.

The Reichbishop then formed a Moderate Cabinet, but the Lutheran representative was not included. I gather there was a good deal of indecision on the part of the Lutheran representative or those nominating him. This Cabinet revoked the Aryan paragraph and also appointed a Conciliation Committee. The revokation of the Aryan Paragraph was not considered as sufficiently satisfactory by the opposition Bishops on juridical grounds because the Cabinet was not legally constituted. This seemed to Heckel rather a pedantic line to take which betrayed weakness on the part of the opposition. The revokation was of course very decisively opposed by the German Christians.

Then came the Youth question. The Youth leaders and the opposition joined forces and the opposition became increasingly radical and issued an ultimatum demanding the retirement of the Reichbishop. The ultimatum however had the effect of strengthening the German Christian party. On January 4th the Reichbishop issued Emergency Decrees to help in his discipline of the Church and enabling him to move pastors. His purpose was to call attention to the danger of sundering the Church, and actually to unite the Church and recall the Clergy to their chief tasks, which were spiritual. The Reichbishop, according to Heckel, maintained that the Pastors' Emergency League members were giving their attention to Church politics and not to their proper spiritual work.

There did not seem to be any way out of this tangle except through the help of the State. Indeed an appeal was made to the State from both sides, though Heckel would say somewhat inconsistently on the part of the Emergency League. The League and the South German Bishops were in strong contact with the State through Frick, and of course the Reichbishop was also approaching the State.

The next step was an announcement in the Press that Hitler would receive the Reichbishop. This led at once to a demand on the part of the opposition that they should be received. This, said Heckel, was a bad move on the part of the opposition. If they were to see Hitler they should have seen him independently and have got time to put their case to him. Hitler could not see the opposition's point in so short a time. It was too fine a point – too theological. This was the impression that Heckel gave me, though not Heckel's words.

At the conference with Hitler, attended by the Reichbishop and representatives of both sides, General Göring came in with a report from the secret police. What had happened was this. Niemöller had been overheard talking on the telephone to a friend and saying of Hitler, as he was about to go to Hindenburg, 'Now the Chancellor is receiving extreme unction from Hindenburg'. Further, that a memorandum was to be given to Hitler by Hindenburg, Hitler being in an ante-room and receiving the memorandum as orders which had to be obeyed.

This note was read at the conference and Hitler asked Niemöller whether it was true. Niemöller had to say yes. Hitler pointed out that such remarks were intended to cause division between him and Hindenburg, and forbade the placing of barriers between Hindenburg and himself. What was wanted was the strengthening of authority, not the making of cleavages. Hitler probably thought that the Pastors' Emergency League included reactionaries in the political sense. In his speech, Hitler had two points – (1) The German Evangelical Church is young. Our foremost interest is to strengthen the Church and therefore we must strengthen the authority of the office of the Reichbishop. (2) Hitler's deep regret that the Evangelical Church had not gained a great deal more influence when they had a remarkable opportunity of gaining influence in view of the awkward situation of the Roman Catholic Church.

Viewing matters as Hitler did, Hitler was inclined to look upon the controversies between the Reichbishop and the Pastors' Emergency League as controversies about trifles, 'talks about genealogies' and such like. Everybody was asked his opinion in the conference, one by one. In the result Hitler pressed upon the members of the conference that the important thing was to finish the struggle in the Church and to strengthen the institution. The foremost question is how to frame an organisation of the *whole* Church. All taxes go to the Reich Church and the single Churches are financially and in other ways powerless as they are. A stronger contact between the Church and State was necessary for the reorganisation of the Church and State. Therefore, Heckel told me, it would be necessary to find a special Minister for Evangelical Church affairs (I pointed out the difficulty which the appointment of a special Minister of State for the Evangelical Church was likely to cause in view of what had happened and the danger of control and Church subordination.)

After the conference with Hitler, Niemöller put out a report of his own to the effect that the opposition would continue. This was rather resented.

On January 27th an official declaration was issued by the Bishops unanimously deciding to support the Reichbishop. The discussion lasted five hours. There were three elements leading to the unanimous declaration:-

(1) The strong impression received by the Bishops of the personal attitude of Hitler to the Church, and that he was much more related to the Evangelical than the Roman Church. Hindenburg and other personalities, especially Frick and Neurath, were very anxious also for peace in the Church.

(2) The German Christian bishops brought forward a motion that the Aryan paragraph should be given up, and this was adopted unanimously. (This statement was made to me privately and in confidence, but the Reichbishop had charged Heckel to assure me that there was no ground for – further anxiety with regard to the Aryan paragraph.)

(3) The Reichbishop promised to form a proper Cabinet. The important Bishops on the side of the opposition were apparently Meiser of Bavaria and Wurm of Württemberg, and of course there was the much respected Marahrens of Hanover. Meiser and Wurm however, it seemed, were of a rather 'contradictory' disposition. They were both against Bodelschwingh as they were also now, up till this moment, against Müller. With the surrender of the bishops, the Pastors' Emergency League can no longer act. The question is whether it will survive and whether it will continue on political or on spiritual lines. It had no political foresight and was not constructive. When I asked whether the opposition pastors

would be allowed to form a Free Church, the answer was that it might be possible but that it was not likely and the prospects were not hopeful, and that in Bavaria it was impossible. A great part of the German people would be entirely unable to understand the notion of a Free Church.

With regard to the attitude of Life and Work and myself, Heckel said that what they would like would be theological discussions in Life and Work on various points at issue. Oecumenical resolutions endangered the unity of the Church, and also (he said) hurt rather than helped the Opposition. Oecumenical relations were a great strength to the German Church and they would be very sorry to lose them, though Heckel and his friends sometimes had considerable difficulties in preserving them in face of the opposition to interference from foreign Churches by many of the Church authorities in Germany. They said that they did not want manifestoes or letters publicly exchanged in the press. And if Bishop Müller were to reply to my last letter he would be rather sharp[7]: and they wished to avoid this. They were very anxious that I should promise to keep silence. I said that it was not possible to make such a promise without any regard to what might happen in Germany. I said that I would not speak except with a real sense of responsibility and after taking care, but that an unqualified promise was impossible. Heckel said that often the authorities in the German Church did not realise what the points are which are felt as dangerous outside Germany, and that they would be glad to have those points indicated to them privately. What, for example, is meant by dictatorship? I pointed out what appeared to be the autocracy of the Reichbishop and his ability to make decrees and suspend them at his will. They pointed out that these were 'emergency decrees' and it seemed to them that that made a real difference. I also asked about the secret police. Göring is a Protestant and seeing that Hitler is a Catholic, he (Göring) likes to assume to himself a sort of position of patron for the Evangelical Church. He was a strong supporter of Hossenfelder, a point which had made dealing with Hossenfelder after the meeting at the Sport-Palace rather difficult. He and Bishop Müller had not seen eye to eye altogether. Bishop Müller had tried to be tactical, hence his complimentary telegram on Göring's birthday and, to a certain extent, his flattery of Göring.

When I asked about Bodelschwingh they said he was free. The best of the Bishops is Marahrens – altogether the best I gathered from what they said, and a man that they would personally prefer to everybody as Reichbishop. But they did not say so, in so many words. They remarked that the Germans were not so ready to speak about foreign Churches as foreign Churches were to speak about them! One very important statement was made. Heckel said that the foreign Churches have a clear right to interfere in the case of heresies, but they said that heresy is not involved here – I think this was meant especially with regard to coercion. They suggested that silence for six months would be wise. It was impossible to understand the German Church situation from outside, that during the next few months a period of pacification was to go forward and that when that was over it would be more possible to form a fair judgement.

7 Bell wrote to Müller on 18 Jan. 1934, deploring the new coercive decrees by which Müller sought to impose his authority on the church. He also sent a copy of the letter to President von Hindenburg. On 29 Jan. the administrative committee of Life and Work met at Chichester and endorsed the letter.

Two further statements:

(1) Heckel is to write me a letter with regard to the Aryan paragraph, and I asked him to make it as positive as he could and as permanent in its effects, so that I might, at my discretion, communicate it to other Churches. This they were anxious I should do, but I said whether I could or not would depend on what such a letter contained.[8]

(2) They then asked for a statement to the Press. They submitted a draft which stated that it was agreed that the *task* of the oecumenical movement was to discuss theological questions. I could not accept this and ultimately agreed on the following form:-

'The Bishop of Chichester on Friday received representatives of the German Evangelical Church in London.

In connexion with the correspondence which has passed during the last month between the Reichbishop and the Bishop of Chichester as President of the Universal Christian Council for Life and Work, it was agreed to promote a common study in a frank and brotherly spirit of various problems now before the Churches, including the investigation of the religious and theological principles involved, under the auspices of the Universal Christian Council.'

In the course of my conversation I gave Heckel a paper containing six points, as points which gave great anxiety to foreign Churches. He took them and said that he would write to me fully with regard to them when he got back to Berlin. The points are as follows:-

1. The prohibition of opposition to actions or decrees objectionable on spiritual grounds.

2. The power taken by the Reichbishop to abolish posts, enact or suspend, at his simple unfettered discretion.

3. The use of the police to help the suppression of opponents.

4. The dismissal of pastors because of their opposition to a German Christian policy.

5. The putting of State considerations above religious considerations, and especially above the principle of the freedom of the Gospel.

6. The grave danger of the Church being used as the instrument of the National Socialist Party; and being absorbed by the State.

G.C.

6 BISHOP BATTY TO BISHOP BELL, 16 FEBRUARY 1934

My dear Bishop,

I shall be most grateful if you will keep me in touch with the efforts your Council is making to help our brethren in Germany. I am doing all I can personally to bring home to Müller and the others the real grief we feel in the C[hurch] of E[ngland] at the reports which reach us.

It will help me to know what others are doing.

Yours very sincerely

Staunton Fulham

---

8 Heckel's letter to Bell, dated 21 Feb. 1934, pleaded that the bishop should cease his interference in German church affairs, and argued that Bell's letters to the *Times* did harm to those he sought to support.

7   MEMORANDUM BY ARCHBISHOP LANG, 1 MAY 1934

GERMAN EVANGELICAL CHURCH

I saw Dr. 't Hooft, General Secretary of the Student Christian Movement, at Lambeth on May 1st 1934. He pressed the importance of the opposition meeting which had been held at Ulm ten days ago. The Bishop of Bavaria on behalf of the Free Synods of Westphalia, Rhineland, Württemberg, Baden, and Bavaria had definitely decided not to support the *Reichsbischof*. This position is also taken by the bishops of Württemberg and Baden and represents a considerable unification of the opposition. Dr. 't Hooft thinks it probable that the issue will be either two main blocks in separation of Western and Eastern Germany or that the Government may interfere and treat all in opposition as enemies of the State. He thinks this is quite possible and regards Dr. Jaeger's close association with General Göring as sinister. He considers that it would be (to use his words) a tragedy if at the present time any contact with the *Reichsbischof* should be made as this would be exploited against all who care for a free and non-political church. It must be remembered that Müller is still a patron of the German Christians. He wished that there could be some expression of sympathy with the principles for which the opposition was contending.

    With regard to what Chichester said about Dr. 't Hooft assisting in the draft of any pronouncement after the conference of May 14th,[9] Dr. 't Hooft would be again in London at the end of May, and the usual address of the Student Christian Movement would find him.
C.C.

8   DEAN BATE TO BISHOP BELL, 4 JUNE 1934

My dear Bishop,

    I hope to be able to send with this letter a large part of my report from Berlin. I am going on to complete the sketch of my impressions at the Hermsdorf discussions, and will send you this further matter in a day or two: but since the Archbp. of Canterbury, whom I saw last week, has asked me to let him have something written before the meeting of Convocation, it seemed only proper to hurry forward & try to put something, however imperfect, in your hands at the same time.

    The Archbp. of York is coming here for a conversation tomorrow, and I will see that a copy of my type-script is given to him.

    The declarations of Barmen are indeed *stimuli et clavi*:[10] they challenge the very essence of Deutscher Xtentum at every point. I have pro-Nazi pamphlets by professing Lutherans which exemplify to the full every 'heresy' which is denounced. I was stupid enough not to bring back what Gogarten has written on that side, as a strict Lutheran, but I am sending for it now.
Ever yours sincerely
H.N. Bate

---

9 The council of Life and Work was to meet at Fanö in Denmark in Aug. 1934
10 A stimulus and a key.

9   REPORT ON A VISIT TO GERMANY BY H.N. BATE, 21-6 MAY 1934

Report on a Visit to Germany by H.N. Bate,
May 21 – 26, 1934.

1. *Theological discussions at Hermsdorf*

The conversations between Roman Catholic and Lutheran theologians, continuing and enlarging those of a smaller group at Marburg, took place, by the kindness of the Roman Bishop of Berlin at his diocesan seminary in Hermsdorf, a northern suburb of Berlin. I was given to understand that they were arranged with the approval of the Papal Nuncio.[11] The Bishop, Dr. Bares, did not appear in person; but both he and the Principal of the Seminary had made generous arrangements for the comfort of those who took part in the proceedings. We were provided with meals, which we all took together, from morning till late evening, and the contribution which we were permitted to make can hardly have covered the cost of such generous entertainment; half of the spacious building in which the Seminary is housed was given to us, together with the freedom of the garden, for rest & conversation; in every way we were treated most generously as welcome guests.

Our Chairman throughout was Dr. Paul Simon, Dompropst of Paderborn, a clear-minded, quiet priest, full of wisdom and kindliness. With him on the Roman side were two of the leading priests of the Hedwigskirche in Berlin, Domkapitular Mgr. Dr. Banasch and Domvikar Dr. Prange; Dr. Parsch of Klosterneuberg near Vienna (the only Austrian present), Dr. Pinsk, editor of *Liturgisches Leben*, Dr. Grosche of Vochem near Cologne, Professor Romano Guardini, who teaches and supervises Roman students in the University of Berlin – a layman of most notable intellectual and spiritual power – Herr Rosenmüller, also a layman, teaching at Münster, Pater Winzer of Maria-Laach, Professor Koch, an acute Canonist from Breslau, and Dr. Max Pribilla S.J. of Munich, who edits *Stimmen der Zeit* and has written copiously on the problems of Reunion. Nearly all of these, – I cannot speak with accuracy about Pribilla and Grosche – have in common a keen interest in the Liturgical movement, to which Dr. Prinsk and Pater Winzer are making contributions of very great value. I was profoundly impressed by the clarity and earnestness of their thinking; a more able group, and a more attractive one, it would be hard to imagine; their courtesy also, and their candid good humour in discussion, were alike admirable.

On the Protestant side there were present Dr. Heiler, Professor in Marburg, but now *versetzt*, i.e. under an indefinite sentence of removal, Pf. Ritter, also of Marburg, a real prophet of Lutheran 'hoch-kirchlich'[12] ideals, and his valiant supporter Dr. Stählin of Münster; to these three, as also to Frau Paula Schäfer, everything that was said from the standpoint of the Liturgical Movement was obviously most welcome. With them, however, were representatives of Lutheran orthodoxy in the more widely-accepted form; Pf. Beta of Oschersleben, and Pf. Schulz of Barmen, a man of wonderful gifts as a speaker and a popular leader,

11 Monsignore Cesare Orsenigo.
12 High church. In the Anglican world the high church tradition identifies a movement which has strong liturgical affinities with the Roman Catholic Church. Its use here to describe German Lutherans is striking, and it possibly arises because of the movement within German Lutheranism to create bishops.

who has just carried through the organization of the Confessional Synod for the whole of Germany at Barmen. With these, and one or two more whose names do not appear in my notes, were two representatives of the Church of Sweden, the Pastor of the Swedish Church in Berlin, Herr Birger Forell, and Professor Nygren of Lund. Nygren, Stählin and Ritter stand out beyond all the rest, in my recollection, as the most effective spokesmen for the varieties of Lutheran opinion. Heiler was on one or two occasions quite first-rate; but his position is (as is well-known) somewhat embarrassed, and this made itself felt in much of what he was able to say. As compared with the steady acuteness of Nygren, and the impassioned directness of Ritter, his interventions in debate were not completely effective. Yet on the whole, from very various angles, the Lutheran case was stated & argued with complete frankness, with astonishing dialectical skill, and with unclouded charity.

I was present as a guest at all the discussions except one, and Mr. Cragg, our Embassy Chaplain, whose kindness to me was invaluable, was with us three times. I was urged once or twice to speak as an Anglican, and I did venture to intervene at times with a question; but apart from one comparatively short speech I thought it best to leave the discussions to take their natural form as the exposition of two main divergent streams of thought, without bringing into the arena a 'third confession', so to say, and attracting attention to the commonsense syntheses which are congenial to the Anglican mind. I was all the more disposed to keep in the background because so many points were raised to which an Anglican (of any description) could not give any impartial answer, but must needs say 'our judgement here goes entirely with that of our Roman brethren.'

The first discussion was prefaced by a word or two from Banasch and Heiler. Banasch laid stress on the completely non-political character of the gathering; Heiler explained its origin in an address given by Guardini to the students of Marburg, and took occasion to develop the view that since the Confession of Augsburg was meant to be an *eirenikon*,[13] the quest for unity lies at the heart of Lutheranism in its undegenerate form.

Dr. Parsch and Pf. Beta then introduced the subject of Catholic and Evangelical 'Frommigkeit' or εὐσέβεια.[14] The former spoke very simply of the Church as the home in which faith, life eternal, grace and duty are the leading notes, of its function as the Christ-bearer, and of the normal Christian life which beats in unison with the Church's rhythm; of the hindrances which scholasticism and casuistry have opposed to the realisation of this ideal, of the wrong perspective in which popular devotion has placed it, and of the liturgical movement as a return to its true simplicity. Pf. Beta, on the other hand, soon lost sight of the theme in an abstract exposition of Justification and Grace; he failed to tell us what evangelical piety really is, but intimated that it regarded the Catholic life as too much externalized in a mechanism of means of grace.

Stählin then tried to bring us back to the subject, putting the questions – as Guardini also did, but without adequate response – 'what is it that makes the average Protestant glad that he is not a Catholic?' and 'if there is one heart in Protestantism or its opposite, how is that heart related to underlying dogmatic principle?' Naturally, discussion ranged then round externality – in fact and

13 A proposal tending to reconcile differences.
14 Spirituality, piousness or devoutness.

Sacrament – and the nature of belief. Ritter asked whether Catholicism was in fact content with a merely formal submissive assent to an institution, – the obvious answer was given – and the Lutherans agreed on their side that in a 'theology of the Word' they would embrace every mode of the Divine self-expression, alike in fact and in book and in Sacrament.

This rather wandering conversation was filled out admirably late in the following day by Heiler, who depicted the inner life of Catholic and Protestant, and the subjective and objective elements in each, much as he has done in his *Katholizismus*.[15]

The second day was given to the crucial subject of Grace and justification, Nygren opening for the Lutherans and Koch for the Catholics.

Nygren, whose address was full of the thoughts which he has developed in *Eros and Agape*,[16] made the point that the supreme concern of Christian religion and theology is to be theo-centric and not ego-centric. He held that the term 'justification' comes indeed from an ego-centric *milieu*; but that it was purged of this taint by St. Paul, to whom early Catholic thought and worship were in that respect faithful; while later, e.g. in Augustine's doctrine of *caritas*,[17] elements derived from the Pagan Eros and not from the Christian Agape of God crept in, and thus the way was opened for the scholastic conception of *fides caritate formata*.[18]

But Nygren would not maintain that the Catholic thought is ego-centric. To him, the *differentia* between Protestantism and Catholicism is that while the latter rests on sanctity imparted, the former is centred upon communion with God on the basis of sin, i.e. as the gift of pure grace; communion in which a man knows himself to be *simul iustus et peccator*,[19] and rests, *sola fide*, not upon his own *caritas* but upon God's *agape*.

Koch's statement was certainly wholly theo-centric. He is a Thomist[20] of distinction, and therefore orderly and clear at all points. The root of grace, in his exposition, is to be found in man's creation for an end, i.e. out of nothing for fellowship with God; that end being frustrated, it can only be realised through a re-creative act, by which, man adding nothing, *ex iniusto fit iustus*.[21] The working of grace is the imparting of super-nature, i.e. not of a new relationship to God but of a new creation.

The cleavage between Koch and Nygren appeared most clearly in Koch's insistence that what the New Testament says about life in Christ, and being risen with Christ cannot be fully squared with *simul iustus et peccator*; that for the Catholic it is not just the act and moment in which God lays hold of a man, but the man's continuous life in and from God which constitutes the notion of grace; while over against the Lutheran fear of mechanical transactions he balanced the thought that (a) it is hard to employ the language of causality without appearing

15 Friedrich Heiler, *Der Katholizmus* (1923). The study considers the early history of the Roman Catholic Church sympathetically, but adopts a more critical view of the Council of Trent (1545–63) and subsequent developments.
16 Anders Nygren, *Eros and agape* (1930).
17 Charity.
18 Faith is formed by charity or love.
19 At the same time a just man and a sinner.
20 i.e. a philosophical disciple of St Thomas Aquinas.
21 By faith alone an unjust man is made just.

to speak in terms of mechanism, while in fact (b) the appropriation of grace belongs entirely to the sphere of will: there is no grace which is not also a task or challenge.

I could not summarize the discussion which ensued. In part it was a Lutheran affair, turning on the question whether Nygren's presentation was not a 'reduced' picture, and whether Luther's own teaching was not in fact far less forensic than that of his *epigoni*.[22] In the end, however, it all came back to the critical phrase *simul iustus et peccator*, which Ritter tried to defend as safeguarding the necessity for 'fear and trembling'. The finest of the Catholic protests came from Winzer; I recall one dilemma of his:- 'either you must deny that grace is a *qualitas inhaerens*,[23] and so become a Barthian, or you must admit that justification is an inner act which takes up the whole man in his moral nature, *facit uelle*,[24] a gift from which a man then lives in spontaneity'.

[To be continued][25]

2. The general situation.

Obviously the remarkable thing in the discussions which I have thus summarized is the fact that they were held at all, that they were begun, continued and ended in kindliness and in the desire for fuller mutual understanding. It must be centuries since such a thing was possible in Germany. That it has been possible now must be due in large measure to the critical situation in which Christianity as a whole now finds itself over there. This was not admitted in so many words at Hermsdorf; the speakers were most careful to steer clear of politics; but in private conversation it became clear that everyone present, Roman and Lutheran alike, was gravely anxious.

The dominant factor in the background of the situation is the logic of the totalitarian state. Day by day the *Völkischer Beobachter*[26] proclaims this doctrine. It is capturing the realm of law: jurists are being summoned to schools in which they are taught that the People's necessities are the only source of legal right -'Recht ist was dem Volke dient.'[27] It must needs claim to dominate religion also. Logically there can only be one Church, as there is one blood, one soil, one *Reich*. Religion can only exist within this one fabric if it is unified as one of its organs, and made subservient to its central idea. That Catholicism can be made the one religion, or be made thus subservient, is obviously out of the question; and the Romans at Hermsdorf were all gravely concerned as to the future attitude of the Reich to the Vatican. Some of them regarded it as not impossible that the Reich would force Catholicism into a position in which the *Concordat* would be denounced, and Rome be represented as an anti-German International. On the other hand, Protestantism (a) cannot be made to acknowledge its subservience without severe measures of compulsion, and (b) cannot be unified for the ends of the State except by external force.

The Government & the Reichsbischof are at the moment concerned with (b). Jäger, who appears to have displaced the very able and acute Oberheid, is pushing

22 Offspring or followers.
23 Inherent quality.
24 Created by the will.
25 No continuation of the report appears to exist in the Lambeth Palace collections.
26 The official newspaper of the National Socialist movement. It was edited by Alfred Rosenberg.
27 Justice is what serves the people.

through the unified constitution which is to bring Protestantism as a whole inside the totalitarian mechanism. But meanwhile the Opposition has succeeded in bringing off a counter-stroke. The movement for local Free Synods has given place to a Bekenntnis-Synode[28] for the whole of Germany. This was being arranged while I was in Berlin, and how it was done without press, post or telephone is a mystery. But it has been done, thanks largely to the fiery zeal of Pf. Schulz;[29] the *Times* has published its declarations, and every one of these ends with an anathema against some element of the totalitarian logic. A more uncompromising defiance could not have been offered to Jäger and the Reichsbischof.

With that defiance, I doubt not, all the Protestants at Hermsdorf would associate themselves, with the determination to carry it through to the end. I have no means for estimating the extent and weight of the adherence which the Barmen Synod will command. But it is important to point out that the forces which will combine in the hope of rendering it futile are many and various.

They are all, in a sense, religious; the 'heresy refuted' in No. 1 of the Barmen declarations underlies them all. On the extreme left wing is the definitely non-Christian force which exalts the German God and him alone; but, allied with this in practice though not in principle, there are many shades of opinion, ranging from left to right, through the *Deutsche Volkskirche* and the *Deutsche Glaubensbewegung* up to the orthodoxy of those who can either equate the totalitarian and the evangelical creeds or endeavour to prove them to be compatible with each other. It is important to realize that among those who write and speak for what is in effect a *Deutsches Christentum* many strictly orthodox Lutherans are to be found, as well as the quasi- and the semi-orthodox. Thus Gogarten is proclaiming that National-Socialism is a 'tutor unto Christ' for Germany; Hirsch, whose Lutheranism is genuine though reduced, would equate the spirit of unquestioning national service with the bearing of the Cross; and Eger, a still more diluted Lutheran, teaches that Lutheranism must abandon either its confessions or its claim to be the German religion. I wish I knew the pamphlet-literature of this type more fully; but from what I know, I judge that semi-Lutheranism is preponderant, i.e. the desire to preserve only a minimum of the evangelical tradition, and to throw over its classical confessional expressions.

It is against this mixed and menacing multitude that Pfarrer Notbund[30] and the Barmen Synod have taken their stand.

Meanwhile, although for the time there has been less overt action against orthodox pastors, no one in the Not-Bund dreams of peace. Professors such as Hermelink and Heiler are being *versetzt*: theological students are being drafted one by one into *Dienstlager*[31] where they will be subject to German-Christian instruction only; those who adhere to orthodoxy (see Mr. Cragg's last memorandum sent to the Council for Foreign Relations[32]) have been refused ordination by the 'Bishop' of Berlin, Eckhart.

28 The synod of the Confessional Church.
29 Pfarrer Georg Schulz wrote the report on the 'Practical Work' of the church for the Barmen synod.
30 The Pastors' Emergency League.
31 Official work camps.
32 Cragg's last memorandum to the Council on Foreign Relations (number 38) was dated 30 May 1934. A copy may be found in Lambeth Palace Library, Bell Papers, 5, fos. 499–50.

In short, the outlook is complex and most disquieting. To measure the forces which give ground for any hopefulness is beyond my power. But it is clear at least that the totalitarian dogma is confronted with the certainty of conflict with an united Catholicism, and of resolute resistance from the, as yet, incalculable body of conviction which was represented at Barmen.
H.N.B.

10   BISHOP BATTY TO ARCHBISHOP LANG, 4 AUGUST 1934

My dear Archbishop,
    You asked me to let you know of any authentic cases of persecution by the State of German Pastors. What is known as the Schwerin Trial of 7 Mecklenburg Pastors is now reported fully in the *Junge Kirche*.[33] They were accused of criticising the State for illegal interference in Church affairs. Terms of imprisonment of 6, 4 & 3 months were inflicted with heavy fines. Other cases will probably follow.
    Pray do not trouble to acknowledge this.
Yours sincerely and dutifully
Staunton Fulham

    The article in the '*Times*' today on the Russian famine bears out much that I heard whilst there.

11   BISHOP BATTY TO BISHOP BELL, 15 AUGUST 1934

My dear Bishop,
    Ebbutt the '*Times*' correspondent brought Dr. Michael, who is the foreign correspondent of the Emergency League to see me today. He told me a sad story of 40 Pastors banished by the police from their parishes. 6 in Frankfurt were imprisoned until they signed an undertaking that they would not enter their parishes again. He feels sure that a strong protest from outside direct to Hitler would secure the dismissal of Müller.
    I have not been very keen on too much interference but all my information points to the fact that in October there will be unification by force and in the words of Jaeger, a subordination of Christian to racial values.
    Your Conference[34] may be able to do something and if a protest is sent, Hitler would be deeply impressed if it could be said that the Archbishop[s] of Canterbury and of Upsala approved of it. Michael's name must not be mentioned as if it were known to the authorities that he was doing this work he would certainly be interned.
    I was in Germany a few days ago and believe Michael's information to be trustworthy.
    It is a most distressing situation, 6,000 will not take the new oath. Unless Hitler has some idea of the indignation in other parts of Christendom, they will meet severe treatment. I hope to go to Germany in October.
Yours very sincerely
Staunton Fulham

33 The journal of the *Neue Reformatische Bewegung*, edited by Hanns Lilje.
34 The council of Life and Work assembled for its conference at Fanö in Denmark on 24 Aug. 1934.

12 MEMORANDUM BY BISHOP BELL, 6 NOVEMBER 1934

Confidential

Interview with Herr Joachim von Ribbentrop
6 November 1934

———

I met von Ribbentrop as Weigall's[35] guest at the Athenaeum, and we had three hours' talk. He is an able business man of, I should think, 45, who knows England well and has had dealings with England for some 25 years. He likes sport and is having a holiday in this country. At the same time he is seeing Arthur Henderson,[36] Lord Cecil[37] and others about Disarmament, and making other opportunities for private conversation on questions of German policy. He is a close personal friend of Hitler. It was in his house that Hitler met von Papen, and the decision was formed to make Hitler Chancellor. He said that Hindenburg refused to make Hitler Chancellor, and there were some very difficult moments. On one such occasion Hitler brought his fist down with a bang and said 'Fools! Don't they realise that I am a Conservative of the Conservatives!'

Von Ribbentrop spoke as a layman and did not profess to be *au fait* with theological questions. His main point was that Hitler had saved Christianity. 'Why', Hitler asked, 'did not the Churches outside Germany, in the midst of our struggle against Communism in the last fifteen years, lift up their voices, when their help would have been far more potent?' I explained what had been said and done by the Archbishop and others, including the Universal Council in its smaller way, with regard to Bolshevism in Russia.[38] I made it plain that I realised that the German Church was, in large parts of it, in a state of semi-death, but I pointed out that it was very strong just where the Confessional Synod was strong, in Bavaria, Württemberg, Westphalia, parts of Berlin and Hanover. Was it not common sense, I asked, for Hitler, if he wanted the masses to be brought to Christianity, to use the help of the Church where it was strongest, rather than to bring in new creatures altogether? Von Ribbentrop, and Hitler with him, I think were sceptical about the ability of the Church to get at the masses. He said more than once that it was a question of technique, how to get Christianity across to the masses. He said that millions of Germans were in a state of desperate poverty and depression, confined in their miserable tenements. They could not understand the language of the ordinary Church, so new methods must be devised, getting hold of them out of doors in the open air, and so on. He even suggested that the Churches might well be filled as a result of the new movement, but that there were not enough Churches to accommodate all the multitudes that ought to be brought in. Did the German Church realise the urgency of the matter and the need of new measures being taken? We talked about the so-called National Church. I agreed that there were eccentric people in Germany whose ideas about

35 Sidney Weigall was a businessman with links with official circles in Germany.
36 Labour party leader and British representative at the disarmament conference in Geneva.
37 Lord Cecil of Chelwood (1864–1958), president of the League of Nations Association 1923–1945, Nobel Peace Prize winner 1937.
38 For Archbishop Davidson's reaction to the persecution of the Russian Church see G.K.A. Bell, *Randall Davidson, archbishop of Canterbury* (London, 1952 edn.), pp. 1067–86. The response of Archbishop Lang is noted by J.G. Lockhart, in *Cosmo Gordon Lang* (London, 1949), p. 381.

uniting the Faith Movement, the Protestants and the Catholics in one great organization called a National Church, might not perhaps be very seriously regarded. But the influence of much present education on the young, without the help of the Church, was dangerous. And more important, I said that the National Socialist system was such as not really to brook any other point of view in the State, and that the real fear of a National Church was of a Church which put a religious complexion on the National Socialist system and said 'Ditto', in religious language, to National Socialism; that such a Church was not really what we meant by a Church, and that some measure of independence was necessary in a proper Church. He appreciated the point of this, but he kept saying that the great battle was with Communism, and that nothing must be allowed to interfere with this battle; that you did not know what people like bishops and Church leaders would say if you tolerated a measure of independence. I pointed out what the Archbishop of Canterbury had done in the way of criticising the Government with regard to Disarmament, with regard to the Irish Troubles[39] and on many public occasions – how the present and the late Archbishop had claimed the right of speaking freely on public and political questions. This puzzled von Ribbentrop a great deal, and he did not think such an attitude would be possible in Germany. I asked whether, to take an instance of independent criticism, it would be possible for a Church leader to speak – though not necessarily in Church – about public affairs, in the same sort of way as von Papen had spoken at Marburg? He thought that that was an unfortunate speech, and was not very encouraging about the analogy. I pressed that perhaps one of the reasons why the Church had been so out of touch with the people in Germany was the great chasm between Lutheran theology and religion, and ordinary social and political interests. He thought there might be something in this.

He said that it was most important that some arrangement should be come to with regard to the future of the German Church. If only the right head of the Church could be found; it was a question of personality. Of course such a head of the Church must be a hundred-per-cent pro-Hitler. From what he said, clearly Bishop Müller is not to be quite easily thrown over. Why should not Müller remain, and have a strong man doing the work with him in a general vague way behind, as Reichbishop? He stressed the fact that Müller was Hitler's personal friend, and trusted by him; and where was another such man to be found? He was obviously afraid of the particularism of some of the Church leaders in Bavaria and Württemberg. He said that the unification of the Church was vital. I said that I was certain that the Church leaders like Koch were thoroughly convinced of the necessity of unification, and that there was no going back on their part to separate Churches. They claimed (and he took this point as an important point) that the Constitution of the National Synod which had been agreed in July last year, had been entirely thrown overboard by the Reichbishop, but that there was no reason why it should not be the basis of a proper unification to-day. I said that the Opposition leaders had no confidence in Müller and did not trust him, and I did not see the possibility of reconciliation under him as Reichbishop. Further, that there was a great deal of tidying up to be done; so

39 For Archbishop Davidson's response to the Irish controversy see Bell, *Randall Davidson*, pp. 1055–66.

much confusion had been brought about that it would be good to have an interval of straightening things out, with the help perhaps of a lawyer or two on the Church side; that, given time, a man fit to be Reichbishop could emerge. I asked about von Bodelschwingh and he did not rule him out by any means, though I do not know that he knew very much about him. I said I thought it would be quite reasonable that Hitler should claim the right of veto. He was very much interested in the English method of appointing Bishops which gave the Crown so much power.

He obviously distrusted some of the leaders of the Opposition, and told me a curious story about Pastor Niemöller. He is in Niemöller's parish at Dahlem. He has not himself been much of a Churchman, though he is now a German Christian, but his children have been christened by Niemöller. In July 1933 he wanted his youngest girl christened, and asked Niemöller to tea with himself and his wife. They discussed matters in a friendly way in which Ribbentrop said that 'in that chair' (pointing to a chair) Hitler sat when it was decided that he should be Chancellor. Niemöller braced himself up and assumed an attitude of reserve. Then Frau von Ribbentrop said something about the German Christians, asking whether there was not something in what they stood for, in a way asking for information. They were not German Christians then themselves. And they both noticed that Niemöller's reserve became all the stronger, and that there was a sort of atmosphere of hostility. They did not understand it. They made proposals for the baptism of the child. It was arranged that the arrangements should go forward, subject to a convenient date. Niemöller left, and they tried, a day or two later, to fix a day on the telephone, but though they tried several times, they could never get hold of Niemöller personally; Niemöller did not make any appointment for the baptism so the baptism lapsed and the child is not yet christened. This has obviously affected von Ribbentrop's feelings towards Niemöller. I said that I could not understand such action on Niemöller's part. I thought that possibly at the moment when they were discussing the christening, feeling was very acute owing to the election and the influence Hitler had exerted to secure the return of German Christians. But he obviously looked upon Niemöller as an opponent of National Socialists and Hitler.

We talked also about Concentration Camps a little. I asked whether he had come across Wyndham Deedes[40] who came to Berlin last Spring with a letter from the Archbishop of York.[41] At first he said 'Was that the letter about Oberammergau, protesting against the use of the swastika at the Oberammergau Festival?'[42] He thought that such a protest was unfortunate as the swastika was the

40 Sir Wyndham Deedes (1883–1956), distinguished public servant and administrator in the Middle East before his return to England.
41 At the suggestion of the German educationalist Kurt Hahn, Archbishop Temple, Bishop Bell and a number of eminent lawyers had, at the end of 1933, collected reports of persecution and torture in German concentration camps. These provided the basis for a memorandum of protest which was taken to Berlin by Deedes and Geoffrey Winthrop Young at the beginning of 1934 to place in Hitler's own hands. This proved impossible, but the two emissaries took the document to a number of government departments before returning to England, certain that their visit had created a stir in official circles. For a full account see Andrew Chandler, 'The Church of England and Nazi Germany 1933–1945', Ph.D. dissertation, University of Cambridge, 1991, pp. 31–40.
42 A performance of the Passion of Christ took place in Oberammergau, in Upper Bavaria, every ten years. In 1934 an extra performance was put on to mark the 300th anniversary of the first play in 1634.

national flag of Germany. I said no, it was about the Concentration Camps, and roughly explained the contents of the letter. He said no, he had not heard of this, though he seemed to recollect in a vague sort of way the fact that some messenger had come. He said that in England the whole Communist question was entirely misunderstood; that there were only 2000 or 3000 persons in the Concentration Camps; that the vast majority of these were Communists guilty of definite crimes, of really bad character – though there were a few intellectual leaders. He said that there were undoubtedly things which one might not wish to happen, but Hitler was fighting a great battle with Communism and that in such a battle, certain things might be done which would not be done in peaceable times or in a peaceable country. He said that Hitler was a great statesman and that in later years, with a proper perspective, people would look on these things in an entirely different way, and would see that Hitler really had saved Europe.

He said that Hitler claimed to have added to the numbers of the Church since National Socialism had come in, by several hundred thousands of Church members. He also said that Hitler's method of action was rather by intuition than by systematic consideration of every possible detail. Von Ribbentrop would say something to him of which he might not take any notice at the time. Then some weeks later he would say 'You remember saying so-and-so? I have done so-and-so.'

When our talk ended I said that I hoped von Ribbentrop might some day come to Chichester. He was very friendly and said that he thought it would be very useful for us to keep in touch with one another. I had the impression that he would very likely write again, or want to see me if some difficulty arose, and that he really did want to see a way through the German Church question, though not really sensitive enough to the inner nature of the conflict, or alive to the spiritual independence of a Christian Church. But he was a friendly man and the talk was useful.

One point I should have made much plainer at the beginning of my memorandum. Von Ribbentrop said repeatedly that the fundamental thing was to save the nation. Hitler had saved and was saving the nation. If there were no nation there would be no Church. This he regarded as fundamental. He also pointed out the great financial difficulty which would be involved if Church people were compelled to raise their own funds supposing the State denied them financial assistance, though I pointed out that presumably the State financial assistance was in lieu of ancient Church endowments which the State had long since taken over.

13   ARCHBISHOP LANG TO BISHOP BELL, 7 NOVEMBER 1934

PRIVATE.

My dear George,

I think I had better send you a very rough and hasty Memorandum which I made of a long conversation with von Ribbentrop this afternoon. It will serve at least to show the kind of subjects which we discussed – much the same as you had already discussed with him. He seemed to me to be sincere and

straightforward, and I presume we may take it that he is in the confidence of Hitler himself.
Yours
Cosmo Cantuar

14   MEMORANDUM BY ARCHBISHOP LANG, 7 NOVEMBER 1934

GERMAN CHURCH CONFLICT.

I saw Herr von Ribbentrop, who is in the intimate circles which surround Herr Hitler, at his own desire at Lambeth on Wednesday, November 7th 1934.

He is an agreeable and obviously able business man making no profession of being ecclesiastical in his knowledge or sympathies but an eager apologist for Herr Hitler and his policy.

The points which he stressed were mainly these – The fact that Hitler had rescued Germany from Communism and therefore should be regarded as having saved it for Christianity; that the unification of the Church must be regarded as involved in the unification of the State; that the principle in Hitler's mind was 'No nation, no Church'; that the Church was to give spiritual guidance and inspiration to the nation; that for the present in this stage of evolution, scarcely to be distinguished yet from revolution, there must be some ultimate direction of Church affairs acceptable to Hitler himself; that Hitler's hope was that this Church would bring to Germany a form of modern Christianity suitable to its traditions and needs, etc., etc.

We did not discuss directly the position of the Roman Catholic Church, though I pointed out that I was as much concerned with the freedom of the R.C. as of the Evangelical Church.

I made obvious comments upon his statements but these were sincere and courteous.

He emphasised the great desire of Hitler to be on good terms with this country.

Having some reason to think that our conversation might reach Hitler I pressed my view as to the inability of Bishop Müller to carry out his responsibilities and said that I hoped that his activities would be so long suspended as to lead to his withdrawal and that Hitler would give time to the Evangelical Church to compose its own differences, to present some scheme of unification which he could at least consider, and to intimate to him some person as chief administrator of the Church who would be acceptable both to the Church and to himself.

I was careful to point out that my public concern was not with the internal constitution of the Evangelical Church but only with the use of coercive measures towards it; and I also tried to show why Christians outside Germany were concerned about the character of this new Germanic Christianity.
C.C.

1935

CHRONOLOGY

11 January:	Hitler meets Müller.
13 January:	A plebiscite takes place in the Saar and the province is returned to Germany.
February:	The *Deutsche Christen* move against Müller.
1 February:	The Anglo-German conference on German rearmament takes place.
27 February:	Hitler meets Müller again. The idea that a member of the Reich cabinet be appointed *Minister in evangelicis* is discussed.
March:	Over 700 Prussian pastors are arrested and briefly detained.
11 March:	A new law establishes departments for church finances in Prussia.
16 March:	Conscription is introduced in Germany and the disarmament clauses of the Versailles Treaty are rejected.
28 March:	Pastor Grossmann in Berlin is sent to a concentration camp at Dachau.
April:	State grants to the church are withheld in Baden.
10 April:	The Provisional Church Government makes an appeal to Hitler.
24 April:	A new decree closes down a number of German newspapers.
26 April:	A rally of the German Faith movement is held at the *Sportpalast* in Berlin.
27 April:	Pastors in Wuppertal send a telegram of protest to Hitler voicing their concern about the growth of paganism.
14 May:	Rudolf Hess speaks of the church dispute in Stockholm.
3 June:	The *Times* publishes a letter by Bishop Bell deploring the 'internal War' being waged against Christianity in Germany.
4–6 June:	The third Confessing synod meets in Augsburg.
5 June:	Archbishop Lang expresses his concern about the German church to the Church Assembly.
18 June:	The Anglo-German Naval Agreement is signed.

26 June:	The German government transfers legal disputes in the church from the courts to a new bureau, the *Beschlussstelle in kirchlichen Rechtsangelegenheiten* in the Ministry of the Interior.
16 July:	The establishment of a new Reich Ministry for Church Affairs under Hanns Kerrl is announced.
16 July:	Interior minister Frick prohibits registrars from permitting 'mixed' marriages.
22 July:	Frick announces to the state governments that the administration of church affairs will now be transferred to Kerrl's ministry.
24 July:	Hitler appoints Ribbentrop ambassador to London.
4 August:	Kerrl assumes responsibility over the *Beschlussstelle in kirchlichen Rechtsangelegenheiten*.
18–25 August:	The executive committee of Life and Work meets at Chamby-sur-Montreux in Switzerland.
21 August:	Kerrl meets Müller and other churchmen sympathetic to the *Deutsche Christen*.
23 August:	Kerrl meets leaders of the Confessing Church and tells them that he will not tolerate further disputes in the church.
26–30 August:	The first Evangelical Week takes place in Hanover.
September:	Bell visits Germany.
15 September:	Two new laws define and legalize discrimination against Jews and 'non-Aryans': the Reich Citizenship Law and the Law for the Protection of German Blood and German Honour.
24 September:	The Prussian Confessional synod meets in Berlin and rejects the work of the new bureau and the attacks on Jewish Christians. The Law for the Safeguarding of the German Evangelical Church is published.
14 October:	The Reich's Church Committee is created. It is chaired by Zöllner. The Confessing synod refuses to recognize it.
28 October:	The propaganda ministry imposes censorship before publication on church publications.
November:	Two confessing colleges are prohibited by the police.
4 November:	Kerrl announces a relaxation of restrictions on the church press.
14 November:	The first supplementary decree to the Reich Citizenship Law dismisses Jews from public service.
20 November:	The fourth report of the Council on Foreign Relations is

submitted to the Church Assembly. A debate on the persecution of the Jews in Germany follows.

28 November: The trust funds of the Confessing Church are confiscated. Kerrl threatens dissolution of the movement.

2 December: Kerrl assumes dictatorial powers over the church by abolishing executive or administrative functions by church organizations.

4 December: The Berlin-Brandenburg Confessing synod protests against Kerrl's act of 2 December. Niemöller is prohibited from public speaking.

6 December: Marahrens, bishop of Hanover, pledges his support for Kerrl.

1935

1 MEMORANDUM BY BISHOP BELL, 20 SEPTEMBER 1935

INTERVIEW WITH RUDOLF HESS
Munich. Friday September 20th, 1935

Dr. Gerll[1] drove us from Hinderlang to Munich – a beautiful drive under the Bavarian hills of some 120 miles or more. We drove in Hess' car and with us was Hof Prediger Schairer, a retired old-fashioned Lutheran pastor of Wiesdbaden. We reached Hess' private house, 48 Harthauserstrasse, about 4.15. There was an S.S. man in front of the small gate leading up a lane to the house – a nice house with a garden. We were received by Hess and his wife in the drawing room. He was a man of about 43, very dark and with a somewhat literary and student look about him. I had been told that he had an inferiority complex and this was represented by a certain shyness and diffidence, and there was also a touch of slight melancholy perhaps in his face. He looked anxious. His wife was about 5 years younger, a blonde, a nice straightforward-looking woman who spoke English. We all had tea together and the conversation soon turned to the Church question. I said that I had learnt a good deal at Hinderlang in different ways. I spoke about what I thought the unfairness of charging the Lutheran Church with being a political party to the extent that the Catholics were. I also said that I felt that Hitler's statement at Nuremberg on the church question, if given full reality on both sides, was a statement with much hope in it for a solution of the problems. The point on which foreign opinion was uncertain, and also friends of mine in the Confessional Church were uncertain, was, I said, whether Hitler wished to make the State absolute, bringing the Church right under the State, or was willing to give the Church a full place within its own frontiers in the life of the nation. Hess said that there was no doubt whatever that the answer was the latter. There was a very definite wish for the Christian religion and for giving the Churches a full place of their own in the nation. I realised the imperfections of the Churches, but I said that the Churches of the world had a great battle to fight against the things which were hostile to Christianity, and they wanted the full strength of the German Evangelical Church in this common fight. This point was a very important point as it turned out. Frau Hess, who had been somewhat critical before I said this, said 'Oh, that is why foreign Churches are interested in our Church conflict.' and she and Hess fully agreed that it was the business of the Churches to unite their forces against anti-God and anti-Christianity. I said that the Confessional Church, I knew, was most anxious to make its contribution to the national life, and that it seemed hard that it could not be encouraged to do so. Hess made a further point emphatically, that Rosenberg was purely an individual with an individual point of view, and that Hitler had told him to keep his individual point of view

1 A medical doctor and a member of Hess's social circle.

out of his work for the Party and the State. He further said (and this was important) that Hitler had very recently ordered the S.S. and the S.A. to cease to meddle in Church questions. When I asked whether Hitler had given this order publicly, he said 'No' but it had been put into the circulars sent to the S.S. and the S.A. men. He repeated that Hitler did not wish force to be used and that he did not wish to meddle in the Confessional question and would maintain that he had not. I also mentioned the Oxford Conference of 1937 and said that I was most anxious that the German Church should play its full share in this conference, and he agreed with this.

At this point the conversation closed as Hitler was arriving from Berlin to take part in a very important conference on Foreign policy at Hess' house. I had a few words with Frau Hess, who said 'What a pity it is that you and my husband do not speak the same language! He ought to have heard you.' She saw, I felt, something of the meaning of a Church as opposed to Christianity vaguely. She assured me that the individual opinions of the German people would not and could not be quelled, that thirty Germans had thirty different Heavens and Hells and would always have them. Just as we were leaving I asked whether I might write to Hess, and she warmly welcomed the idea and said it was much better to put it in writing and begged me to write to the private address and not to the Brown House.[2] We parted in a friendly way. It was emphasised that this was only an introduction and that I must come again and see Hess and generally keep up with him. Dr. Gerll was very emphatic on the importance of mutual understanding and continued association between us.

We walked down the lane out to the car and saw Gerll and one of the Nazi men at the double. They got to the door just as Hitler passed in a car, followed by another car. He was sitting on the driver's side and I arrived just in time to see the back of his head. They said that he looked very worried and that one of his worries was this Church question which he was most anxious to see solved.

2   MEMORANDUM BY BISHOP BELL, 28 SEPTEMBER 1935

Interview with Reichminister Kerrl
(Written September 28, 1935)

I met Kerrl, by Rosenberg's kind arrangement, at dinner at Rosenberg's house where there was a party for my wife and myself. Kerrl was a vigorous voluble man of 50 or so, stoutish with a small moustache and a reddish face, not very cultivated looking but full of gusto. After dinner he and Rosenberg (for most of the time) and Herr Schmidt, a first class interpreter from the Foreign Office, and Count von Durckheim and I, sat in Rosenberg's study. After a few general remarks, Kerrl said 'And what interests the Bishop in our German situation?' I then spoke of my long friendship with German churchmen from 1919, of the Stockholm conference, of the Anglo-German Theological conferences, of the Universal Christian Council and of the Oxford Conference, and of the great importance of having the German Church fully represented in the fight in which the Churches should unite their forces against the enemies of Christianity. Our conversation lasted nearly two hours. We did not get away until about twenty

2 The official centre of the National Socialist Party in Munich.

to twelve, but I need not go through the whole discussion. The important points made were that Kerrl again emphatically assured me of Hitler's wish to give the Confessional Church a full and living place in the national life, and that there was no question of the absolute State over the Church, or the Church coming down with a hammer and saying 'Believe this doctrine, walk in this way' and so on. He said that in Hitler's view his National Socialism was a form of political government and that it was no more necessary for the Church to declare National Socialism to be incompatible with the Christian religion than it had been four hundred years ago necessary for the Church to declare that the theory of Copernicus was incompatible with the Catholic faith. Time would show the value of the National Socialist form of government.

He said that Hitler had referred to pastors or priests rather than to organisations, as interfering in politics.

He impressed upon me that he was a religious man and a sincere Christian, and that he wished to approach the whole matter from that point of view. He said that Rosenberg, so far as his views went, must be regarded as a private person, and that he had been told not to bring his views into his work.[3] He also said, when I asked him the direct question, 'National Socialism is not a religion but a form of government.' He said that there was no intention whatever on the part of the State to impose a State religion, but to provide an order or a frame within which the Church could give its living witness. There had at one time been an idea of a united national Church in Germany comprising Catholics and Protestants. He had known this was impossible from the outset and the idea was regarded as quite impractical now and any hope there had been of such a united Church had been abandoned. He said that he had his own ideas with regard to the manner of framing this order for the Church, that he had explained them to Bodelschwingh and that Bodelschwingh, for whom he had a great admiration and liking, had said 'If those are your lines I will collaborate with you.'

Our talk ended, after I had emphasised the points made by him about freedom for the Church and the importance of the collaboration with Bodelschwingh, by a reference on Kerrl's part to the need of our two countries understanding one another, and he welcomed my enquiries and was obviously thoroughly genuine in his appreciation. He said indeed that I might have been a German Pastor talking the whole thing over with him.

3   MEMORANDUM BY BISHOP BELL, 23 SEPTEMBER 1935

Memorandum by Bishop Bell
Interview with Bishop Marahrens at the Bishop's House, Hanover.
Monday 23 September 1935.

On Saturday, September 21st, I had a long talk with Hans Lilje, telling him of my conversation at Hinderlang and also with Hess. He and Koch had already pressed upon me at Munich the importance of my going to Berlin and seeing Ribbentrop and Kerrl, and they had also wished me to see Hess. He also was very anxious that I should see Bishop Marahrens. So he arranged that we should

---

3   Rosenberg had become the *bête noir* of Christians in Germany and Britain alike for his notoriously anti-Christian work, *Der Mythos. des 20. Jahrhunderts. Eine Wertung der seelisch-geistigen Gestaltenkämpfe unserer Zeit* (Munich, 1930).

stop at Hanover on Monday on our way from Berlin to The Hague. We arrived at the Bishop's House on Monday soon after 2. The Bishop has been Bishop of Hanover ten years and is a Hanover man. He will be 60 on October 11th. He and his wife and my wife and Lilje and I were taken upstairs to the drawing room and sat round a table and had coffee and cake in a ceremonious way. The Bishop is a tall, very dignified-looking man, rather of the old school, and the contrast between him and these modern men of Hitler must be very great. He struck me as on the old side altogether, but he was very dignified and most courteous and charming. After the ceremonies of coffee, Hetty was taken for a drive by Mrs. Marahrens, a very nice woman with a bright blue eye, a little younger than the Bishop, and I was taken into his study by the Bishop and Lilje. We had only an hour, and I told the Bishop first my satisfaction about the oecumenical co-operation as Koch had told me. Then I made it plain that my interviews with Hess and Kerrl had been undertaken with Koch's strong approval, and that I was an observer only and that there were many complications behind; and further that what I had to report from my conversation with Hess and Kerrl could only be regarded as elements in the situation; of the value or otherwise of them they would be able to judge, but I thought they ought to know. I then spoke about my general impression derived from Hinderlang; next of my talk with Hess and then of my talk with Kerrl. I made it plain that I realised that politics and the wish for Anglo-German friendship undoubtedly affected the situation, and that one might make use of this fact in the interests of the Church. I told him about the letter I was proposing to write to Hess, and asked him whether he thought it would be a good thing to write such a letter. He replied that he thought it would be a good thing to write such a letter, that he felt the letter should point out the longing of the Church to take its part in the life of the nation without any hesitation, and that the chance ought to be given to the Church. 'We want to help the State, we want to preach the Gospel without politics', but the situation was extremely complicated and dangerous, he said, and that they had to do the best they could in very difficult circumstances, and it was possible that an order might be given them which would prevent them from living their proper life. He said that the German Christians had introduced politics into the whole question and that this was the root of all the evil. He obviously felt very strongly about the German Christians. He said that he believed that there was much goodwill on the part of the State but a great lack of knowledge. Hess and others did not know what a Church was. The Church is vitally necessary and they did not understand what that meant. There were many forces against goodwill. Would Kerrl be able to bring his goodwill into effect. He had seen Kerrl once himself alone. He gave one or two instances of the daily difficulties, German Christians demanding a German Christian Pastor whose views were mainly political. He spoke of complaints pouring into the Ministry and being disregarded. He obviously felt rather sore about the way in which the State was treating the Confessional Church in practice. I think also that younger men, more impatient than Marahrens, felt, as Lilje made plain to me, a good deal of indignation that foreign observers could get access in this way to the Ministry while they could be treated with incivility and put off constantly. The Bishop spoke very gratefully both of the oecumenical relations and the way in which they and myself had helped the German Church. He strongly wished to maintain these links. He parted with a blessing and gave one the impression of a fine, Godly old man in a difficult day. I made it plain that I would keep an attitude of considerable reserve, and he was quite clear that was most necessary. G.C.

4   BISHOP BATTY TO ARCHBISHOP LANG, 2 NOVEMBER 1935

My dear Archbishop

I have just returned from Latvia Poland & Germany. I enclose some brief notes of interesting interviews I had in Berlin.

It is most important that at the present moment the Church of England should not express any sort of approval of the work of Herr Kerrl's Unification Committee and I regret the leader in the 'Guardian' of Oct 25th.[4]

Yours sincerely and dutifully

Staunton Fulham

5   MEMORANDUM BY BISHOP BATTY, OCTOBER 1935

Berlin October 1935

I had a long interview with Pf. Jacobi, President of the Brandenburg Confessional Church and probably the most influential man in the dispute at the present moment. He is a powerful speaker and advocate and the Police have seized his passport as they fear the influence he would have if he went abroad.

I asked him to state his objection to the Conciliation Committee set up by Herr Kerrl. He said it was a purely nominated committee comprised of men whom the Government could coerce into agreement. It has three 'representatives' of the Confessional Church upon it but not one of these would have been elected if the Church had been asked to select men to represent it. He anticipated the Committee would draw up a scheme of unification and then compel obedience to it. The position eventually would be worse.

Unfortunately Herr Kerrl was in the west of Germany but assured me that his Chief of Staff could speak on his behalf. His Chief of Staff is Herr Ditter who was one of the ADCs[5] to the Kaiser on his *last* visit to England.

He was in full military uniform and the whole office gave me the impression of a Court martial sitting on the Church.

I spent an hour with him and questioned him closely on reports I had heard. I regret to say that he assured me that some which I knew to be true had no foundation in fact. He denied, for instance, that any pastors had been arrested.

I especially pressed him on the 24th Article of the Party Programme, viz 'The Nationalistic Socialistic State is founded on Positive Christianity'. I asked for the Nazi definition of Positive Christianity but could get no satisfactory reply. He stated that they recognised that dogmatic agreement was not possible and so aimed at a religion [which] would be of practical value in the lives of the people, they were encountering difficulties owing to the attitude of the Roman Church with regard to the Marriage Laws. He explained that the work of Herr Kerrl

---

4 The leading article in *The Guardian* on 25 Oct. 1935 had welcomed the creation of the new Reich church committee under Zöllner. There is evidence to suggest that its author was Duncan-Jones.

5 Aide-de-camp.

was only provisional and directly the Church had been unified it would be left to manage its own affairs.

I said that he must be aware that there was strong opposition to the work of the Committee on the ground that it was not representative and asked how they would deal with those who refused to recognise the authority of the Committee. He refused to commit himself on this point or to allow that the Committee was not representative.

We discussed other matters such as, the Baptism of Converted Jews, the Press Censorship and the deplorable feeling created in England by what we believed to be a persecution of those whose only offence was to hold fast to the Christian faith as set forth in the Confession of Augsburg.

My view of the situation is that about 5% of the clergy support the Nazi idea of unification. About 35% belong to the Confessional Church and the remaining 60% are going on with their work and awaiting events. It is the latter body that Herr Kerrl hopes to bring to see his point of view. In considering these figures it must be remembered that the 35% includes most of the leaders in thought and action including a large majority of the pastors in the great cities and important Churches. I fear that the Confessional Church will have to face a fierce struggle in the near future but I am still of opinion that their consistency combined with spirituality and sound learning will triumph over the bludgeon in the end.

I must add that in all my interviews I stated that I regarded any information given me as confidential but reserved the right to inform Your Grace of what I had done.

Staunton Fulham.

6   BISHOP BATTY TO BISHOP BELL, 27 NOVEMBER 1935

Private & Confidential

My dear Bishop.

I have just received the memorandum on Germany from Douglas.[6]

About a fortnight ago I had interviews with the Confessional leaders, including Jacobi, in Berlin and afterwards spent over an hour at Kerrl's office obtaining unsatisfactory answers to my questions. Incidentally, the '*Times*' correspondent[7] wrote to me afterwards to say that a very untrue account of my visit was being circulated by the office.

The impression left upon my mind was that a doctrinal dispute in the Church of England could as usefully be referred to a Court Martial at the War Office.

The Confessional Church deserves our sympathy. It is putting up a good fight for the essentials of the Christian faith but in the German fashion [have] no sense of diplomacy. I did not send any account of my visit to the Council as it would have been too risky to send out 40 copies.

My great desire is that at the time we should not do anything which might seem to weaken that moral support which the Confessional Church values very highly.

Kerrl is splendid on paper for foreign consumption but he has not yet done anything to justify the hopes held out.

6 Canon J.A. Douglas, the chairman of the Council on Foreign Relations.
7 The Berlin correspondent of the *Times* was Norman Ebbutt.

The Confessional Church feel strongly that the 'representatives' of their body on the Unification Committee do not represent them and were of course nominated by Kerrl.

I am off to Geneva on Friday but hope to be back in England by Dec 12th.

The Italian Ambassador in Berlin described the sanctions to me as 'mosquitoes in the garden of EDEN' and I shall be interested to hear more about them on the spot.[8]

Yours very sincerely
Staunton Fulham

---

8 Italian forces had invaded Abyssinia in 1935. The League of Nations sought to respond by applying sanctions against Italy. These proved fruitless, and were withdrawn on 4 July 1936. The Italian ambassador to Berlin was Bernardo Attolico (1880–1942).

1936

CHRONOLOGY

19 January:	Niemöller publishes *Die Staatskirche ist da*. Copies of the leaflet are confiscated.
21 January:	Kerrl addresses a gathering at Hanover.
10 February:	*Gestapo* actions are placed above the law.
14 February:	A new appeal court for disciplinary cases formed by the Reich's Church Committee.
17 February:	The Reich Confessing synod at Oeynhausen. The Provisional Church Administration splits over its response to the committees.
7 March:	The Rhineland is reoccupied by German forces and the Locarno treaty is repudiated.
13 March:	The Confessing executive is re-formed, but without representatives from Bavaria, Württemberg, Hanover, Saxony and Mecklenburg.
22 March:	The creation of a new council and executive of a 'Lutheran Church of Germany', by the churches unrepresented in the new executive of the Confessing Church.
27 March:	Reventlow leaves the German Faith Movement. Hauer also resigns.
15 May:	High state officials in Germany are prohibited from holding office in any church body.
28 May:	The Second Provisional Government of the Confessing Church agrees to endorse an appeal to Hitler, complaining of the anti-Christian character of party leaders, the disruption of church order, the antisemitism of a government which presses the claims of blood, race and soil, the restrictions placed on church publications and the absolute claims of the state.
4 June:	The memorandum of 28 May 1936 is submitted to the Reich chancellory.
17 June:	Himmler is appointed head of the German police.
19 June:	The administrative committee of Life and Work meets at

	Paris and discusses representation at the forthcoming Oxford Conference.
July:	The memorandum of 28 May is published by the press abroad.
24 July:	Ribbentrop is appointed ambassador to London.
August:	The Confessing movement organizes a pulpit protest against paganism.
1 August:	The Olympic Games open in Berlin.
6 October:	Weissler and Tillich are arrested for leaking the 28 May memorandum to the press.
November–December:	The abdication crisis in Britain.
1 November:	The Rome-Berlin Axis is announced.
13 November:	A third man, Werner Koch, is arrested for leaking the 28 May memorandum to the press.
19–20 November:	The Reich Church Committee meets in Berlin.
25 November:	Germany and Japan sign the Anti-Comintern Pact.
13 December:	Archbishop Lang broadcasts an address in the wake of Edward VIII's abdication.
23 December:	The Prussian Confessing synod demands the resignation of Kerrl and his administration.
29 December:	The *Times* publishes a further letter reporting on developments in the church struggle by Bishop Bell.

1936

1 MEMORANDUM BY BISHOP BATTY, 26 NOVEMBER 1936

Private and Confidential

Report on a visit to Germany, November, 1936

The main groups in the Evangelical Church are as follows:-

1. The *Reichskirche* managed by the Reich and Regional Committees appointed by Herr Kerrl. Dr. Zoellner is the head of this group.

2. The Lutheran *Rat* or Council mainly composed of Lutheran Churches in Hanover, Bavaria, Württemberg and Saxony. This Council tries to occupy a middle position between the Confessional Church and the State appointed Church Committee. It appears to be on fairly good terms with Dr. Zoellner but the Confessional Church does not recognise it. This Council is recognised by Bishops Meiser and Wurm and Professor Lilje.

3. The Confessional or *Bekenntnis* Church led by Drs. Niemöller, Jacobi and others is utterly opposed to the State Committees.

4. The *Deutsche Christen* movement led by Dr. Rehm. They claim to support the Confession of Augsburg and Dr. Zoellner has announced that the movement is not heretical. They are very bitter opponents of the Confessional Church.

5. The *Deutsche Christen* movement has split. The most important group has formed the National Church of Thuringia. This appears to be making progress and may become an important factor in the situation. It is led by a forceful personality Dr. Leffler. They repudiate all Confessions of Faith on the ground that they cause strife. Dr. Zoellner regards this body as heretical. It is difficult to ascertain exactly their doctrinal position as they simply state that they will have nothing to do with creeds but intend to build up a Church in the spirit of Jesus Christ. Reichsbishop Müller has now joined this Church.

I had interviews with most of the leaders of the various groups including Dr. Niemöller, Dr. Wienecke, Professor Mashe, Professor Lilje and Bishop Hossenfelder. The last named I do not take very seriously but felt it admissable to include him amongst those I saw.

I gathered that the Confessional Church stands alone. The four groups opposed to it all expressed the same opinion that it could never be the German Church as like the Roman Church it was international and political. I asked why 'political' and the answer was that its leaders desire to have a Church as a power beside the state.

I will not recapitulate much that I have already told your Grace but upon one important fact all parties agreed viz that Hitler will soon be compelled to speak and give his decision.

With regard to this he is in a very awkward position. He can take two steps -

1. He can proclaim a German Church into which all will be compelled to come.

2. He can sever the connection between Church and State.

If he does (1) the Confessional Church will certainly resist and in the words of Niemöller become the Church of the Catacombs. He must also risk a large swing over to the Confessional Church if a crisis is created.

If he adopts (2) it will be the severest blow the totalitarian ideal has had and would probably lead to further contacts between the Churches in Germany, England and Sweden undermining the Pan German hopes.

Such is the position at the moment, the next important development will come when Hitler speaks.

2 MEMORANDUM BY A.J. MACDONALD, DECEMBER 1936 (DATED 23 MARCH 1937)

PRIVATE AND CONFIDENTIAL

THE CHURCH OF ENGLAND COUNCIL ON FOREIGN RELATIONS

———

German Evangelical Church Discussions

———

Itinerary of a Tour made in
Hamburg – Berlin – Leipzig – Wittenberg
December 1st–10th 1936
by
Dr. A.J. Macdonald

———

Dec 1st

	Arrival at Hamburg, 3.7. Guest of *Friedrich-Stammer Gesellschaft*[1] at *Vierjahreszeit* Hotel.
4 p.m.	Interviewed by Prof. Berber at the Institute and Library of Foreign Publications.
5 p.m.	Tea and long discussion with Pastor Dettman of the Confessional Church.
8 p.m.	Dined with Dr. Burchard-Motz at his house.

2nd

11 a.m.	Long interview with Pastor Rothe, Head of the Free Church (Lutheran) Settlement for sick and imbecile poor, and so on, adults and children.
1.30 p.m.	Lunch at Old Merchants' House with Dr. Burchard-Motz and *Herr* Arning. Tour of Hamburg shops, especially those owned by Jews.
3.30 p.m.	Interview with *Herr* J. Kirston (private business).
4.30 p.m.	Tea and discussion with Pastor Ottmer (*Deutsche Christen*).
7 p.m.	Dined at hotel with *Herr* Arning, and with him to opera 'Tosca'.

———

1 Unidentified. It is likely that it was a protestant welfare association or domestic mission.

3rd

12.26 p.m.   Arrival in Berlin. Guest of Baron Dufour von Feronce, formerly Counsellor of the German Embassy, London, and German Minister at Belgrade. Luncheon and discussion with Baron von der Ropp on programme for visit.

4 p.m.   Visit to Dr. Lilje, Secretary of the *Lutherbund*.[2]

8 p.m.   Visit to a Pastor of the *Bekenntnis Kirche* party and his friends.

4th

10.30 a.m.   Interview *Freiherr* von Langenhahn of Vienna, on affairs in Austria.

11.30 a.m.   Discussion with *Herr* Bäuerle, Dr. Diesel and Baron Dufour von Feronce at the Stöcker Hospiz.

1.15 p.m.   Lunch at the Anglo-German Club with *Herr* Seyferth and *Herr* Fischer (of the Propaganda Ministry). Later, conversation with Count Durckheim and *Herr* Gottfriedsen.

4.30 p.m.   Discussion with a number of *Bekenntnis Kirche* Pastors.

8.00 p.m.   Address to the Theological Faculty of Berlin University. Professors Deissmann, Wobbermin and Bertholet present.

December 5th

10 a.m.   Visit to the headquarters of the *Winterhelfe* organisation,[3] and to the distributing station in Neue Schönhauser Strasse.

11.30 a.m.   Visit to the Secretary of State, Dr. Dieckhoff.

4 p.m.   Walk along Unter den Linden and other streets for the *Winterhelfe* street collection.

7.30 p.m.   Dinner at Baron Dufour's house. Present Dr. Simons (ex-President of the Leipzig High Court, and ex-Foreign Minister), Count Bernstorff, *Ober kirchenräte*[4] Dr. Stahn and Dr. Wahl, and others.

6th

10. a.m.   Service in the *Dom*: Preacher D. Döring. Afternoon visit to Potsdam and *Sans Souci*.

7 p.m.   Addressed a congregational meeting at Velten (Pastor Brutschke).

December 7th

10 a.m.   Visited the headquarters of the *Hitler Jugend*. Lunch with *Herr* Fricke at the *Hitler Jugend*

---

2 The Luther Society.
3 'Winter help' was a National Socialist social work scheme to help the elderly and vulnerable in the community.
4 Member of a church council.

Club at Wannsee.

5 p.m. Tea with Baroness von Schäffer-Bernstein and leaders of Evangelical Women's Work.

8 p.m. Dinner at Esplanade Hotel with the *Mitteleuropaischen Wirtschaftstalt* (industrial and financial leaders of central and south Germany).

8th

11.15 a.m. Visit to *Reichs Minister* Kerrl. Dr. Stahn present.

12.15 a.m. Visit to Dr. Zöllner. Dr. Wahl present.

12.45 a.m. Visit to Bishop Heckel and *Konsistorialrat*[5] Dr. Banke.

1.30 p.m. Lunch with Dr. Krummacher and Dr. Wahl.

3 p.m. Visit to the Berlin Zoo.

6.30 p.m. Visit to Pastor Niemöller, Dr. Böhm and Dr. Julius Rieger (from London).

8.30 p.m. Bible class at Stöcker's Hall (Pastor Dannenbaum).

9th

10.30 a.m. Dr. Burchard-Motz of Hamburg at Esplanade Hotel.

12 noon Lunch with *Oberregierungsrat*[6] Leffler (Leader of the Thuringian Deutsche Christen) at the *Habsburger Hof*.

5 p.m. Arrival at Leipzig. Interview with Professors Gerber, Beyer, Sommerlatt and others at the Rendtorff House (*Gustav Adolf Verein*).[7] Address to the students.

8 p.m. Addressed the theology faculty (professors and students of Leipzig University at the *Weinachsfest Mensa*,[8] Professor Bornkamm in the Chair.

November 10th

9.30 a.m. Visit to Thomas Kirche (Leipzig).

11.19 a.m. Arrival at Wittenberg. Visits to *Lutherhaus*, *Stadtkirche*, *Schlosskirche* with Lic. Oscar Tulin. Addressed students in the Seminar.

6.30 p.m. Arrived back at Berlin.

7.30 p.m. Dinner with Baron von der Ropp.

The conclusions offered in this report on the situation in the German Church dispute are not based entirely or even mainly upon observations made during my ten days' visit at the beginning of December 1936. They had been to a large extent formed by a close study of documentary evidence since the dispute began

5 Member of a church consistory.
6 Senior civil servant.
7 Founded in 1832, and reorganized in 1842, the Gustav Adolf Verein was concerned with the spiritual welfare of German protestants living in the diaspora.
8 The student refectory at the university.

three years previously, and partly during longer visits to Germany in 1933 and 1934. But my visit last December supplied fresh evidence for the conviction already held that in the German Church dispute, and in every other human dispute, there are and have been, at any rate for eighteen months past, two sides to the question.

I am anxious, also, to emphasise this proviso: *for eighteen months past*, because down to the point when *Herr* Kerrl and Dr. Zöllner took office in the autumn of 1935, there is no doubt that the Pastors' League, numbering at that time over 7,000 members, and the *Bekenntnis* or Confessional Church party were fighting against measures which threatened the freedom of Church life, and perhaps the integrity of the Christian faith.

However, by the autumn of 1935, after the failure of Dr. Jäger's drive in Württemberg and Bavaria, police action was almost entirely withdrawn, save in a few instances where it was proved that the pastor had indulged in unwise political speech or writing. A new situation was created when Bishops Marahrens, Wurm and Meiser called upon their pastors in Hanover, Württemberg and Bavaria to cooperate with the Committees about to be set up by *Herr* Kerrl. The result was that by December 1936 only 3,000 of the 19,000 pastors, of all shades of theological or ecclesiastical opinion in the *Deutsche Evangelische Kirche*, were standing out in opposition. The great majority were working quietly and effectively in their parishes. This is a significant fact which had not, perhaps, been sufficiently noticed in this country.

During my ten days' tour I had lengthy interviews with pastors and laymen representing all types of Church opinion, Confessional Church, *Deutsche Christen*, Free Church, as well as representatives of the large body of Lutheran pastors, whose theological views differ but little from those held by pronounced members of the Confessional Party, but who have not been drawn into the controversy, or who have abandoned it during the last year or two, in order to concentrate upon quiet work in their parishes.

If the representatives of this class of Lutheran pastor, whom I met in Hamburg and Berlin, or its neighbourhood are typical of the great majority of pastors no longer in opposition to the Reich ecclesiastical authorities, there appears to be ground for a more hopeful view of the whole situation, in spite of apparently sharp differences, which, since my visit, have been manifested between leading personalities at headquarters.

I found evidence that pastors who teach the whole Lutheran faith have not been hindered in their work from the beginning of the dispute. In other cases pastors who were formerly engaged in it, have long since abandoned it, and are conducting progressive work in their parishes. Some of them testified, that even amongst the children no hindrances had been placed in the way of their ministry. In one case a member of the National Socialist Party has sent his children to the Lutheran pastor to be prepared for confirmation. In another case the official leader of the local branch of *Hitler Jugend* work amongst girls cooperates with the pastor in the instruction of her charges. Occasionally I saw members of the National Socialist Party, in the uniform of the party or wearing its badges, present at public worship, or religious meetings, obviously taking part as devout Christian people.

In no single case could I find any evidence, even when members of the militant *Bekenntnis* party were questioned, of any interference on the part of the civil authorities, when the pastor confined his preaching and teaching to the preaching of the Gospel. The trouble arises in those cases where the pastor feels it necessary to apply this teaching in the form of sharp criticism of the present *regime* in Germany.

The evidence of pastors belonging to the Huguenot Church[9] and the Lutheran *Frei Kirche*[10] supported these conclusions. At no point, since the very beginning of the troubles, had any opposition or criticism been offered to their labours. Their social work, as well as direct spiritual ministry, has been conducted without interference or hindrance. In one of these cases a pastor, of vigorous personality and pronounced fundamentalist views, is carrying on a magnificent evangelistic work in the centre of Berlin but he tempers evangelical zeal with tactful consideration for prejudices which might break out into criticism.

In all these cases the value of a conciliatory attitude, and the avoidance of a provocative attitude, appears to reap a reward – freedom to do the work of a Christian pastor, evangelist and minister.

On the other hand I came across clear evidence of a forthright, uncompromising spirit in the attitude of several members of the Confessional Church Party. In one case this appeared to be the reaction of a personality hardly suited to the ministerial office, a highly-strung and now disheartened pastor, who would probably find himself ill at ease in any ministerial sphere. Such a one gathers a small circle of lay folk of a similar type around him and the vigour of their combined protests is apt to be out of proportion to the difficulties originally experienced, but tends to call into action opposition and hostility which might have been avoided by a more conciliatory and tactful attitude.

At the same time, there are pastors belonging to the *Bekenntnis* party, men of mild temperament, though of pronounced theological views, whose opposition to the *Reich* ecclesiastical administration is as definite as that of the more radical critics, but who express themselves with less violence. However, they appeared to me to be mainly senior men, whose habits of thought had become fixed, and so no longer adaptable to new ideas and methods.

Pastor Niemöller has the quiet, firm, courteous presence of an officer of the British Senior Service. His theological views are clear cut and simple, as might be expected in the case of an ex-naval officer. Yet he has the martyr spirit, and honestly believes that he is engaged in a cause as vital as that upheld by Martin Luther. His personality is such that he would fill any church, no matter what gospel he preached. But my impression of him was that so gifted and so well-equipped a pastor could, by conciliation and by a fair attempt to estimate the difficulties of others, achieve a great deal to heal the wounds in the German Evangelical Church. Since my last visit to Germany a striking illustration of Dr. Niemöller's tendency to exacerbate an already difficult situation occurred when

9 The German Huguenot Church was a church with its roots in early sixteenth century French Calvinism. Granted freedom of worship in France by the Edict of Nantes in 1598, some 300,000 Huguenots fled to other parts of Europe when the edict was revoked in 1685. Some settled in Prussia. By the twentieth century the Huguenot Church was only a very small Christian sect.

10 The Free Churches of Germany were little more than sects, and largely disregarded by politicians and other church leaders alike, although the Association of Evangelical Free Churches was negotiating with the *Deutsche Christen* party towards the end of 1933. Ernst Helmreich discusses their fortunes in the Third Reich in *The German churches under Hitler* (Detroit, 1979), pp. 369–87.

he is reported to have said to his congregation at Dahlem 'Our Leader is the golden calf round which the people dance'. Among the *Deutsche Christen*, I found a similar type of pastor, gifted mentally and physically, natural leaders, whose views on the Old Testament were no more pronounced than that of Liberal Evangelicals or Modern Churchmen[11] in this country, yet holding orthodox views on the Person and ministry of Christ, loyal to the Scriptural doctrine of Atonement and Resurrection. In one case, at least, such a leader does not appear to have been wisely handled by some of the church authorities, although in another case, it appeared that a rather bluff, and not too-well educated pastor of this party, might with justice be misunderstood by people of orthodox theological views. It appeared that with sympathetic treatment many of the *Deutsche Christen* might be won over to some understanding whereby the sharpness of their criticism of the Confessional party might be refined away and a return to quiet ministerial work secured.

Indeed, one of the fundamental causes of the failure of *Herr* Kerrl's Ministry to bring about a larger measure of reconciliation than it has secured in many quarters, lies in a radical centrifugal tendency and policy among the different parties or movements or 'fronts' engaged in the dispute, is significant. [sic] I had the unhappy feeling that there is no deep-rooted desire for conciliation, but rather an instinct to continue a fight well begun, well maintained, but now of obsolete moral and religious significance. In reply to my suggestion that these leaders should quietly meet together and, in an atmosphere of charity and prayer, try to understand each other's points of view and so compose their own difficulties as well as to try to understand the most difficult situation which confronts the central *Reich* ecclesiastical ministry, I found a disinclination to entertain such an idea. Although the idea of 'leadership' and of following a lead appears to be thoroughly understood and appreciated in political matters in Germany to-day, the absence of a proper recognition of these principles in ecclesiastical matters, appears to be one of the chief causes of the continuance of the Church dispute. This is very natural in a Church organised on non-episcopal lines. Leadership, where it exists, can only be local. But the great need of the situation is that the local leaders should realise that a willingness to follow the lead of the territorial bishops, and, in turn, of the central administration, would do much to ease the existing tension. Indeed in those territorial churches where such a lead is followed, peaceful conditions have for a considerable time been maintained. The splitting-up of the German Evangelical Church into conflicting sections is the result very largely of the absence in many areas of a well-established system of bishops who might have given such counsel, at different points in the dispute, as would have secured the support of the local leaders.

Another apparent need is that the pastors should confine themselves to a simple preaching of the Gospel, such as I heard in the *Dom* at Berlin one Sunday morning, leaving politics aside and trusting to the Gospel word to win its way. Modern Germany, like modern England, requires to be re-evangelised, and so long as that need exists, the pastors have a full programme before them. To say,

---

11 Conservative theologians often referred to the *Deutsche Christen* as a German expression of Modernism, perceiving that their wish to diminish a core a traditional doctrinal beliefs and embrace new currents of opinion made such a connexion convincing. Macdonald's reference to 'liberal evangelicals' is more surprising, but is probably intended to make the same broad point.

as some pastors said to me, that Gospel preaching is not enough suggests a failure to understand, not merely the present situation, but the proper function of the ministerial office. A pastor is called to the preaching of the Word and the ministry of the Sacraments. If these are not enough, then the responsibility is no longer his. He is certainly not called upon to introduce another content or method into his preaching. But, I found, in several cases, that such a ministry does fill the churches and create peace in the parishes.

These impressions were confirmed after my interviews with leading laymen. During the course of half an hour's talk on December 8th with *Herr* Kerrl, who told me that he was converted to Christ at the age of thirteen and had read his New Testament ever since, the minister said that conditions in the world to-day resemble those in the Roman Empire 2,000 years ago. Everything is in ruins and now, as then, delivery can come only through Christ. The great act of Christ was to lead men back to God. Christ did not introduce a new religion, but He negotiated for men an approach to God. There is no need to compare Hitler with Christ, indeed there is no comparison between them, but Hitler had been sent by God, and authorised by Him to raise up the German people from the ruin in which it stood, and to make possible for it a new historical future. In addition, Hitler had attempted to make clear to the German people that God is there, although in wide areas the conception of him had completely disappeared. Many Germans had abandoned the idea of God altogether. It was fatal that the Church had not grasped its duty. It opposed itself to the National Socialist endeavour and was lacking in a physical understanding of the People [*Volk*]. It adhered much more strongly to its own dogmatic opinions instead of to the single great duty of only preaching Christ again to men, and of bringing Him close to them. What do the people know of confessions and dogmas? When they have again accepted Christ, there will then be an opportunity for them to understand these things. (i.e. confessions and dogmas). Therefore the pastors must leave aside everything which obscures the figure of Christ or makes it difficult to understand Him. It is fatal that the churches are in opposition and hold their own views to be more important than Christ and His life and teaching. In place of Him they prefer to talk of Abraham and Old Testament personalities, and are excited if the people are backward in the understanding of such things.

The Jewish question is especially prominent. Mommsen described the Jews as 'the ferment of decomposition'.[12] They are indeed the medium of destructive ideas in the modern world through the *Aufklärung* (eighteenth century theological liberalism),[13] Marxism and Bolshevism. They have overthrown Russia to the ground. Therefore it is difficult for the German people, before it has recognised Christ, to occupy itself with Old Testament figures, or with human conceptions.

He (*Herr* Kerrl) strives honourably on behalf of the Church. They should unite with him and with Hitler's great struggle. But it is all very difficult while good will is lacking in many clergymen, both Roman Catholic and Confessional.

He concluded by saying that he would be very grateful if an understanding

12 With Leopold von Ranke, Theodor Mommsen (1817–1903) was the greatest German secular historian of the nineteenth century. His international reputation rested upon his *Römische Geschichte*, a major work which was never completed. He was awarded the Nobel Prize for literature in 1902.
13 The Enlightenment of the eighteenth century.

of this situation could be aroused in England and if an honourable understanding between the two peoples could be established.

The value of this statement by *Herr* Kerrl on the urgency of bringing the German people back to a knowledge of God, by simply preaching Christ to them has been seriously diminished, if not entirely nullified by a pronouncement made by him on February 13th, 1937. In passing, the date of this pronouncement should be carefully noticed for reasons which will be given below. On that date he is reported to have said 'Bishop von Galen and Mr. Zöllner wanted to bring home to me what Christianity really was, that it was a question of the acknowledgement of Jesus as the Son of God. That is ridiculous, quite unessential. All that matters is to let the character of Jesus work upon one, to translate Christianity into action. In the course of history an *Apostolicum*[14] has been built up. That the recognition of this *Apostolicum* should be a token of Christianity is nonsense. There has risen a new authority as to what Christ and Christianity really is. This new authority is Adolf Hitler. I do not want by this to attribute divinity to Hitler. God speaks through men, through history, through living words. If this which has been said before had been recognised there would have been no split between Christianity and National Socialism. All could have worked together to carry out the will of God, which is to secure the survival of our people. Therefore a way must be found to get away from the isolation and endangering of the German Protestant Church.'

Elsewhere in the address *Herr* Kerrl says that he proposes to rule without Church Committees, either national or provincial, and that individual members of the Church could henceforth 'place themselves under the direct authority of the Church Ministry' (Kerrl's Ministry at Berlin). Moreover he said 'Under no circumstances will there be elections. Nor would they have any success'.

Two days after the delivery of this address to the Presidents of the Provincial Church Committees – an address outlining the policy which *Herr* Kerrl was about to promulgate – *Herr* Hitler on February 15th brushed it aside and announced that elections would take place: 'the Church shall now, in complete liberty and along the lines determined by the congregations themselves, give itself a new Constitution, and therewith a new organisation. I authorise the Reich Minister for Church Affairs, with this object in view, to prepare the election of a General Synod and take all the necessary measures'. In a word, the Führer brushed aside the proposals made in *Herr* Kerrl's address of February 13th and by implication any expressions in it, practical or theological or otherwise. Thus *Herr* Kerrl's statement criticising the doctrine of the divine Sonship of Christ, was not approved by the Führer. It is, therefore, no longer germane to the controversy. It falls back into the limbo of discredited sayings and incidents, and ought no longer to be regarded and appraised as possessing current significance in the dispute. Yet, nearly a month after it was uttered, it has been set forth in the British secular and theological press as a statement representing the latest attitude of the National Socialist government on this vital doctrinal question.

Moreover, coming from *Herr* Kerrl the statement, although serious, should, in justice, have been discounted by the fact that *Herr* Kerrl is in no sense a theologian, not competent to give an opinion on a theological point. He was appointed to assist in the practical work of framing a new church constitution.

14 Apostolic authority.

The failure to achieve this, completed by the resignation of Dr. Zöllner the day before, [February 12th] lies behind his speech on February 13th. His main difficulty is not Christology, but quite clearly the fear that the Roman Church, and the Evangelical Church following in its track, are attempting to set up a State within a State: 'Witness the inflammatory speech of the Pope against National Socialism to the pilgrims who visited Rome. If a Catholic Bishop came to the Pope and said: "We want to do everything to create good relations with the State", then we would be much more inclined to listen to complaints. Our party and our leader want to have perfectly good relations with the Christian Confessions. We stick to the speeches of our leader at Potsdam and elsewhere. But the Church must recognise the primacy of the State. That ought not to be difficult, as the party expressly represents Positive Christianity ... If however, the Church wants to be a State within the State, then the Church will soon find itself standing alone and isolated ... The fundamental principle is: the peoples are the handiwork of God. Imperialism and curialism are both in conflict with those principles, and with the nation.'

These practical questions form the burden of *Herr* Kerrl's address on February 13th and his most unfortunate Christological reference should not be allowed to have the importance and significance which have been assigned to it.

Herr Kerrl impressed me as belonging to a type of Christian layman with whom many of us are familiar in this country. A robust and kindly personality, a man doing his best in a difficult situation, and ready to meet sympathy with sympathy. For example, in the summer of 1936 he secured a grant of M.30,000 for the erection of a Greek Orthodox Church in Berlin.[15] His views on the attitude of the Confessional Church, on the Jews, and on Bolshevism I found to be generally held by other laymen and, indeed, on the Jewish and Russian questions by the pastors as well. In a conversation with a former President of the High Court of Justice an almost identical attitude and account of the situation was presented to me. The same views were expressed by an ex-ambassador. Here are devout men, who contend that with growing experience the rough corners of administrative action are being smoothed away, and they all deplore the fact that the pastors do not make allowances and try to work with the few church authorities. This state of affairs is especially regrettable since, they say, the pastors as Christian leaders should now shew an example in conciliation, and a desire to co-operate in the difficult task of preaching Christ anew to Germany.

An opinion is growing among the lay folk, that a solution of their difficulties will come only if the laymen – church officials and others -assume more responsibility in church affairs. This appeared to be the conviction of several leading business men, as well as of officials at the different ministries.

Bishop Heckel, the head of the foreign relations department of the German Evangelical Church, appears to be carrying on a policy exactly suited to the needs of the situation. While loyally supporting the Government on all political matters, and on all questions of church organisation, he avoids raising issues on points of sharp theological difference, and seizes every opportunity to shew

15 In Mar. 1936 the Orthodox church was recognized as a public corporation. The ministry of church affairs provided 15,000 marks to assist the building of a new church in Berlin, and encouraged the Labour Front and the foreign office to provide sums of 20,000 marks and 3,000 marks respectively. Hitler was invited to contribute to the fund, but declined.

friendship and kindly Christian brotherhood to all who approach him. His care of me when I was in hospital and afterwards was extremely generous. He has written a most important pamphlet on the coming conferences at Oxford and Edinburgh[16] which ought to be translated and read by everyone.

Bishop Marahrens very kindly met me at the railway station at Hanover on my return journey and stayed until the train left. He sent cordial greetings to the Anglican Church. We had little opportunity for close discussion, but he told me that the situation in the Church questions was still fluid and that it was unsafe to prophesy about it. He impressed me as being a leader with most of the qualities which the situation requires, personal, spiritual and mental, a man of great vigour of body and mind.

There is no space to report at length of my long interviews with officials at the Foreign Office, Propaganda Ministry (Dr. Goebbel's office), at the *Hitler Jugend* headquarters and at the Winter Help headquarters. But the personnel in every case impressed me as a fine body of bright, honest young men, trying to do their duty. They resembled the best type of boy scout master and scout assistant commissioner in this country. At each of these Ministries the idea was prevalent that the Confessional Church minority, like the Roman Church, was not backing up the Government's efforts to restore prosperity to the German people. At the *Hitler Jugend* office I was informed that the Movement only takes charge of the children for fourteen week-ends in the year, and while I was in Berlin, *Herr* Baldur von Schirach issued an order that during the other Sundays of the year the children are not to be engaged in *Hitler Jugend* activities during the hours of Church services on Sunday. In their scheme of instruction a very large part is occupied with physical exercises and organised games. I received the impression that any intelligent and tactful pastor should be able to co-operate with these bright open hearted young men.

There can be little doubt that the reports of the *Times* Berlin correspondent, down to the time of my visit, have represented a one-sided view of the church question. Little attempt has been made to ascertain and set forth in the English press the exact aims and policy of *Herr* Kerrl's Ministry, or of the Prussian Church departments supervised by Bishop Heckel and *Herr* Banke. These reports cause misunderstanding between the two countries and are strongly resented by all types of people in Germany. Even when reporting facts, an unkind twist often appears to be given to the statement. For example a full report of the Winter Help organisation and of the annual Street Collection on December 5th when 5½ million Marks were gathered in, would have made a column of interesting matter, and a sympathetic report would have done something to shew the human side of National Socialism to people in England. The Berlin correspondent of the *Times* gave it some three inches with an unkind sneer at the end that this was propaganda. If feeding hungry, and clothing needy people is mere propaganda, then I think all the social and charitable work in the world is discredited. On the afternoon of the great street collection (December 5th) I saw no compul-

---

16 Heckel attempted to oversee German preparations for the Oxford conference, first appointing Heinz-Dietrich Wendland and then Friedrich Wilhelm Krummacher and Eugen Gerstenmaier to co-ordinate contributions. A book of essays edited by Eugen Gerstenmaier, *Kirche, Volk, und Staat. Stimmen der Deutschen evangelische Kirche zur Oxforder Weltkirchenkonferenz* (Berlin, 1937), which included Heckel's own article, was still published for the conference.

sion exercised against the public to compel them to contribute. Berlin was in a happy holiday mood and people were contributing with the greatest willingness.

I ought perhaps to report that I addressed the theological faculties of the Universities of Berlin and Leipzig, when the professoriate was present as well as the students; and also theological colleges in Leipzig and Wittenberg. I gave short addresses to parochial gatherings in and outside Berlin.

If we may rely upon Bishop Heckel's statement that only some 3,000 of the 19,000 pastors are now standing out in opposition to the existing ecclesiastical organisation, it would seem that we should be very cautious in intervening in the dispute at the present time. Critical letters to the press and manifestos forwarded to Germany, which may have been helpful at an earlier stage in the controversy, are now regarded as a hinderance even by people who formerly welcomed this kind of intervention.

Herr Kerrl's Ministry is due to retire this autumn, though of course it may be continued in office. In the meantime, it will be wise if we leave the conflicting parties to themselves, hoping that yet more of the minority may find some means of co-operating with the Church authorities. Certainly the regulations made for Church finance, clergy discipline, and such matters, throughout the past year appear to be sound and helpful to clergy and laity alike.

On the merits of the case in dispute between Reich Minister Kerrl and Dr. Zöllner it is hardly fitting for a foreign observer to comment. But it did appear to me, when in Berlin, that possibly the veteran theologian and lay-minded Minister might have difficulty in understanding each other – difficulty which not infrequently occurs when strong personalities differ on administrative points. On one point Dr. Zöllner appeared to me to have missed an opportunity when he declined to interview Pastor Leffler the able and active young leader of the Thuringian German Christians.

One of Dr. Zöllner's chief reasons for resignation appears to be the failure of *Herr* Kerrl's Ministry to create church committees in certain specified areas. However, in the official gazette of the German Evangelical Church, dated 23rd December 1936, the difficulties which hindered the formation of a unified ecclesiastical administration have been set forth in detail. It is clear that the fundamental trouble has been the existence, sometimes in the same area – notably in Hanover – of two types of Church organisation, the Lutheran based upon the Congregationalist principle of local autonomy, but directed sometimes by Deans and Provosts, who are permanent officials; and the Reformed based upon local synods, which are Presbyterian in character.

The official gazette points out that three methods of election of the new territorial synods are possible: (1) direct, election by the members of the churches; (2) election by the local congregations; and (3) election through the local synods (presbyterian). The first method was regarded as impracticable since it would be an attempt to revive the process of parliamentary voting which has broken down in Germany. The third method would work very well in areas where the Reformed Church flourishes, and this method might also be adopted elsewhere, but for the fact that in Lutheran districts the local synod is not sufficiently central, nor is it of sufficient significance in church life to be entrusted with the election of representatives to the territorial synod. Probably it would be better to base the election in these areas upon the local congregations and to introduce a system partly of election by them, and partly by nomination.

Thus a double system of election appeared to be contemplated, although the gazette made it clear that the ideal system would be election in the first instance by local election committees to the local synod or presbytery, and from this body to the territorial church synod. Apparently the election of the National Church synod would be in the hands of the ten territorial church synods.

This statement is not quoted as a draft of what the new constitution will actually be, but in order to illustrate the difficulties which *Herr* Kerrl's Ministry has had to face on the question of the formation of a new church constitution.

At the headquarters of the Prussian Church the view is held officially that *Herr* Hitler's intervention now offers to the Church an excellent opportunity of putting its house in order. The hope has been expressed that the leaders of the minority opposition will make a sympathetic attempt to co-operate in the elections. Responsible Church leaders have expressed the hope that opinion outside Germany will make it clear that there are limits to the support which a minority has a right to expect from friends abroad on this question. There is a very real danger that a majority of earnest Church people will not come to the polls. Pastor Niemöller is reported to have announced that the Berlin-Dahlem group of the *Bekenntnis Kirche* will not vote. If a mere fraction of the members of the German Evangelical Church record their votes, the Church will be faced by the possibility of being brushed aside as of no importance, on the ground that it represents a small minority of the German people. I have it on good authority that the Party desires a complete and honest vote, which will reveal the true strength of the German Evangelical Church.

In conclusion, it is becoming more and more clear that the Führer's demand for unity in the Evangelical Church, in order that it might become the National Church of Germany, was and is grounded upon an accurate estimate of the practical needs of German life and religion. But such a unity can only be achieved, and such a National Church can only come into being when the Government realise that the Church in Germany must be a Christian Church, preaching faith in Jesus Christ as Son of God, incarnate among men, dying on the Cross and rising from the dead: living under the guidance of the Divine Spirit, and offering spiritual service to the German people. If the Government opens the way for the foundation of such a National Church, then it can afford to disregard minorities on either side, whether extremist Confessional churchmen or extremist German Christians, who would gradually dwindle into the position of mere sects. A German government which attempted a solution of the church dispute along these lines would soon rally the sympathy and support of sober opinion abroad.

A.J. MACDONALD
23rd March, 1937.

1937

CHRONOLOGY

1 January:	Protest by the Confessing Church against the exclusion of students on its church training courses from the universities.
9 January:	The Reich's Church Committee announces that nine Lübeck pastors have been arrested.
30 January:	The *Reichstag* extends the Enabling Law for four more years.
February:	Zöllner tries to visit the nine pastors of Lübeck, but is prevented by the police.
13 February:	The Reich's Church Committee resigns.
15 February:	Hitler meets Kerrl at Berchtesgaden. He orders free elections in the church.
19 February:	Friedrich Weissler dies in Sachsenhausen camp.
22 February:	Hitler meets Kerrl again.
26 February:	The Confessing synod states its conditions for participation in the election.
2 March:	Hitler passes to Frick the regulation of the election.
11 March:	The *Times* publishes a letter from a number of churchpeople protesting against the death of Weissler.
14 March:	The papal encyclical, *Mit brennender Sorge* is published. It criticizes the German government for repeatedly breaking its word in the concordat.
20 March:	Dr Werner, head of the church chancery, assumes the administration of the church until the election.
24 March:	The *Times* publishes a letter from Bishop Bell warning the German state not to interfere in the forthcoming church elections and drawing attention to the papal encyclical.
April:	The *Deutsche Christen* meet at Oberhausen.
6 April:	A new interim Reich church administration is appointed jointly by the Lutheran and Confessing churches.
20 April:	Hermann Muhs is appointed secretary of state in the Ministry for Church Affairs.

June:	Frick criminalizes the contribution of money to the Confessing church, or any other church organization not recognized by Kerrl.
22 June:	The seventh report of the Council on Foreign Relations is submitted to the Church Assembly. Controversy follows.
25 June:	Kerrl assumes responsibility over all church finances in Germany.
1 July:	Niemöller is arrested.
5–6 July:	Confessing and Lutheran leaders meet at Cassel and appeal to the state for a personal hearing.
11 July:	A declaration prepared at Cassel is read out in the churches.
12–26 July:	The international conference on Church, Community and State takes place at Oxford. German representatives are absent.
17 July:	A new Anglo-German naval agreement is announced.
3–18 August:	The second world conference on Faith and Order takes place at Edinburgh.
29 August:	A second declaration observing the state's refusal to respond to the Cassel declaration is read in the churches.
17 October:	The Prussian superior court declares that the Confessing Church is not a legal part of the German Evangelical Church.
6 November:	Italy joins the Anti-Comintern Pact.
7 November:	A protest against the writings of Rosenberg and warning that confidence in Hitler is fragile, signed by ninety-six Lutheran and Confessing pastors, is held back from public declaration after Goebbels threatens charges of treason.
11 December:	Kerrl confirms the appointment of Werner, made on 20 March.

1937

1 MEMORANDUM BY BISHOP BELL, FEBRUARY 1937

Private and Confidential
Visit to Berlin
January 28 – February 1, 1937

I left Harwich on the evening of January 27th, and arrived in Berlin on Thursday, January 28th, at 4.30 p.m. Here Professor Adolf Keller met me. We first went to the office of the Society of Friends to arrange an interview, and then to the Furstenhof Hotel, Potzdamerplatz. Keller had been in touch with the British Embassy about a possible introduction to Baron von Neurath whom he wanted me to see, so I called there and saw Sir Eric Phipps. He was very kind but said that anything in the nature of political intervention was very much resented, and he could not give me an introduction unless on the instructions of the Foreign Office. He thought that if it were desired to see Baron von Neurath I ought to write a personal letter myself. He himself thought that as Ribbentrop was nearer the Führer it would be better to get in touch with him.

In the evening, after dinner, Hanns Lilje came.

January 28. Talk with Hanns Lilje. Lilje had made most of the plans for seeing people, and had taken great trouble. He was anxious that I should see Baron von Neurath and said he had reason to believe that an interview would be welcomed by the Baron. It was agreed that I should write personally to him. Lilje said that the situation in the Church was much more serious than it had been. In particular the two leading now in the Church Ministry were hostile and were very dangerous. He mentioned Muhs and Schimanowsky – an ex-Pastor who had left the Church and was now in charge of the Police Department in the Church Ministry. Lilje also laid special stress on the suppression of the Evangelical Weeks.[1] They were not actually forbidden as such, but they were made impossible, or deprived of their speakers. Thus Lilje had himself just been forbidden, that morning, through the Secret Police under orders from the Church Ministry, to enter the Province of Schleswig-Holstein for five weeks. The Evangelical Week due there was not forbidden, nor was his preaching forbidden, but he himself forbidden to enter. So Bishop Meiser had been forbidden to preach at Erfurt, and Bishop Marahrens had been forbidden to go to Lübeck. Evangelical Weeks now, so I understood from Lilje, were being suppressed because they endangered religious peace. The Church Ministry refused to help in the case of dismissed Pastors at Lübeck. The Seminary at Elberfeld (a Confessional Semin-

---

1 The programme of Evangelical Weeks, public gatherings in which clergy and laity met to discuss religious questions, began with an assembly at Hanover in August 1935. Widely supported, the series soon attracted the attention of the police and at the end of 1936 two meetings, planned to take place at Nuremberg and Erfurt in January 1937, were banned. Controversy ensued. Between January and August 1937 six Evangelical Weeks and three Evangelical Days were prohibited.

ary) was suppressed, and the penalty of 'relegation' was threatened against all taking part in theological courses which were managed by the Confessional Church. 'Relegation' involved rejection from all Universities. Lilje mentioned that the Theological Faculties were good at certain Universities, such as Tübingen, Erlangen, Leipzig, and in part Göttingen; but not good at Berlin, Bonn, Heidelberg, Giessen.

The new movement, he believed, was a movement of 'separation from the Church and Christianity'. The Führer gave this slogan recently at Fogelsang – a training centre of youth leaders. Sixteen hundred men left the Church recently together at Rostock, and the Führer has told leading men to leave the Church. There is thus a steady and deliberately encouraged departure from the Church.

In the matter of the Oxford delegation, Lilje pointed out the need of protection for those who went there. He said that Meiser and Marahrens had both been very much attacked in Germany for disloyalty after their visit to America before Christmas.

January 29th. Interview with Miss Collyer and Professor Martin, both of the Friends. A long conversation, mainly about Ossietsky[2] whose health was better, but who did not, as far as they could see, apparently wish for special help from foreigners. They said that E. Fuchs[3] estimated the number of political prisoners in concentration camps as between fifty and sixty thousand.

Interview with Dr. Zoellner, President of the Reich Church Committee, accompanied by Bishop Heckel and Dr. Wahl, at 12 noon at Marchstrasse. We had a long and very discursive conversation, almost entirely about the Oxford delegation. Zoellner had really forgotten the main point about his agreement at Chamby. He was personally kindly, but he was obviously much too old for his job now. He said that his birthday was tomorrow (January 30th) when he would be 77. It is not really necessary to go over the whole discussion. But he said that it was impossible to allow any suggestions from Praeses Koch, except as material for the Nominations Committee which would choose the whole delegation. He obviously wanted to choose some of the Confessional Church representatives himself, and to reserve his freedom. He insisted that the Church was now pretty fully organized, and that where there were not Bishops recognized by the Reich Church Committee there were deputy leaders, and that these deputy leaders took the place of the Bishops in any common council. He was very anxious that Oxford should not be an arena for the Church conflict. He said that permission to leave for a foreign land could only come from the State which would scrutinize the names of the delegates. He pointed out that the Foreign Office of the Church (Heckel's department) was specially qualified to consider competence for oecumenical work. We parted shortly before 2. and arranged to meet again on Sunday. Nothing was said about his relations with Kerrl which I knew from Keller and from Lilje had become extremely critical.

Interview with Bishop Marahrens at 3 p.m. This was at the office of the Lutheran Council. Bishop Marahrens said that there were great difficulties, and that it was perhaps impossible to go to Oxford at all. He said that they had their

---

2 Carl von Ossietzky (3 Oct. 1889–3 May 1938), socialist journalist and winner of the 1935 Nobel Peace Prize. An unflinching critic of the National Socialists, Ossietzky died in a concentration camp after many years in and out of prison.
3 Possibly Ernst Fuchs, theologian and historian of the New Testament.

own problems to settle with the State, and they wanted to settle them. How could they be fairly discussed at Oxford? 'We might be afterwards attacked for treason.' He said the situation was much more serious in Germany than before. The forces which were unfriendly to Christianity were now more powerful, and the movement against was deliberate and unsteady. The forces friendly to Christianity were still existing but they were weaker, and they were unable to apply themselves fully to the situation. He did not think much could be done from outside. He realised that Ribbentrop was making propaganda in England to show that the State was favourable to religion, and it might be true that the State was, as such, not formally hostile; but it was the Party that did the propaganda. It would be quite true to declare that influences hostile to Christianity in public life were encouraged. It would not be true to say that Germany itself was hostile or was anti- Christian. Bishop Marahrens was very friendly, but he was feeling the seriousness of the situation in the German Church very keenly.

Interview with Pastor Niemöller, at 5. Keller and I went on to Dahlem and met Pastor Niemöller in the house of a lady who was an old friend in Egypt of Keller's – a member of Niemöller's congregation. Niemöller was entirely different make and quality from Marahrens. He was somewhat slight, and a man of great vividness. Our talk together, which lasted nearly 2 hours, was a real inspiration. He was like a man on fire, but smiling and friendly all the time; and a man of very great faith. He was not just a fighter, though he was that too. He said that faith was greater than organization, and that there had been too much interest in organization everywhere; but we must not begin with that. He had two fundamental principles – Matthew XVI 'Thou art the Christ, the Son of the Living God', and Matthew XXVIII 'Go ye out therefore and teach all nations, baptising them in the name of the Father and of the Son and of the Holy Ghost'. He refused to agree that he was simply concerned with some secondary confession. Those were the two fundamental principles for which he stood. Now the Church was being persecuted, but he emphasised the fact that the life of a Christian was a life with an obligation. With the National Socialists their convictions were an obligation and all other things were secondary. So many Churchmen were luke-warm and with them their Churchmanship was secondary. As to help in other countries, he said 'You have your own problem of Church and State, and everyone should tackle it in his own country.' He was altogether most friendly and warm-hearted. We could not have had a happier or more illuminating talk. I asked about Ribbentrop, who lives in his parish. Mrs. Ribbentrop, née Henckel, rather detached from the Church; as a girl of sixteen had refused to join the Evangelical Church. Ribbentrop, when he married her, left the Church. In 1932 their two elder children, aged about 14 and 15, much influenced by a nurse, desired baptism. This was arranged for by Niemöller after consultation with the Church authorities, while of course the Ribbentrops could not act as sponsors. In 1932 Ribbentrop asked for re-admission to the Church. Niemöller asked 'Do you believe in Christ as your Saviour?'. When Ribbentrop said 'No', Niemöller said 'Then you cannot be admitted. There are too many already in the Church like that.' Ribbentrop quite understood and smiled. He had often been in Ribbentrop's house. Their views on National Socialism were the same. In 1934 Ribbentrop wished his baby christened, and made the same request for re-admission, and gave the same answer and was again refused. There was no loss of friendship.

Niemöller said that the situation in the Church was much worse, and that there were many difficulties in his own congregation. One of his own colleagues sided with the Reich Church Committee.

Supper with Lilje and Dr. Breit, the President of the Lutheran Council. We had nearly three hours together, Dr. and Mrs. Lilje entertaining us. Dr. Breit is a man of about 60. He impressed one as a man of great seriousness and also real ability. He comes from Munich. He said that the policy of the Lutheran council was not political. They adopted the Barmen statement so far as theological decision was concerned. The only disagreement was on how to behave vis-a-vis the State Church Committee. There was no theological principle involved. The difference between the Lutheran Council and the Provisional Church Government was to be explained by the difference of background. The intact Churches which the Lutheran Council mainly represented, had a tradition behind them. The 'destroyed' churches (which had suffered from the coercive measures of 1933) had no tradition. Breit would say to the provisional Church Government 'You cannot solve the whole problem by giving it up. You preserve your beautiful theology as correct, but at a price.' It is quite true, he said, that there is a danger of over-stressing the attitude to the State set out in Romans XIII, but while the Lutheran Articles said that the State office holder was to be respected, yet if the State went wrong the Church was to oppose the State. He thought that Dahlem had given up too easily and readily all hope of keeping the Christian tradition and the State together. He maintained that we are not permitted to give up the Christian idea of a State. 'We (the Lutheran Council) have a pious *tradition*. Dahlem has a pious adventure. Dahlem is indeed a Church of faith.' The Lutheran Councils were now much more in the battlefield than, apparently, Dahlem, and he instanced the attacks on Meiser and Lilje. The unification of the Church which had started in 1933 had produced 56 Churches in place of the existing 28. The Lutheran Council had arisen and said that it wished to do away with territorial boundaries and to have a single Church, and that it had been founded with this object in 1935.

The Lutheran Council had not authorised the Reich Church Committee to act for it in the matter of the anti-Christian propaganda, but had made certain conditions. A serious tension had arisen between Kerrl and Zoellner. In that situation the Church Committee had found itself in a vacuum. This produced a dangerous position. Should the Church Committee now resign? Some thought that it should resign, but the Lutheran leaders said 'No. The State will say that you have resigned, and will then take much more drastic measures. We (the Lutheran Council) will give you ecclesiastical authority if you feel obliged to oppose the State, and only so far as you act ecclesiastically.'

As we parted Breit said that he felt like a man in prison; that he was most grateful for the visit, and that our coming was like the coming of one from Jerusalem to Babylon.

Saturday, January 30th. Interview with Baron von Thadden and Pastor Eberhard Müller. Müller was Lilje's successor as Secretary of the Student Movement, and was now Secretary of the Evangelical Weeks of which Baron von Thadden was Chairman. They were the result of some academical associations started by Marahrens. After the split in the Confessional Church, the Weeks went on as a spiritual tie binding both sections together. Both parties thus were present at Stuttgart. Collaboration on a spiritual basis was easier. Some ten thousand people had been reached through these Weeks, and they did missionary work amongst the people, also occupying territory which had been occupied by German Christians. They were now attacked by the Church Ministry, particularly by Schimanowsky. The struggle began last October. At Flensberg both Asmussen and Henrich were forbidden to speak. Asmussen stayed away, but Henrich went and was arrested, but was liberated after an appeal from Bodelschwingh. Schimanowsky became very menacing, and he and Muhs can take any measures they like against the Weeks. It seemed that Weeks now under preparation had been forbidden, but that one at Nuremberg had been allowed in part, while Dortmund, which had been allowed, had been finally forbidden. Speakers were sometimes allowed to speak on a religious subject. But can the Church allow its missionary work to be forbidden?

The Southern Bishops were applied to by them for authorisation, and the Lutheran Council on January 29th, i.e. the previous day, invited Müller and von Thadden to declare that measures taken against the Evangelical Weeks would be measures taken against the Church itself. The leaders of the National Socialist party declared that lay preachers were not church officers, and that they could therefore only be political opponents. The Provisional Church Government (and apparently the Church Committee too) were likely to declare that attacks on the Evangelical Weeks were attacks on the Church. If the Church Committee made this declaration, they would probably continue, they expect, in spite of preventive measures. Their work was, they insisted, a spiritual work. It consisted of a preaching of the Word, a statement of doctrine, an application of Christianity to the circumstances of to-day, apologetics against Rosenberg. The real objection to them was that they were gaining ground, especially over the German Christians. They asked parents to make a stand against the paganisation of youth. At the larger gatherings there were sometimes four thousand present; at the smaller, fifteen hundred. They made a special appeal to youth. They represented the real evangelistic work of the Church, taking the place of the old forms.

They said that the nomination of Muhs in the Reich Church Ministry meant that the State would not tolerate any other influence than the State. Kerrl was no longer the exponent of National Socialism in the sphere of the Church. The nomination of Muhs was the real cause of the split between the Church Committee and Zoellner. Zoellner said he could not work with Muhs. Kerrl then said that members of the Church Committee would no longer be invited to deal with Church affairs. It was true that 'positive Christianity' was still held by some members of the Party, but the revolutionary element was gaining ground. Zoellner was at present in a transitional position. The time would come for his removal. Zoellner is said to have declared at Lübeck that he would be more rigid now against Kerrl. Zoellner's precarious position was a reason for the rigid attitude of Niemöller. Zoellner was not objected to personally by him and his friends, but he was regarded as a manoeuvre of the State. Baron von Thadden was himself a member of the Provisional Church Government executive.

To a question how were the wounds to be healed, the Baron said that yesterday there had been a meeting of Southern Bishops at Ulm, with the approval of the Provisional Church Government. Some 'intact' churches[4] were obliged by their

---

4 The 'intact' *Landeskirchen* were the churches of Bavaria, Württemberg and Hanover, where church organization and administration remained in place under the Lutheran bishops, Wurm, Meiser and Marahrens.

existing constitutions to have some relations with the State. In the 'destroyed' churches'[5] territory they were confronted with a hostile State (South and West of Germany more Christian than North. In the East there was a real revival movement in the country. In mid-Germany there was less Christian life than elsewhere.) In the party the stratum of the dispossessed old bourgeois was lifted up again, and found a new means of existence in a large army. Similarly the old commercial travellers had become Generals, Majors etc. As to the general rearmament, the Baron said that after the disappointments of the post-War years it had become a conviction that in order to have influence in the political world, you must have an army. Now that Germany has power, Russia is interested. But the military party were not eager for war. Military strength was thought to be decisive for exercising influence in the world. This impression was confirmed by the treatment of Memel, when the League of Nations did nothing to help an unarmed Germany.[6] The Baron was himself an agriculturalist, and he spoke of the inter-relation of the economic and the military problem in Germany. He said that Germany was not interested in any war in Europe, though Alsace, he said, constituted some sort of problem. He was formally convinced that if Germany were given better economic conditions, it would be willing to enter into the general political field of Europe.

How can foreign Churches help? There should be a stronger activity on their part, but everything must be done to avoid the impression of a conspiracy. The leadership of the German Church was as patriotic as that of the Church in England. He suggested that two questions should be combined: (1) A will to help Germany, and (2) A struggle against the anti-Christian propaganda. The Church of England should declare that there was a *communio sanctorum* also in the non-Roman world. Mussolini had managed to cancel the German law suits against Roman Catholic priests, and the Ministry of Justice had accordingly cancelled the law suits against the Evangelical pastors. The Roman law suits were mostly on morals; the Evangelical were mostly about the Oath.[7] It was painful for them that Rome was so strong, and that the Evangelicals were divided. The impression prevails with the Government that the Roman Church is a real Church. Hitler said in some castle recently 'The Roman Church is a Church with which one can have dealings. The Evangelical Church is a heap of sects which can be neglected.' The Baron said if Central Europe is to be saved at all, the Christian State must find a solution on a very large scale in the way of large help to Germany and other countries, and do it on the grounds of Christian communion so far as the churches are concerned.

Interview with Praeses Koch. Little was said about the Oxford delegation. He would take that up with Zoellner. But Koch was very greatly worried because of the publication of the letter to the Führer at Whitsuntide. He said that in the declaration of the Provisional Church Government in the pulpits at the end of August they had said that it was against their instructions and wishes that the

5 The 'destroyed' churches were those which were led by the councils of brethren of the Confessing Church established by the first provisional government of the church at the Dahlem synod of Oct. 1934.
6 The loss of Memel, located on the Baltic, had long been a grievance to Germans after the Great War, and the League of Nations was sternly judged for failing to resolve the question. German forces occupied it in Mar. 1939.
7 i.e. the civil servants' oath.

matter of the letter had been known abroad. There were two people who were involved in the selling of the letter to the foreign Press. One was Weissler – a full Jew who was in the office of the Provisional Church Government; the other was Tillich, who sold it for 150 marks.[8] The German Christians were now spreading it abroad that Koch and his friends were guilty of high treason. How had Bishop Ammundsen and the English bishops seen the letter? Forell was charged with being the channel. I said that Forell would be in Berlin next week; and he said that he would ask him himself. He was obviously very much afraid that extreme measures might be taken against himself, as had been threatened, according to a Dutch journalist, in 1934 when Koch had been given to understand that if he went to Fanö he would suffer the same fate as Röhm.[9] But the Government hesitated to proceed on the basis of rumours. Koch thought that my letter to Hess about Christmas probably had something to do with the delay in acting. The *Stürmer*[10] had prepared a special number on the whole subject, but it had not yet been allowed to appear. The German Christians had announced that they would publish the general charge of high treason in a Sunday paper on February 14th. Every day brought anxiety. The first signs of a charge impending against him came soon after August 23, 1936. He had seen Weissler's collaborator at the beginning of August and had said that he was very sorry for the leakage – it was not their fault – and had written to the Minister of Justice who was proposing to make an official enquiry. So far nothing had actually happened. It was the Basel newspaper which had published the letter, and Koch had pointed out that the editor could not give his contributor away.

Turning to the general situation, Koch said that the time may come when the churches abroad may manifest communion with the Churches here. Koch quoted Hitler's remarks 'One has to count with the Roman Catholic Church, but the Evangelical Church is a heap of sects.' Koch said that united the Evangelical Church were a strong body. The situation was much worse in the last few months, and the Provisional Church Government was suffering from the stigma of this publication. He expects sooner or later a strong attack on the whole Evangelical Church. The declaration from Churches outside would be most useful, and it should be so devised as to protect the Confessional Church, though possibly Zoellner might object to some expression which had that object in view. He thought it not likely that the attack would come immediately, as Hitler has other sorrows. He thought that the persecution should be even more visible than it is now to justify even smaller actions. 'The little dogs will be let loose soon.' He showed me a typescript attack on the Provisional Church Government which Dr. Ley's *Arbeitfront* was circulating. He also quoted a remark made by Rector Horstmanbunde (whose son was a Confessional Pastor). He was a German Christian, and had said publicly at Bad Oeynhausen 'I have come to the den of lions, but I am not afraid to charge Koch with high treason.'[11]

8 On 6 Oct. 1936 Friedrich Weissler and Ernst Tillich were arrested for making public the memorandum to Hitler which was drawn up by the second provisional church government of the Confessing Church on 28 May 1936. Weissler died in Sachsenhausen concentration camp on 19 Feb. 1937. Tillich was released in 1939.
9 Ernst Röhm, the leader of the S.A., was murdered in the purge of the movement of June 1934.
10 A journal published by the National Socialist Party and edited by Julius Streicher. It was notorious for its vicious antisemitism and violent language and imagery.
11 The Confessing synod of Bad Oeynhausen, 17 Feb. 1936.

A declaration was not wanted at the moment from the Administrative Commit-tee.[12] These things cannot be repeated. When I asked at what moment it would be wanted, he said that he thought that now the German Christians had failed, and the Church Committee had failed, in dealing with the Church, that there would be an appeal to the people to quit the Church and forsake Christianity. In Westphalia quite recently the law for raising taxes by the Church tax with the authority of the State had been cancelled. This was of great importance because it was in an industrial area. The Roman Catholic bishop had however succeeded in getting the tax continued for the Roman Catholics. With regard to Hitler's attitude, Koch said that it is certainly Hitler's desire, but you cannot quote his words, that members of the official administration should quit the Church. Though nothing has been publicly ordered in fact many officials are quitting the Church – policemen and so forth. At Dortmund on one day a hundred left, beginning with the Burgomeister.

Praeses Koch said it was a great support my coming to see him. It was a difficult life for him, the same anxiety every day. We then lunched together in the Hotel, and during luncheon listened for nearly two hours to Hitler's speech to the Reichstag.[13]

Interview with Dr. Böhm and Otto Dibelius. We talked about the non-Aryan question. They said that the search for a pastor was difficult.[14] A man called Gordon, married with no children, was suggested, but this turned out to be unlikely for he did not seem the kind of man who would be a settler rather than a salaried pastor to settlers. We talked of the delegation to Oxford. At the Faith and Order Meeting at Clarens it was apparently settled that the Church Committee should not send officially to Edinburgh, but less officially, as in 1927 to Lausanne. Zoellner, Lange, Deissmann and Dibelius were considering names. This del-egation will probably mature. With regard to Oxford nothing was settled, but conferences had been held by Zoellner and the Provisional Church Government. When Zoellner was reminded of the arrangement made at Chamby he said he had forgotten. The real difficulty is now – what will the Church situation be in July 1937? They wanted to know who would choose the speakers at Oxford. Would it be the individual delegations? And who would take the devotions? They feared apparently that suggestions for German spokesmen and leaders would be left to Zoellner, if he came. I said that these were all matters for the Conference itself, and the Programme or Business Committee. The situation in the Church was worse. Muhs was like Jaeger. The result would be that the possibility of sending a delegation to Oxford was less likely. Meiser and the Lutheran Bishops would think of not going to Oxford but sending a declaration that they are persecuted by the State – they could not come, as Oxford would be certain to be watched by the secret police. The same issue lies before the Provisional Church Government; if they did not go, Zoellner would not go. There was to be a Convention of the Provisional Church Government in April for the study of certain questions, and a brochure of about 70 pages would be

12 i.e. the administrative committee of Life and Work.
13 30 Jan. 1937 was the fourth anniversary of Hitler's coming to power. In this anniversary speech he sought to reassure Poland that he respected its right to exist.
14 A pastor was needed for the establishment of a community of resettled refugees in Columbia. The first refugees left for Popoyan on 16 Feb. 1937, but the venture proved a failure and it was abandoned in 1941.

produced after the Convention and would be available for Oxford. It would deal with special points arising out of the Provisional Church Government, e.g. Church and People, the Community, etc. Supposing they were able to go to Oxford, the question would be then how to get English pounds. What would the economic situation be in July? They were all obliged to save a percentage on the expenditure of 1936; thus orders had been given to save 25% of fat, 50% of metals, 10% of paper. The question however of approaching the Government for financial facilities would be raised after (and if) the delegation had been chosen. One possible way of helping for English pounds might be the printing of *communio* in Germany.[15]

The situation was much more serious, as has already been stated. In the National Socialist State there were two currents, (1) Those who wished for a compromise between National Socialism and Christianity, (2) Those who wished *ecraser l'infame*. They had been struggling against each other which should win. In the Autumn of 1935, with the appointment of Kerrl, the first of these currents was still strong. Now there was no doubt that the second was much stronger. The newspapers of the S.S. and S.A. always contained articles against the Christian faith. Now numbers of big Party men were leaving the Church. It was all being done conspicuously. Muhs belonged to the radical wing. He had given the ordinary notice to the Ministry of Justice that he would leave the Church, when he was appointed to a post in Kerrl's ministry. As there was an interval between giving notice and the notice taking effect, he had withdrawn his notice. But it did not alter his attitude. When Dibelius, or somebody, said to Zoellner 'You are serving an anti-Christian State', Zoellner said 'The State which elected me was not anti-Christian – now it is.' The future of the Church situation depended on the political situation and especially on foreign policy, and not least relations with England. The visit of the Catholic Bishops to Rome was of great importance. The Meeting at Fulda in January was an extraordinary Meeting. It was said that Mussolini had promised help to the German Cardinals on condition they supported his candidate for the Papacy. But whatever the truth of that, something was going on.[16] Cardinal Bertram was very anti-Nazi. If the Roman Church problem is assisted or solved, this would help with the Evangelical Church problem. Also the future of the Evangelical Church must depend on public opinion in England.

There are two secondary points to remember – (1) The State looks on the Evangelical Church as a trouble-maker; (2) The Fascists, the Bolsheviks, the Nazis can only develop on one line, i.e. must always be sharper. Its inner principle drives it on and it cannot stop. So Otto Dibelius. Böhm said that there were two phases of the State's attitude to the Church – (1) The political phase, with a view to getting power over the Church; (2) The philosophical phase, viz. to educate the children in National Socialist ways. The real intentions of the

15 Unidentified. It is likely that this was an ecumenical journal or report published by the Life and Work movement.

16 Immediately after the Fulda conference of 12–13 Jan. 1937 the three German cardinals, Bertram, Faulhaber and Schulte, and bishops Galen and Preysing, travelled to Rome to urge that the pope make a public statement on the situation facing the Roman Catholic Church in Germany. Consequently, Faulhaber, Secretary of State Pacelli, and Pope Pius XI set to work on a new encyclical expressing their concerns: *Mit Brennender Sorge*. This was issued on 14 Mar. 1937. It would mark a turning point in the history of the Roman Catholic Church in the Third Reich.

State still lay behind a veil. Much importance must be attached to the Castles of Orders (like religious orders) for the training of the leaders; also the non-Confessional elementary schools, called the 'Adolf Hitler' schools, were very important, and the method of the party was very clever. They did not just promulgate a new law, but purported to consult the people with a view to getting *neutral* schools.

National Socialism has always had a struggle – long before it came into power. It must fight. The Church alone exists now on any other side. Therefore it must fight the Church.

They asked me about Macdonald and his visit to Germany. Did I know that Von der Ropp was in the Secret Service of Germany five or six years ago? This has been established as a fact, when he first came forward in Christian work a little while back.

On Saturday evening at 6.30 Keller and I went to the Opera and heard 'The Meistersingers'. The Opera House was packed.

Sunday, January 31, from 9.30 to 12.30, Keller and I had a long interview with Dr. Spiero of the Paulusbunde and Fraulein Friedenthal of the Provisional Church Government, on the non-Aryan question. There is a separate Memorandum about this.[17]

On Sunday afternoon (following a short visit to Hugh Green[18]) we went out to see *Professor Seeberg*. He is sympathetic to the German Christians, but whereas he had been Dean of the Faculty (I suppose after Deissmann's disappearance) he was no longer Dean, having given way, as he put it, 'to wilder men'. He was very friendly. He had no use for Karl Barth. He said that Hitler's religion was a combine of a sort of mystical symbolism and the enlightenment. The mystical symbolism had always an appeal to Germans, notably as found in Eckhardt, Jacob Böhme, and Goethe.[19] In a way they were seeking Christianity without the Church. When I asked what 'positive Christianity' meant, he said Rust had answered the same question, when he asked it, by saying it meant ethics. He said that his own point of departure was the Incarnation. The Incarnation was not limited precisely to one moment, but it followed from the Incarnation that God reveals Himself in life. But he added he did not mean by this, revealed Himself in Hitler. He was about to produce a new volume dealing with the theology of Luther, I think from this point of view. I asked how many students of theology there were in the University. He said that in 1933 there were altogether 1000 theological students in Berlin University, and 600 taking his course. This year there were 150 only in his course, and that would soon drop to 60. When I asked why, he said that the academic life was discouraged, and that soldiering absorbed many people: but there were some members of good families who were studying theology. He said that the Confessional Church stated that the University and State examination was not necessary. So far as he

---

17 See document 4 in this chapter.
18 Unidentified.
19 Meister Eckhardt (1260–1327), Dominican mystic whose writings were revived by the German romantic movement in the late eighteenth and early nineteenth centuries. Jakob Böhme (1575–1624), Lutheran theosophical mystic also favoured by the romantic writers. Johann Wolfgang von Goethe (1749–1832), great German romantic writer of literature, particularly known in England for his play *Faust*. It is perhaps surprising to find his name here.

was concerned, he felt that his first task was to keep the theological faculty alive in the university, and his second task to keep it alive internationally.

Interview with Zoellner, with Heckel and Wahl. We went on, driven by young Seeberg, a theological student, to Zoellner, in his private house, arriving an hour late. We had a good long talk, but not a very important one. I felt more and more that Zoellner was not up to the task – forgetful and repeating himself. He said the Party but not the State was anti-Christian; but he spent a lot of time in explaining the course of some Conference in the previous few days with the Provisional Church Government. He had hoped to come to an agreement with them for co-operation in Christian work, but they had insisted that the Confession of Barmen must be accepted in every detail. When Zoellner said he could accept a good deal of it, and he could accept the spirit of the whole, they said the discussion could not proceed. He gave me a dossier about this. I said that I was very much puzzled by this, and I felt that there must be something behind. That could not be the real reason. I thought that Heckel and Wahl agreed about this.

Zoellner said that there had been a sharpening of the situation in the Church, due to (1) the irritation of the Führer because of the intransigence of the Provisional Church Government, and (2) the growth of the national idealism of an anti-Christian kind represented by Rosenberg. Zoellner felt very sore. He felt that if the Provisional Church Government had played up a year ago, he could have succeeded in solving the Church question in three months, and he said he would guarantee that he could have done. The declaration by the Provisional Church Government read in the Churches on August 23, with the claim of the individual pastor to decide as to what State action was right, and to judge the State (so Zoellner represented), was intolerable to Hitler. Zoellner again quoted Hitler's remark about the Evangelical Church being 'a heap of sects'. He said that Dibelius had actually told Zoellner that if he and Marahrens were to inform Hitler that they two were united on behalf of the Evangelical Church, he (Dibelius) would telegraph to Hitler that Z[oellner] and M[arahrens] had no authority to speak for the Church. This, Zoellner said, was intolerable.

Wahl told me afterwards that Zoellner was negotiating with the Hitler Youth leaders for the protection of Sunday and for the protection of Evangelical youth from an anti-Christian *Weltanschauung*. I remarked to Wahl afterwards that though I had suggested that I wanted to know something about the difficulties in the Reich Church Ministry, and had said so on the Friday, Zoellner had not dealt with this. Wahl said that that was probably due to his having received an unexpectedly friendly telegram from Kerrl for his birthday the previous day, which led Zoellner to hope for better relationships; so he did not want to deal with that question while such a possibility existed. Zoellner went off to the theatre at 6.30. Keller and I went on to our next appointment.

Interview with Superintendent Diestel at his house. Herr Diestel and his wife gave us supper, and we saw his daughter Renate, a girl of about 15. We had a very good talk of a general kind. Diestel made a point which Lilje had already made, and which is, I think, fundamental with regard to Zoellner. Zoellner had never been in the persecution of the Church. He had not therefore the experience of those hard times which enabled him to enter into the feelings of those who had, and to see the real crisis. Diestel also said that Zoellner was rather too near the German Christians. There were certain German Christians, like I think Rahm,[20]

---

20 Wilhelm Rehm was *Deutsche Christen* leader in Württemberg.

who were a dangerous influence upon Zoellner. Also Zoellner had not protected the Confessional pastors enough. Diestel said agreement between Zoellner and the Provisional Church Government was really impossible. Diestel made some interesting remarks about the present position of Church and State. The modern world has left the position of a State built upon Christian principles. There was no such thing now as a Christian State. There were new ideologies, and it was now for individuals to fashion their lives on Christian principles. The same applied to the idea of a colony of non-Aryan Christians with other Christians abroad. What Government would take them? Governments now asked 'How much money have you got?' – not 'What principles?'. Anything can be had for money now. The idea of building civilization on Christian principles was no good, according to present notions.

Interview with Gustav von Bodelschwingh. We waited for him till about 11.30 p.m. at the Hospice, to which he was coming after a journey by train. He was the brother of the Von B[odelschwingh] who had been elected Reich Bishop. He was a fine man, simple and very real. He was very much against the Provisional Church Government. He said 'Niemöller and Koch do not understand the State.' Karl Barth's influence was fatal. Niemöller and Co. had never spoken a word of gratitude for what Hitler had done for Germany. He had only blamed him for his faults. Thus he had said Hitler had slain a thousand but only owned to 79, at the time of the 'purge'. Let Hitler say so, and say he was sorry that he had lied. But there was no mark of penitence on the Church's part. The Church itself has sinned much. Let it say so. Von B[odelschwingh] knew Reichbishop Müller and had been very greatly opposed to his appointment, and had protested insistently, by letter and by waiting outside the State Ministry or the Chancellor's House, against Müller's reception by Hitler. He said 'What the Church wants is a father, and there is no father for the Church in Germany.' To Koch and Niemöller he would say 'Resign if you disagree with the State, (i.e. Hitler). My father resigned his office of Finance Minister when Bismarck wished to go to war with Austria.' All that was happening was a judgement on the Church. The Church must not make a political party (as the Catholics had done). In opposing Rosenberg it must use the method of penetration. Further, the Church must not measure the State by a Christian standard. The State was to be regarded as a scourge for the Church. It was unfair to expect it to be measured by ordinary Christian principles. The State had become authoritarian, the Church remained democratic but it should (so I gathered) become authoritarian too. We had much discussion about how far the State was free to act on non-Christian principles, and whether there could be no John the Baptist protesting against the State and justified in doing so. Von B. poured out his soul. He was deeply religious. He said that his brother was coming more round to his position. He said that he had known two geniuses in his life – one his father, the other a great locomotive engineer, Schmidt, and he felt that he was guided by the sort of instincts by which they would have been guided.

Monday, February 1st. Interview with W. Gros, a non-Aryan sculptor, who told me his story, described in a letter from myself to Leiper and to Glick.[21]

---

21 A full account of Bell's interview with the sculptor Wilhelm Gros may be found in his letter to David Glick, substantially reproduced in Ronald Jasper, *George Bell, bishop of Chichester* (London, 1967), pp. 138–9.

Interview with Graf Durckheim. Durckheim rang me up, as I had written to tell Ribbentrop that I was in Berlin but said particularly I did not want anything. I had half an hour with him. He was obviously not best pleased that I should have been seeing so many of the Church leaders. He said that my letter to the *'Times'* had harmed the Church.[22] He felt that the State would become harder to the Church as things went on, and he also quoted Siegmund Schultze's bitter complaint that the Allies had conceded to a militarised Germany what they had refused to a civilised Germany. He said that it was easy to pick out a few perfectly true facts and to quote them out of all relation to the general position of Germany, and thus give an entirely untrue view of Germany. I referred to the anti-Christian propaganda as a very important point; also to the encouragement now being given to party leaders and others to leave the Church; also to the attacks on the Evangelical Weeks, and the attacks on Bishops Meiser and Marahrens after their visit to America.

Interview with Dr. Lilje and Otto Dibelius. We lunched together. I asked Dibelius about Zoellner's accusation that it was on inability to agree on Barmen that proposals for co-operation had broken down. He said that that was really ridiculous. Zoellner managed the Conference very badly and could easily have got a basis of agreement, but he is too old and obstinate. He also ridiculed the idea that he (Otto Dibelius) had threatened to send a telegram to Hitler. He said Zoellner's obstinacy and forgetfulness was a very great difficulty. I emphasised the fact that the Barmen theses would be difficult for English theologians, and that they certainly would never understand failure to agree on a broad basis because Barmen was considered a position to be held in all its Particles at all costs. He quite agreed. He said that the line to be taken now was that the Provisional Church Government and the Lutheran Council should agree together (which should not be difficult) and present their agreement to Zoellner. I saw Dibelius upstairs. When we went down and joined Lilje we talked about Durckheim's conversation. They both took the view that the very fact that Durckheim had criticised my letter had shown its great value. There was no criticism possible within Germany; therefore none of which the Government need be afraid. The only criticism available was outside Germany and they had to pay attention to that. Dr. Dibelius also said that it would be a very impressive and a very useful act if, at the great Service in St. Paul's Cathedral between the Oxford and Edinburgh Conferences in the Summer, a very special point could be made in a sermon by the Archbishop of Canterbury that all the Christian Churches represented at that Service and those Conferences stood together under the Cross of Christ.

Lilje saw me off at the station, as did Keller. I told him what Dibelius had said about agreement with the Lutheran Council. He said it was for the Provisional Church Government to make the first move as they had treated the Lutheran Council rather badly.

We then said goodbye, and I arrived at Chichester on February 2nd at 11 a.m. G.C.

---

22 Bell's letter to the *Times*, 27 Mar. 1937, p. 13e. Durckheim was Ribbentrop's deputy in Berlin.

2   BISHOP HEADLAM TO THE GERMAN AMBASSADOR, JOACHIM VON RIBBENTROP, FEBRUARY 1937

Your Excellency,

I must thank you for the long and interesting conversation that I had with you yesterday. It emboldens me to write and express more fully what I tried to say to you. That I do the more readily because I believe that I represent and understand the views of many people in this country who are most inclined to sympathise with your country. It is to a large extent the more religious minded among us who have felt the injustice with which your country has been treated, a treatment at variance with our traditions.

Now, with all that you said to me yesterday about the aim of your Chancellor to restore the unity and prestige of your country, and to build up its economic life, we should sympathise fully, and again with its desire to re-create the wholesome traditions of German life, for which we have had a great admiration. But when this desire is interpreted in the terms of 'blood and soil', and when, as some of your people seem to do, the German God is contrasted with the Christian God, then we dissent because we believe that the greatest factor in building up the traditions of the German people has been the Christian religion.

Now, as I say, the great body of religious-minded people in this country sympathise with the aims of your Chancellor in restoring the life of the nation in all its aspects; but what has done so much harm in just those circles that sympathise most with you has been the treatment of the German Church and the Roman Catholics, and the suppression of religious education.

(1) As to the treatment of the Church we have followed with close attention the history of this trouble, and have done our best to get accurate information from all sides. It has always seemed to us that your Chancellor was wiser and more sympathetic than some members of the Party; but there seemed to be other forces far less wise at work. The Confessional Church has seemed to me much too narrow in its outlook, but it has been driven into that position by the unwise action of Reich Bishop Müller. What we feel is that the Christian Church should be free from State interference, and that in that way it will be best able to benefit the nation.

(2) Although there is much that we dislike in the Roman Catholic Church and in its policy, we think that anything which seems like coercion, or can be described as 'persecution', is wrong. Moreover, all experience shows that the Roman Catholic Church is most dangerous when it is attacked. All Christians believe that 'the powers that be are ordained of God',[23] and are ready to support the established government unless it interferes with Christian liberty. Also, the opposition of the State throws the Church into the hands of its ultramontane element.[24]

(3) Christian liberty means in particular, both for the Protestant and Roman Catholic Churches, freedom for religious education. While we quite understand your desire to train up a disciplined body of young people in physical fitness, we gather that there is a movement for suppressing religious education in Chris-

---

23 Romans xiii. 1.
24 A view within Roman Catholicism which emphasizes the central authority of the papal curia over national powers.

tian schools, and that seems to us contrary to the just treatment of the Christian Church.

I was very much interested in what you said about your conversations with the Chancellor on the revolution taking place in religious ideas. As I have already suggested, many of us will feel that your Confessional Church meant a presentation of the Christian religion out of harmony with the thoughts of the day. We in this country are always trying to teach Christianity in a manner which may be in harmony with what is true in modern thought, and may meet the needs of the day; and that we believe the Church will always do automatically if it is left free and unfettered. I feel sure that to be in close harmony with both the theoretical and practical Christian movements in this country at the present day would be a great help to people who in your country are working at the same problems and would be a help also to us.

Now, may I say something in conclusion about the Conferences to be held in this country this year? Life and Work at Oxford in July, Faith and Order at Edinburgh in August. There will be collected together at these two Conferences religious leaders and theologians from all the countries and Churches of the world except, unfortunately, the Roman Catholics. It will be a great misfortune if Germany does not take a part in such a conference, or if representatives are not allowed to come from all the different parties in the Church. It is quite true that things critical of this country will be said; but if Germany is not represented it will be very injurious, I am sure, to its reputation. The conference at Oxford is concerned with Christianity in relation to the life and work of the community, and includes all those matters which concern its beneficent action in the world. The conference at Edinburgh will be concerned with definitely religious and theological questions. It avoids all references to anything political. Its influence will be more indirect; but I am not certain that ultimately it will not be found more important for all those problems which you and your Chancellor were discussing; for Germany not to be represented or to be represented imperfectly in these conferences would be a great misfortune for the rest of the world, which has learnt so much from your country in the past; for it would prevent your country being able to exert its proper influence, and I think it would be a misfortune for Germany itself.

I must apologise for the great length of my letter and for speaking so plainly, but you said that you must speak frankly and I, also, have tried to be frank as well as sympathetic.

Believe me,
Your Excellency,
Yours most faithfully
A.C. Gloucester

3   BISHOP BELL TO ARCHBISHOP LANG, 12 FEBRUARY 1937

Private

My dear Lord Archbishop,

I had a most interesting and instructive four days in Berlin, January 28th to February 1st. I saw a large number of Church leaders and others. In particular I saw Dr. Zoellner, the head of the Reich Church Committee; Bishop Marahrens of Hanover; Dr. Breit, President of the Lutheran Council for Germany; Praeses

Koch, Otto Dibelius, and Dr. Böhm, all of the Confessional Church; Pastor Niemöller, the famous minister of Dahlem; also Gustav von Bodelschwingh; Professor Seeberg of the University of Berlin, Graf Durckheim who is Ribbentrop's representative in Berlin, Dr. Lilje, the Secretary of the Lutheran Council, and others. I also saw the British Ambassador[25] and had a talk with him; and I had three hours with the representatives of the non-Aryan Christians.

I gave your Grace's messages where I thought it discreet to do so, and in particular to the non-Aryan Christians who received the assurance of your Grace's sympathy with very great appreciation. I think it will interest you too to know how often reference was made to the abdication crisis and to the influence of the Church – not so much in direct intervention, so to speak, as in the religious influence on popular opinion which the standards of the Church secured: and of course pre-eminently to your own broadcast address.[26] Praeses Koch told me how constantly he read your utterances in the *Times* which he takes in, and how great an admiration he has for you.

With regard to the general position of the German Evangelical Church, and indeed Christianity generally in Germany, things have altered for the worse in the last three months. The radical trend is clearly gaining ground, and the more moderate trend, which the appointment of the Reich Church Committee in October 1935 represented, has lost considerably. All the Church groups were agreed upon this. Dr. Zoellner has a great struggle in his own Ministry with the officials of that Ministry. Kerrl is not a very strong person in himself, I gather, but very recently two strong Party men have been introduced into leading positions – one an ex-Pastor Schimanowsky, who is in charge of the Police Department in the Church Ministry (what a Department to have!); and the other Muhs who is the Permanent Secretary, and had given notice that he wished to quit the Church. Others in the Lutheran Council and in the Confessional movement regarded themselves as in prison, metaphorically speaking, and it was very pathetic to find how pessimistic they were. Zoellner, alas! is far too old for his responsible post. I do not mean necessarily old in years – he was 77 actually on January 29th – but he had already retired from active work when he was recalled by the State, and he cannot get away from old ideas and old prejudices, and is very forgetful. It was really most pathetic.

They all enormously value the sympathy of the Church of England, and it is a great support to them to know that they are watched and encouraged.

With regard to the non-Aryan Christians, their position is lamentable I fear. Things are worse and worse for them. They see no future in Germany. I enclose a Memorandum with regard to their position which your Grace may care to read at leisure, and I do wish that one could do something to help them.

I write this letter so that you may have something at any rate as a token of my having visited Germany, though I hope that one of these days I may be able to speak more personally *viva voce* about it all.

Yours very sincerely and dutifully

George Cicestr.

25 Sir Eric Phipps.
26 Lang's broadcast of 13 Dec. 1936, after the abdication of Edward VIII, was widely considered a mistake in England itself. See J.G. Lockhart, *Cosmo Gordon Lang* (London, 1949), pp. 396–407.

4   MEMORANDUM BY BISHOP BELL, FEBRUARY 1937

NON-ARYAN CHRISTIANS.

Interview with *Dr. Spiero*, (head of the Paulusbunde, 10 Kurfurstdann, Berlin-halensee) and *Fraulein Friedenthal*, (Secretary of the Department of the Provisional Church Government dealing with Non-Aryan Christians, under Dr. Albert, Friedorgstr. 11, Berlin-Dahlem).

––––––––

We had three hours together on Sunday morning, January 31st, 1937, and went over the whole situation. They told me that there were 400,000 Jews in Germany, and there was a possibility that the non-Aryan Christians, i.e. those with at least one grandparent non-Aryan, were 1,000,000.

According to the law, both a man and his wife must have four Aryan grandparents in order to be employed as a State official, physician, dentist, teacher, professor, architect, engineer, artist, musician, officer or under-officer in the army.

Further, a man and his wife must have Aryan grandparents going back to 1800 in order to be a lawyer, an editor or press-man, a peasant landowner, or a member of the Party. The certificate of baptism seems to be of material importance with regard to this last category – 1800. Those who lived in 1800 must have been baptised before 1800 to be qualified. Further, though theoretically there is an opening for non-Aryan Christians in industry not connected with the State and in some banks not connected with the State, and though Schacht,[27] on October 24th, 1936, sent a proclamation to this effect, the practice was usually different, as the doors were in reality for the most part closed.

The position of the non-Aryan Christians is much worse than the Jews'. They have no international organization behind them, and no great men representing them. It is worst of all for the young. The older ones can complete courses on which they entered, and the adults have sometimes been pensioned when they have been turned out. But the younger generation cannot enter upon a profession, such as medicine, though they are allowed to study for the profession. Those who are in the universities at present can complete their course, but they cannot take up posts. There is a difference between the full non-Aryan and the 'Crossing'. The full non-Aryan Christian is one who has four full Jewish grandparents. The 'Crossings' are those with one or two Jewish grandparents. The full non-Aryan Christian may not serve in the army or in the *Arbeitdienst*. The 'Crossings' have some rights. They may show a flag, they may have Aryan servants under 45, they may vote for the Reichstag; they must serve in the army though they cannot be officers. Of those who have passed Matriculation, the 'Crossings' can study without limitation. A limited number of the full non-Aryan Christians can study. They can enter for the College examination, e.g. for medicine, but they cannot take the State examination.

Non-Aryan Christians are allowed to go into Jewish business firms, but these Jewish firms naturally take full dues. If their fathers have no farm, farming is impossible for them. Other careers that are impossible are illustration, writing,

27 Hjalmar Schacht (1887–1970), president of the *Reichsbank* (1933–9) and economics minister (1934–7).

acting, cinema, singing, orchestra. They are not allowed to give private lessons, except with permission, to non-Aryan pupils. Non-Aryan teachers only may teach non-Aryan children. There are some non-Aryan Christian schools. In some Jewish schools there are some non-Aryan Christian teachers and children, but these schools present a real difficulty, because the Jewish schools are Zionist schools. The non-Aryan Christian parents do not know what will happen to their children. In some, but not in all, public schools, non-Aryan children are treated kindly. The schools are bad in Heidelberg and in various smaller towns in the provinces, while the conditions are better in Berlin and Hamburg. If it is asked 'Why should there not be non-Aryan Christian schools as such?', the answer given by many non-Aryan Christians is that this involves a classification as non-Aryan Christians, which they dislike.

A still more difficult situation for the young will be created by the new law which comes into force at Easter, saying that all boys and girls, from 10 to 18, must be in the Hitler Youth. Non-Aryan Christians will not be allowed to be members. It is quite possible that 'Crossings' will also not be allowed. Yet the Hitler Youth is in future to be the channel through which entry is made into the whole of German life. Thus the course for an ordinary German boy or girl is, first Hitler Youth, then either the S.A. (Brownshirts) or S.S. (Blackshirts), (the latter being an armed or semi-armed body, unlike the former, and being carefully selected, numbering between 20,000 to 30,000, and the corps out of which Hitler's bodyguard is chosen, and admission is only possible to those who can trace Aryan grandparents up to 1800), then six months in the *Arbeitdienst* and two years in the army; and of course everybody will join the Party. To be ruled out of these organizations by race, closes all opportunities of life in Germany. There is no law indeed that one should go into the S.A., but it is in fact almost as good as a law. The keenness of the feeling against non-Aryan Christians is illustrated by a new law which has just been passed in Magdeburg. Here it is impossible to have a funeral for a Christian non-Aryan. The crematorium is closed to such though it is open for Jews. When an non-Aryan Christian dies, the corpse is left in the house. No undertaker will take it. The Prefect of the Police is sent for by the relatives, and it is for him to decide whether the body is to be buried in the Jewish cemetery or the Christian cemetery. Apparently this is only the case in the one town of Magdeburg at present, but may spread.

What of the future? What are boys and girls to do after Matriculation as well as while they are growing?

Dr. Spiero and Miss Friedenthal were grateful for the opportunities given for education abroad. There are 40 at present in England but they could do with 400, and they have many applications. There is of course the difficulty of a transfer of money, for money would often be available if it could be sent out of Germany. But the really fundamental problem is that of transplantation or settlement out of Germany for many thousands. That is the only opening that they can see with any hope of a future. They believe that in the United States there are great chances for individuals as physicians etc., but they also want great masses of families settled; and settled with other Christians of different nationalities and not simply as a colony of non-Aryans. The principal thing for which they care is that non-Aryans should not be stigmatized. 'Are there not great wide rooms' they asked, 'in which we could settle?', 'Is it possible to go to New Zealand or Australia?'. They would much prefer the British Empire to

South America, and they would be only too glad to be naturalized British citizens, and the community would be in the main a farming community.

The difficulties of finding work will be made still more evident when it is seen that not only is it impossible to nurse or to be a typist etc. in ordinary secular firms, but even in Bethel[28] apparently non-Aryan Christians are not admitted for work. It is also nearly impossible for non-Aryan Christians to get into the Protestant Inner Missions Institutions,[29] because they receive money from the State.

Why is not the German Church doing something?

The answer is that the Provisional Church Government would like to help, but cannot because it is not recognised by the State. The Reich Church Committee could help, and Zoellner ought to speak with Rust and Kerrl. There ought to be an order issued through the influence of the Church that non-Aryan Christian children going to a public school should be treated kindly, and that pastors, who have children's organizations in every community (Gemeinde), should bring both the non-Aryan and other Christians together.

Suggestions for the Administrative Committee.

Write to:-

        (1) Zoellner,
        (2) The Lutheran Council,
        (3) The Provisional Church Government

to say that when the law is in force requiring all children to join the Hitler Youth, then it is a task of the Church to provide for the non-Aryan Christian children who are not allowed to join the Hitler Youth.

It would also be good to write to the same Church representatives asking for admission of non-Aryan Christians to Church institutions e.g. as nurses, deacons, kindergarten instructors, teachers of housewifery; and that no difference should be made by the Church between Aryans and non-Aryans. If they are not allowed to take the State examination, then that of the Church should be accepted.

The Paulusbunde has about 30,000 members. It has to do with charity, legal advice, lessons in foreign language, religious instruction, settlement etc.

G.C.

5   ARCHBISHOP LANG TO BISHOP BELL, 19 FEBRUARY 1937

CONFIDENTIAL

My dear Bishop,

Pray forgive my delay in thanking your for your letter of February 12th about your visit to Germany. My thanks are very real. I read your letter with the greatest interest. It so happens that I had already read a report of a visit from A.J. Macdonald and also had some talk with him here. It was interesting to compare your impressions and his. He of course is critical of the more decisive attitude of people like Niemöller and thinks that they missed a great opportunity when the Church Committees were formed in October 1935. His report which I understand will in some form be issued by the Council on Foreign Relations

---

28 Bethel, near Bielfeld, comprised a theological school, an orphanage and a sanatorium. It was a
    famous charitable institution run by Bodelschwingh.
29 Home missions of the German protestant churches.

seems to go very far even in recognising the merits of many 'German Christians', and I cannot but think that some other interpretation of the situation such as yours may be a necessary addition. Meanwhile of course since you wrote Zoellner and his Church Committee have resigned and Hitler's announcement seems to change the whole situation. I should like very much to have a talk with you and learn what your reaction to Hitler's proposal is.

I was much impressed by your Memorandum about these poor non-Aryan Christians. It is indeed a most distressing position. But it is not easy to see what we can further do to help them except in the way you suggest for your Administrative Committee.

Tell me when you are likely to be in London within the next week or two so that if it is possible you could come here and let me have some full talk with you on the whole matter.

Yours

Cosmo Cantuar.

6   BISHOP HEADLAM TO ARCHBISHOP LANG, 16 APRIL 1937

Private & Confidential.

My dear Archbishop,

. . .

I understand you are going to read Macdonald's report. I think it is one-sided, but I think what he brings out and what one ought to remember is, that the Christian religion is not confined, as some people seem to think, to the Confessional Church. I had a young German staying with me here before Easter, who was really a very devout Christian, and he represents more or less the official Church, and he expresses great astonishment that people like the Dean of Chichester should be such strong partisans for the Confessional Church, for the theology of that Church is something which they could not possibly stand. I think too the absolutely non-compromising attitude taken up by that Church has really hampered the settlement of the position in Germany. Niemöller is a truculent sailor, who was a leader in the submarine warfare, and I think, though his nationalism is not that of Hitler, it would be equally aggressive. I think the partisan character of the interest people seem to take in foreign countries is often rather dangerous. After all Hitler is a person with great power, and I do not think that a policy gratuitously insulting him is likely to work for the peace of Europe.

Yours ever,

A C Gloucester

7   BISHOP HEADLAM TO ARCHBISHOP LANG, 22 APRIL 1937

My dear Archbishop,

I have read Dr. Macdonald's letter. The real difficulty about all these people is, that they will take sides in such a partisan manner. If Macdonald had written his report with discretion, I don't think there would have been any difficulty, and I rather blame myself for not having gone through it with him and suggested alterations. I was very much occupied with other things at the time, and, after all, one desires to trust people like him. But he is really not discreet. He was not discreet, of course, on the Roumanian Commission, and he does not seem to understand how things look to other people. On the other hand, the opposition to him is just as bad. The partisanship of the Dean of Chichester (he has never I think met other people) is quite intolerable, and all the Evangelicals on the Council think that Niemöller and his people stand for Protestantism and, therefore, must be supported. I have already arranged to write a preface to both the reports that we propose to publish, and I will do my best to be reasonable.

Yours ever,

A C Gloucester

1938

CHRONOLOGY

19 January: Archbishop Lang addresses convocation and observes the continuing oppression of Christians in Germany.

25 January: General Blomberg resigns from the general staff of the German army.

February: A.S. Duncan-Jones, dean of Chichester, flies to Berlin to see the trial of Martin Niemöller.

4 February: Ribbentrop is appointed foreign minister and Fritsch is dismissed as commander-in-chief of the army. Hitler assumes personal command over the armed forces.

12 February: Hitler meets Schuschnigg, the prime minister of Austria and forces concessions from the Austrian government.

2 March: Niemöller is acquitted, but immediately taken to a concentration camp.

5 March: Kerrl orders that all ordinances in the church, excepting those concerned with doctrine or ritual, must now be submitted to the Ministry of Church Affairs for approval.

11 March: German forces occupy Austria and the *Anschluss* of the two countries is declared.

29 March: Archbishop Lang speaks on the *Anschluss* in the house of lords.

10 April: A plebiscite in Austria confirms popular support for the *Anschluss*.

20 April: Werner orders that all pastors in the Old Prussian Union should swear an oath to Hitler.

9–13 May: A conference takes place at Utrecht to prepare for the creation of the new World Council of Churches.

14 July: Bishop Headlam criticizes Bishop Henson for his support for Martin Niemöller in a letter to the *Times*.

16 July: Henson replies with a robust riposte.

17 July: Joint Christian and Jewish intercessions take place across England for the persecuted Jews of Germany.

20 July:	Headlam responds with a second letter against Henson in the *Times*.
26 July:	Archbishop Lang and Bishop Bell publish an exchange of letters in the press declaring that Headlam's view do not represent those of the Church of England.
27 July:	Bishop Bell makes his first speech in the house of lords, voicing concern over the refugee crisis.
31 July:	The Confessing synod of the Old Prussian Union recommends pastors to take the new oath of loyalty.
15 September:	The British prime minister, Neville Chamberlain, flies to Berchtesgaden to see Hitler in the light of the crisis in Czechoslovak-German relations.
18 September:	Congregations across England observe a day of prayer during the Sudeten crisis.
22 September:	Chamberlain travels to Bad Godesberg for his second meeting with Hitler.
27 September:	The second Provisional Government of the Confessing Church issues a special order of worship and prayer for peace during the Sudeten crisis.
28 September:	Archbishop Lang broadcasts a call for prayer.
29 September:	The Munich conference of European powers.
30 September:	Agreement is announced at Munich.
2 October:	In England a day of national thanksgiving is observed after the Munich agreement.
5 October:	The German government announces that Jewish passports will be stamped with a 'J'.
29 October:	The Lutheran bishops, Marahrens, Wurm and Meiser, are summoned by Kerrl. The prayer of September is described as treasonable. The bishops are ordered to sign a statement of condemnation. They do so.
7 November:	Ernst vom Rath, legation secretary in the German embassy in Paris, is murdered by a Jewish youth.
9–10 November:	A pogrom against the Jews of Germany and Austria, *Kristallnacht*, takes place after Rath's murder. Ninety-one people are murdered; 191 synagogues are destroyed.
12 November:	The *Times* publishes a letter from Archbishop Lang protesting against the pogrom against the German and Austrian Jews.

1938

1 MEMORANDUM BY BISHOP BELL, APRIL 1938

A Visit to Berlin and Hanover
April 20–22 1938

All the members of the Oecumenical delegation to the German Evangelical Church received telegrams from Bishop Marahrens on Good Friday saying that the conference planned for Easter week had become impracticable.[1] It appeared that Lilje on the Wednesday had seen the head of the cultural department in the Foreign Office who had advised giving it up as inopportune. (English unpopular – Foreign attacks in press on Anschluss). Koechlin and I, nevertheless, after conferring on the telephone, agreed that we two should go personally and see whom we could: telling the others and leaving them to decide on their participation. As a matter of fact we went alone. I arrived on Wednesday morning April 20 – being met by a young pastor (Dr. Rose) and Diestel: Koechlin on Wednesday afternoon. We were busy from the moment of arrival till that of departure, and saw the principal Evangelical Church Leaders. The most official interviews were, (1) on Wednesday night at dinner with Diestel, where we met the Dahlem people, Diestel, Asmussen (president of the Confessional Church Council), von Thadden, Otto Dibelius and another (Gromeysen?[2]); (2) on Thursday morning at Jebenstrasse, with Bishop Heckel and Wahl; (3) on Thursday afternoon at the Lutheran Council office, with Superintendent Breit and Fleisch; (4) on Friday morning at Hanover with Bishop Marahrens. Thus we saw officially and semiofficially all the main elements in the Church; and I also had a long talk with Böhm, in charge of the Oecumenical work for V.K.L.[3] in hospital, and another with Frau Niemöller.

It was most encouraging that everyone made us feel most welcome – and that they were very glad that we had come, after all. It was a very good action on our part, such was the common view. The Oecumenical Council had sent its representatives, and acted up to the Oxford Resolution – even though not on the scale which had been planned. And now those who were more timid said – the delegation problem had been solved, and we believed them. Further, it was most encouraging that everyone expressed a strong desire for the continuance of the oecumenical relationship. And (what was of no little interest) all parties beginning with Böhm – and including Lilje, Asmussen, Otto Dibelius, expressed the wish that we should call on Heckel.

(1) *Oecumenical work.* Every body wished this to be maintained: although it

---

1 A delegation of members of Life and Work was to visit Germany during the Easter week of 1938. The idea was, however, complicated by the incarceration of Martin Niemöller and the *Anschluss* with Austria. The German foreign office discouraged the visit, and so, at the last moment, did Bishop Marahrens. Bell arrived in Berlin with Alphons Koechlin.
2 Unidentified.
3 Unidentified.

was recognised that political conditions in Germany might cause difficulties at the moment. Indeed Dibelius and Böhm both said (with Heckel) that there was no chance of anyone being allowed to go to Utrecht, for example: and asked that the principle of the 'empty chair' to be occupied when they were ready might be accepted regarding future developments. Böhm emphasized the importance of regular visits of brothers from other churches for mutual information. 1937 had been a good year, and many such visits had taken place. Professors and Pastors should come to Germany, discuss theological problems, etc. Ernest Barker[4] would be very welcome. Breit pointed out that there were big psychological difficulties: the Oecumenical Movement was distrusted by the State, it seemed something anonymous, dangerous, intangible – a sort of unknown force not very friendly to Germany. So Dibelius and his friends felt that the present possibilities for the German Church, were simply to work within Germany on the common problems, i.e. doing oecumenical work inside their own nation, as they could not get opportunities outside. There was no real opportunity for German Church to do active work for the Oecumenical Movement. They had to stand there as witnesses for the oecumenical idea in spite of the atmosphere – tide over until a better time came. Breit said, that the main fact that they had to recognise was that State authorities criticised, hampered or destroyed all oecumenical activities wherever they could (see the history of the Oxford delegation), and the church must, therefore, seek to get the way free for such activities. He himself felt that their only constructive contribution was to get as many personal relations as possible with individual churches. Let representatives of single churches pay visits – make the reality of the particular church known to the German Church. The principle of *Una Sancta*[5] was agreed. This plan of getting to know single churches was a sound way to bring it home, the individual foreign church being, as it were, a sector of the Una Sancta. It must be recognised that (out of my own experience in parish life) the Oecumenical Movement is so little real to the members of our congregations – everything possible should be done to make it real to them. Breit added, that theologians were good, and indispensable, but the congregations need another way: and it was a real misfortune that so far the Oecumenical Movement could only be understood as 'something done by theologians'. Bishop Marahrens also laid great emphasis on the necessity of basing the movement on the congregations – there was a real danger not sufficiently appreciated by Heckel, of keeping the special studies apart in the hands of Theologians only, and failing to provide for the rank and file in the parishes. Marahrens himself had had most illuminating oecumenical discussions with his 1100 clergy. So far as the theological work was concerned Heckel had obviously been doing a good deal. He was anxious, he said, that Oxford should not remain a torso. A group of 50 theologians and students were proceeding with 'Life and Work' problems; and another group with 'Faith and Order' problems. The grouping of subjects under the heading 'Church, Community and State', was disagreeable to German thought, as the Oxford Conference was not popular – indeed that kind of heading had been killed. Better to start with the Bible – then the Church – and so come onto Life and Work problems. Or rather (expanding)

---

4 Ernest Barker (1874–1960), professor of political science and fellow of Peterhouse, Cambridge 1928–1939. Barker was a prominent lay member of the Church of England.
5 The universal church.

'Dogmas and Reality', thence onto 'The Doctrine of the Church' (compare 'Doctrine in the Church of England') – and 'The Church and Reality'. Heckel emphasised the importance of giving considerable freedom to the individual church to take what subject it liked or felt most appropriate out of the common field. He said that they wished to discuss especially relations between the confessions – the confessional basis of *Una Sancta*, or the Oecumenical Movement in relation to structural confessional types. In Germany they had the impression that (though Oldham[6] had not intended it) there was far too great centralisation in the preparation for Oxford, the nearer the conference approached. That ought to be avoided in the future. Let each church take what appealed to it most strongly, though, of course, keeping in close touch with the whole Movement. Thus it might be, that 'Education' might mean a great deal more to the Americans than it did to them – and 'Weltanschauung and Faith' a great deal more to the Germans. The main point must be freedom for each church to study the problem or problems most relevant in its own situation, but from the oecumenical point of view. As to subjects in the Oecumenical Movement most likely to appeal to Germans, Dibelius had suggested that Faith and Order might be safer. But Marahrens said, that while it was true that in his clergy conferences issues of faith and order did arouse more interest, it would be a great pity not to keep Life and Work subjects to the fore. And Heckel said that there was no restriction imposed by the state on research. Future relations between German Church and Oecumenical Movement on the research side relatively easy – though freedom in framing the subjects for research should be greater, and so freedom in the bringing of the particular Church's own contribution. Böhm told me that they had received the Oxford Report and were to work on it, by means of conferences, etc. During the last half year oecumenical work has been made impossible by the Secret Police.

(2) *World Council*. There appeared a general agreement that the name proposed (partly owing to the German translation *Weltkirchenrat*) was unfortunate, suggesting a new ecclesiastical power of cosmopolitan kind. Marahrens emphasized this; and urged that the organisation should be as simple as possible. Dibelius said, that to Nazis the World Council was *monstrum horrendum*! Heckel urged the immense importance of marking continuity. Indeed he thought it a great pity to amalgamate Faith and Order and Life and Work in one organisation. The difficulties of cooperation would be much greater if an entirely new organisation was to come into being. Continuance would be much easier if the old line could be followed as far as possible. And as to staff, Heckel thought change ought not to be made until the whole structure of the council was shaped. Much easier to have confidence in Bureau or Council, if you know the men – already well known in this kind of work. Confidence would thus be maintained. A new General Secretary expected, but that he must not be a man like Siegmund Schultze or Tillich – not an extreme man – but he should be a theologian, gifts of organisation, gifts of personality. (Marahrens also stressed the importance of his being a theologian, so giving a proper faith basis to all his work). Heckel seemed to favour the more lawyer like man like Max Huber, as the authority of clergy is waning, that of lawyers is increasing, even in church administration.

6 J.H. Oldham was the prime-mover with Visser 't Hooft in drafting the programme and preparing material for the Oxford conference on Church, Community and State.

Both Heckel and Marahrens are anxious that Schönfeld should remain – they trust him – he is well known; he would be a token of German interest and collaboration; while to drop him would certainly be noticed in Germany. Dibelius, though he did not say so, implied that Schönfeld being more economist than theologian might perhaps be spared.

Utrecht. There seemed no chance of any German delegates. Marahrens spoke as though he might come as one of Committee of 14, but did not wish to endanger his attendance at the Lutheran World Convention Committee just after at Uppsala. He asked if Dr. Nubel (U.S.A.) could deputise for him. This was difficult – but we said that he might be taken into consultation by the Committee of 14. (N.B. Unless Dr. Nubel or some Scandinavian Lutheran in (Oxford) Committee of 7, the Lutheran Church will be unrepresented).

(3) *Bishop Heckel.* His position recognised to have grown in strength. Thus Böhm said his position was strong with Foreign Office and Party: and he was suspected of connexion with the Secret Police and of responsibility for withdrawal of 7 passports. Böhm thought (wrongly it would seem) that Heckel wished to stop [the] Oecumenical Movement because State and Party dislike it. It was clear that Heckel was the necessary channel through which all questions of passports and money for delegations must go. Böhm wished us to challenge Heckel as to whether he considered himself the sole legal representative of the German Evangelical Church – would he go to Utrecht (e.g.) with Dahlem and Lutheran Council? (Marahrens had sent H[eckel] to London for Committee of 14 with a limited mission: H[eckel] had overstepped it – he would not do so again). H[eckel] had refused to sit with the rest for receiving the Oecumenical delegation, had it come in full force. Asmussen also wished us to challenge Heckel as to his claim to represent Evangelical Church solus. Dibelius thought we should inquire Heckel's attitude to future. Would it be an advantage to make a change at Geneva turning research in the Edinburgh direction? as Kerrl's view of the Church's function is that it is to pray and to struggle about dogmas. Dibelius said the Kassel gremium dissociated itself from Heckel. Lilje also wished us to solve the Heckel question. We, however, pointed out that we foreigners could not intervene in what was a purely internal matter. But we would call on Heckel, and discuss future of Oecumenical Movement with him – study, F[aith] and O[rder], Life and Work, Schönfeld, etc.

(4) *Present conditions of 'Evangelical Church'.* Dibelius much the most illuminating here. The Nazis are in high spirits now. The position much more difficult for the Church. But the Church position connected with the political position on a whole. Some people think war very near – if so in interests of unity of nation, concessions might be made to the Church. If Berlin-Rome axis extended to London this also might affect it. All these things make it difficult to tell people the real facts month by month – and the Austrian Anschluss weakened opposition to the State.

Generally speaking there were two lines of attack:- (1) Incessant struggle against the Church and the Faith of Christ. Party leaders constantly leaving the Church – first quarter of 1937 steady stream: 2nd and 3rd quarters a stop, because of the proposed Church election: 4th quarter (election abandoned) more than ever. Nazis have baptisms, marriages, funerals of their own – but felt to be meagre: e.g. at funerals much said about dead man's qualities, not about death. Not felt to be the real thing. (2) Constant going forward with plans for official (or State) Church. Now that Zoellner committees had collapsed, the Party was trying to achieve their aims in an administrative way. But silently, rather than by throwing hundreds of pastors into prison. The old figures of 1933 were reappearing. The old German Christians were being put on to the Church courts and administrative boards. The Party tried to take away confessional pastors when they were displaced – (Pastor Rose told me) by German Christians; private members of the congregation sometimes lent their houses for church services. Difficult to find money for confessional pastors when not recognised. State wished to get young confessional pastors who had been ordained by Confessional Church to undergo new examination – 90 per cent of them refused. The administrative control was exemplified in Austria. A State Board to be set up inside Austrian Church – the proposed General Synod not to be created, but a lawyer appointed by the State to control, with perhaps a bishop without administrative influence. There was also talk in Germany of a Bill to bring clergy under law of treason by making them take the oath and accept the Weltanschauung required of all State officials. There was a wiser situation regarding V.K.L. which was now allowed to have a church office – but its officers were ordered not to leave the districts in which they lived – and so prevented meeting in the office!

Frau Niemöller. My talk with Frau Niemöller was pathetic. She had seen her husband for 45 minutes at the Alexandra Platz prison, whither he had been brought for the purpose from the Sachsenberg Concentration Camp. She had only ten minutes alone with him. For the first ¼ hour he had been dazed – not knowing why he had been wanted – fearing a death in the family. Then he talked – what troubled him most was the uncertainty, how long he would be confined months? years? There was a library in the camp to which he had access. One hour's outdoor exercise per day. No conversation. Solitary confinement. The strain great. Doctor came to see how he was, after the talk with his wife, as the warder heard him say he felt poorly. Only two letters allowed each month. No visitors. She had been permitted to see him as a special favour, because she said she was going into the country for a little while and wanted to see him. She said she was sure he had never been asked to sign any document. His solicitors were with him until his rearrest, and there was no mention of this. She seems very restless. Seemed to like the idea of a holiday in England – when I said we should be most happy to have her and children. But she was anxious – restless. Then her children *needed* a father. She was very fearful lest Niemöller should be forgotten by churches abroad. I assured her this was not the case. We prayed together at the end.

Sir Neville Henderson. I saw him just before leaving Berlin. He was very kind. He emphasised Hitler's objection to foreign interference. Why do your bishops, M.P.s and press interfere in *my German* Church? I shouldn't with Welsh disestablishment.[7] Hitler claimed that there was no country in which the Church was so free as in Germany. Henderson's own view was that there was persecution: that it was specially in Prussia, where the Church had been dead: that it might mean (had brought, I said) religious revival: that Rosenberg was the real black spot. He did not think that Hitler knew all that went on – but what he cared for was *unity of* nation! Two ideas 'nationality' 'socialism' – a genius, though un-educated, except that he had read much history. The Sudeten Deutsch were

7 The Church of England was controversially disestablished in Wales in 1920.

bound sooner or later to join up with Germany -'principle of self-determination'. Henderson deprecated demonstrations! Don't press the Church – wait till the storm rolls by – things will right themselves. Personal contacts and private visits very sound. Come and see me earlier when you next visit Berlin.
G.C.

2   BISHOP HEADLAM TO ARCHBISHOP LANG, 11 JULY 1938

Confidential
My dear Archbishop,

I wish to write a short account of some of my experiences in Germany. I spent altogether ten days there and met and interviewed a very large number of clergy belonging to all parties in the Church. I had with me my niece, Agnes Headlam Morley, who speaks in German as fluently as she does in English. We were treated with the very greatest kindness and hospitality by everyone.

We had a long talk with Von Ribbentrop but, unfortunately, could not see Kerrl as he was out of Berlin. We saw Dibelius and Marahrens of the Confessional Church, Wobbermin and Fabricius and many other Moderate German Christians, Lietzmann and other neutrals and of the Thuringian Church Graf von Korf, a principal pastor in Essen and Landesbischof Schultz of Mecklenburg. Everywhere we found the greatest desire for friendship with this country and friendship with the Church of England; the horror and futility of war was a common subject of discussion. They said England and Germany should work together. I do not think there was any unreality about this.

Parties in the Church: There are about 19,0000 pastors in the Evangelical Church in Germany. Of these a certain number not exceeding 3,000, belong to the Confessional Church. The great majority call themselves either 'neutral' or 'moderate German Christians'. The number of extreme German Christians is not large.

As regards the Confessionals, I think I had better give you an account of a conversation I had with Professor Lietzmann. He said that we made a great mistake in England by concentrating our attention on the confessionals and ignoring the rest of the Church. Much as we might respect them he thought they were mistaken. When Dr. Zöllner's Committee was appointed they had an opportunity of uniting the Church. He knew that that Committee was appointed with the sincere desire of bringing disunion to an end, and they missed an opportunity which would have been good for the wellbeing of the Church. He thought we should give up partisan activity and do all we could to help to create a united German Church.

Dibelius' answer to that would be that Dr. Zöllner's Commission was not intended to be a success; that it was simply a means of getting the Church into the power of the Government, and that their opposition had saved the situation. I believe he was quite wrong.

Secondly, as regards the neutrals: I will give an account of a talk with a young pastor of the name of Kagerah. He spent a year at Westcott House[8] and has

---

8 Westcott House, Cambridge, is a theological college for candidates for ordination in the Church of England. It is named after Brooke Foss Westcott, bishop of Durham, and followed a liberal tradition.

stayed with me at Gloucester. He is now pastor of an important parish in the suburbs of Hamburg. He is not a Confessional and dislikes their theology. He tells me that his parish is a good one. There are about 5,000 people in it. Hardly any of them have left the church. In Germany you have to pay the church tax unless you have formally declared that you have ceased to be a member of the church. Almost everyone in the parish was confirmed, but many of them suffered a good deal from the excessive devotion to physical exercises. They discussed freely with him difficulties raised by the religious teaching they had received in the schools. The church tax in the parish was 10% of the income tax. It was collected and administered by the State. In his parish it amounted to 180,000 Reich Marks. He had no trouble from the Hitler Youth as the local leader was a good Christian.

I had similar accounts from pastors of the Berlin parishes. Many people who left the church under Communist conditions were now returning, and in an ordinary parish the great majority of the young people came for confirmation. That was the case with the working classes even more than with the upper classes.

The Moderate German Christians: I would take for the Moderate German Christians Professor Fabricius. He takes the view that the National Socialist movement represents positive Christianity, and he has written a pamphlet to prove that. He told me that Germany was National Socialist and Christian. Professor Wobbermin, whom I know well, and who has stayed with me in Gloucester, takes the same view. He is said to be working a good deal for the unity of the Church. I asked them both about the Rosenberg movement. They said that it had no real hold on the country at all, and that the various stories we are told about creating a new German religion did not represent anything serious. When I talked to Dibelius about them he said that Fabricius and Wobbermin were good men but they were professors, and did not in the least know what was going on in the world.

The Thuringian Church: I had the opportunity at Cologne of a long talk with two members of the Thuringian Church. We also met at Professor Wobbermin's an enthusiastic pastor who I suppose would say that he belonged to the same party. They are accused of denying the Old Testament, of denying that Our Lord is the Son of God, and of putting Hitler on the same level as Christ. They assured me both statements were entirely untrue. Their view of the Old Testament was that of Luther. They believed in the incarnation; they believed that Jesus Christ was the Son of God; they believed that Christianity is a religion of Love. What they were opposed to was the theology of Karl Barth. They objected to his teaching that there was no revelation of God in Nature; that the nation as it belonged to the world was sinful. They objected to the teaching of the total depravity of the human race. I am bound to say that I think Hitler conferred a great benefit upon Germany in getting Karl Barth out of the country. Personally I look upon his theology as intolerable, and I cannot make out why English people take so much interest in him.

Speaking generally, I do not see that there is any substantial reason why all the parties in the German Church should not unite, and that Christianity would be much stronger if they would.

The Anti-Christian Movement: There are sinister movements behind. It is undoubtedly true that many of the leading Nazis are anti-Christian. That is the case with Himmler, the head of the Secret Police; with Ley, with Rosenberg, with Baldur von Schirach, the head of the Hitler Youth and others, both in the centre and scattered throughout the country. I was told that one of the reasons was that they were all renegade Roman Catholics and did not understand the Evangelical Church at all. The origin of the Anti-Christian movement goes back to the Liberal Movement of the pre-War period. All the different ideas embodied in it had their source there. There are two main theses: the one is that Christianity is a religion which makes men weak, and the other that Christianity throughout German history has inflicted great injuries on Germany. They would instance particularly The Thirty Years' War. On the other hand, I was told by one informant that there was a great deal of discussion on these questions and people asked 'Why has Christianity done England so much good? It seems to have made it strong and has helped in the building up of the Empire.' They are very much impressed with the Imperial attitude of the English Church. Now the danger is that Hitler should associate himself with this party. He has always refused to do so. He has often acted in opposition to them. But if he is irritated by the continued opposition of the Confessional Church and by the activities of the English Bishops he may very likely side with them and use all his influence against the Church. That is why the unity of the Church and a moderate and intelligent policy is so essential.

The Hitler Youth: The danger may come through the Hitler Youth. The whole of the training of the young people of the country is put into the hands of the Hitler Youth and is intended to be intensely national. It can be, and is sometimes, used against Christianity or, at any rate, to injure them. For instance, I was told of a clergyman who last Whitsuntide arranged a camp for all his young people for three days. The object was to give them religious instruction and training. The local leader of the Hitler Youth arranged a parade exactly at the same time. Again, another clergyman had a camp and he went out for a walk with seven of the boys. Eight members of the Secret Police arrested them because they were taking part in sport, and sport was confined to the Hitler Youth. On the other hand, Bishop Marahrens said that his daughter had been a member of the Hitler Youth and it had done her no harm at all. Bishop Heckel said the same thing of his sons. Most of the pastors I spoke to said that no harm was done to their work by the Hitler Youth. It depends upon the local leader. And a local leader who is anti- Christian can make himself very disagreeable. I talked to the Thuringian Christians about this, and they said they quite agreed about the danger. That they always insisted on the necessity of Germany being Christian. That it would be ruined if it was not. That their policy was to work with the Hitler Youth and not oppose it. That if the Church were united there would be very little difficulty; that this anti-Christian movement was really something alien to the German people. The real danger was that Hitler would be driven to associate himself with this movement and the attitude of this country, which seemed to suggest that Democracy, which most Germans look upon as a foolish form of government, was identical with Christianity.

The German Church and the English Church: All sections of the German Church were most anxious for friendship with the Church of England. They were interested in our work in Latvia and Esthonia of which full accounts had appeared in the German newspapers. I explained to them that there was no political aim in this work; that we should be glad to carry on the same conversations with Germany, but that we could not approach any section of the German Church, it must be with a united Germany first. They did not think they were ready. But I think some of them are of opinion that unity amongst themselves could be best attained by conferences with the English Church. It must be remembered that theology and outlook of the German Christians is much more in accordance with our ideas than those of the Confessional Church. The Confessional Church are largely under reformed influence and of the theology of Karl Barth. There would be among them a considerable opposition to episcopacy. I was told by German Christians that when they created their new bishops they had discussed the question of coming to the English Church for their consecration.

The Jewish Question: I always avoid mixing up different subjects of investigation, and we did not talk much about the Jews. But I should like to notice two or three things. It is quite obvious that the mass of the people do not know in the least what has been happening in Austria. Two or three people whom we met who did know were horrified. About three weeks ago the Nazis in Berlin tried on a new drive against the Jews. It created a good deal of indignation among the mass of the people and several people the next day went ostentatiously to Jewish shops to deal there, in order to show they did not sympathise with the movement.

Conclusion: I am sure that the great body of the German people are friendly to this country and do not want war. And the policy of Hitler is equally against it at present. That there is behind a sinister element, just as there was before 1914. I think the policy of continuously scolding and irritating the German people and Hitler is most dangerous. For example: The formation of an exhibition in this country German art will do no good and may help to do harm. The political opposition to National Socialism and the condemnation of Germany for having the sort of government they like naturally does no good. As I have said, there are things they do which we don't like. It is not our business to keep every nation in order. We are by no means immaculate ourselves. Our attitude towards the German Church has been very largely a mistaken one. The important thing is that Hitler should learn to respect Christianity. He will not do that if Christianity is used to oppose National Socialism, and if scatterbrained English divines flirt with Bolshevism.

Yours ever

A C Gloucester

1939

CHRONOLOGY

9 February: The Church Assembly debates religious persecution abroad.

15 March: German forces occupy Prague.

18–21 March: Werner publishes four decrees. The consistories are empowered to transfer pastors against their wishes; parishes lose the right to choose their pastors; minorities in each parish are granted the right to demand the use of the church's premises; dictatorial powers are assumed by the president of the consistory.

20 March: Archbishop Lang speaks on the international situation in the house of lords.

23 March: German forces occupy Memel.

25 March: All Germans between ten and eighteen years of age are conscripted into the *Hitler Jugend*.

22 May: Hitler and Mussolini sign the 'Pact of Steel'.

28 May: The Confessing Church issues a public protest against Werner's four decrees.

5 June: Archbishop Lang and Bishop Bell speak in a debate on the refugee crisis in the house of lords.

11 June: Confessing leaders appeal to all pastors to declare themselves either for the Confessing Church or the *Deutsche Christen* movement.

July: Rust closes the theological schools at the universities of Heidelberg, Leipzig and Rostock.

23 August: The Molotov-Ribbentrop pact is signed, facilitating the invasion of Poland.

1 September: German forces invade Poland.

1 September: Archbishop Lang speaks on the invasion of Poland in the house of lords.

3 September: Great Britain declares war on Germany.

1939

1 BISHOP BELL TO PROFESSOR KARL BARTH, 15 NOVEMBER 1939

My dear Professor Barth,

I owe you apologies for not having written before. There is first, your book 'The Church and the Political Problem'.[1] There is next the two articles in the Christian Century which you kindly sent me.[2] I have read both the book and the articles with great pleasure. The book I have read twice. I read it first very soon after I received it, at the beginning of, or just before the war. I read it again on Armistice Day. I feel myself more and more in agreement with you. I do not say that I am carried all the way, as I ought to be. But what you say about the Church and the political problem does strike me as fundamental truth. I had your book, I remember now, when Markus was here.[3] It came just before his weekend with us. And my first glance at the book, and perhaps assisted by Forell's enquiry of me as to whether you should write a book, if war broke out, on the theological justification of the allies' cause (or some such title) made me think there was too much about war and fighting and bearing arms against the aggressor. But reading it now, I find that the argument is an argument which enjoins the Church to take its side indeed in this great conflict, and not to be silent, but to speak while it does not insist, so to speak, on it being the necessary sequel that Churchmen should enter into the fray as bellatores. And I do thank you very much for your book.

I am also very much interested, as you will not doubt, in your more autographical [sic] papers in the *Christian Century*. They were most stimulating and refreshing. It does make a tremendous difference to me in reading whatever you write now that I know you, and have had you in my house and can call you a friend.

Some English newspapers, following a statement in the *Christian Century*, I suppose, have put it about that Niemöller has offered his services to the German military command. Ehrhardt[4] wrote to the *Daily Telegraph* quoting a letter from you to him, denying this. Then came a statement from Geneva put out in the International Christian Press Service, purporting to come from an authentic source, not precisely described, to the effect that Niemöller had offered his services, but not as an escape from imprisonment, and that this offer had been declined. I cannot think that this statement is true. Hildebrandt says that it is

---

1 The only reference that I have traced is to a German edition, *Die Kirche und die politische Frage von Heute: vortrag gehalten an der versammlung des Schweizerischen evangelischen hilfswerks für die bekennende Kirche in Deutschland in Kirchengemeindhaus Wipkingen* (1939). But Bell did not read German.
2 'How my mind has changed in the last decade', Part 1, *Christian Century*, 13 Sept. 1939; Part 2, 20 Sept. 1939. These two articles argue that the church must adopt a 'political' stance in the world.
3 Markus Barth, born in 1915, was the elder son of Karl Barth.
4 Arnold Ehrhardt was a professor of law and a personal friend of Barth's in Switzerland.

impossible that Niemöller should have made such an offer. He says that it is not only the case that his family would not allow him to volunteer, fearing the fate of von Fritsch,[5] but that if he were to fight with the German military forces, he would be fighting for the upholding of those very things for resistance to which he is in prison. Tell me what you believe and know.

A book has just been published by Sir Alfred Zimmern[6] on spiritual values and world affairs, a review of that book in the Sunday Times the other day, by a very well-known writer, J.A. Spender,[7] said that one of the puzzles which he, Spender, found it difficult to solve, was how leaders in the Confessional Church who resisted Hitler and the regime quite whole-heartedly in Church questions, could yet say that they were loyal followers of Adolf Hitler otherwise. I do not myself believe that there are many Confessional leaders left, if any now, who are infected by that dualism. I think they were at one time, but it must be now many months, or perhaps years, since those who had hopes, blind hopes, of Hitler in the political or economic sphere, have been disillusioned. Surely all of them now feel that Adolf Hitler is one and life is one, and that in every department of it the Fuehrer is to be resisted, and that his ideological principles expressed themselves equally in the persecution of the Church, in the system of concentration camps, and in the seizure of Poland and Czechoslovakia.

With all warmest greetings and please remember me to Markus who I hope is settled down well in his vicariate.[8]

Yours sincerely,

George Cicestr.

2   PROFESSOR KARL BARTH TO BISHOP BELL, 8 DECEMBER 1939

My dear Bishop!

Thank you very much for your kind letter. Please excuse my long silence. Theology, in the middle of the term, gives me a great lot to do. Besides, I had some trouble arising from illness, surgeons etc. It is over, I hope so, and here I am.

You are asking me about Niemöllers last adventure. My information, given to Dr. Ehrhardt and transmitted from him to the *Daily Telegraph*, was correct at this moment. Later my information became — alas — wrong. I know the truth directly from Niemöllers family and from his closest collaborators: he *had* offered his services to the German navy in a preceding moment. The he *drew back* his offer (probably in this moment I received my dementi). Then he *renewed* his offer and had a rather unkind non-acceptance by the admiral Raeder[9] (and this is the statement in the International Chr[istian] Press, mentioned in your letter). These are the facts.

---

5 General Werner von Frisch had been removed from office after false allegations of homosexuality had been made against him by the Gestapo in Feb. 1938.

6 Scholar and writer. Author of *The greatness and decline of Rome* (1907) and, later, *The League of Nations and the rule of law, 1918–1935* (1936).

7 J.A. Spender (1862–1942), journalist and political writer.

8 At this time Markus Barth was working in Zurich as an assistant minister to Paul Vogt, the founder of the 'Swiss Evangelical Society for Aid to the Confessing Church in Germany'.

9 Admiral Erich Raeder, commander in chief of the German navy.

The explanation? Lastly there is no explanation. There are only some considerations:

Niemöller is in *solitary* confinement since nearly two years. He had rarely the opportunity to meet people. He had at no time the opportunity to hear and to speak [to] people in liberty, outside the prison and without the presence of watchmen. The news he got from the outside world were these related in the nefarious papers of the official German press. No one knows exactly, what was happening in his mind and especially, what he thought since the war broke out. It is not impossible, that — not his spiritual but his mental strength was in a certain degree shatered . . . !

But certainly, these circumstances are not entirely solving the question.

Do not forget: 1. Niemöller has always been and certainly remained till today a good — a too good — *German*. He fought very earnestly, deeply convinced of the rightness of the German cause in the war 1914–1918. He fought after the war in the same zealous spirit against the German communists. The he became a minister: a devoted, a very faithful minister. But the old Adam — like the old Adam of us all — never died. Being a spotless lover and promoter of the evangelical message he never ceased to be at the same time a fervent German nationalist. He became a member of the National Socialist party (later he resigned!). He agreed with Hitler — not with his *church* policy but in a considerable degree with his political views, claims and acts. In the first years of church struggle I myself had not seldom to struggle — against this political short-sightedness of Niemöller and of his friends. I wonder, if he ever saw the *unity* in the thoughts and facts of *Hitler* and the *gasp* [sic] in his *own* thoughts and facts. I do not think that he did loose his brain, when he offered his services to Hitler. I think he did simply, what his old Adam told him to do.

Do not forget: 2. Niemöller is a very good—a too good -*Lutheran*. Lutheranism permits and demands to believe in the ultimate reality of this gasp [sic] between an ecclesiastical and a purely political aspect and attitude. Behind and at the bottom of the astonishing act of Niemöller you will find: the lutheran dualism between the kingdom of heaven and the kingdom of unlimited worldly power, between Gospel and Law, between God revealed in Christ and God acting through nature and history. Lutheranism is very adequate to the natural German soul. And: Anima Germanica naturaliter est Lutherana![10] There are a *few* German theologians and Christians, who are chemically free of the ingredient of this doctrine. *There are some*, you can be sure about that! But Niemöller, I fear, was never among these few people. He is able to be killed from Hitler for Christ's sake. But equally he is able to be officer on board of a warship of the same Hitler!! I hope, that Hildebrandt, Niemöller's former assistant, has learned, since he is in England, to take another line.[11] Before, he also was hardly sickening in this hospital.

Dear bishop, our friends of the Confessional Church are Germans and they are Lutherans. There is a little minority of men and women, who — also since the outbroke of the war — see, what is to see, who suffer and hope and (secretly)

10 The German is a natural Lutheran.
11 A friend of Dietrich Bonhoeffer and Martin Niemöller, Hildebrandt found himself classified as a 'Non-Aryan'. He left Germany in 1937 and worked in Cambridge between 1939 and 1951. Bell knew him well.

fight with us. They need our deep sympathy. They need our prayers. A day is coming when they will be visible and audible. And let us love also the others, this poor majority today erring in the fog. They are, believe me, not bad – only too German, only too Lutheran.

There are, also among this majority – Niemöller is a remarkable example – very excellent, very learned and very pious men. The day is coming, when their eyes will be opened. The necessary catastrophy of the Hitler-system can be helpfull to realize this spiritual effect. Much more: the existence of a catholic christian community of faith, love and hope. Much more: the work of the living Word of God, who can not fail to accomplish his gracefull designs among us all: among Swiss and British an[d] also among German sinners.

Meanwhile, dear bishop, you have become with the doctorship of our faculty 'one of ours'.[12] I do not need to say, how glad I am about this fact, about the unanimity of our decision, about your willi[n]gness to accept this little sign of our great admiration for your work and your personality. When a better time is coming, we hope you will come to us and have a look at this city and its inhabitants. I often and gaily remember the evening in your Palace at Chichester an[d] our good conversation. I hope, that I myself have not seen the British shore for the last time. Have a good and blessed Christmas-time, you and all your friends and brethren.

Please do not be hurt by this terrible disabuse of the English language. I never learned it properly but only by reading (the life of archbishop Davidson . . . and also criminal stories!).
Yours very faithfully
Karl Barth

---

12 Bell had been awarded an honorary doctorate by the faculty of divinity at the University of Basle in the autumn of 1938.

BIOGRAPHIES

ENGLAND

Bate, Herbert Newell. Dean.
Born in 1871, Bate was educated at Oxford and remained a significant historian of the early church. From 1920 to 1928 he was a canon at Carlisle, and from 1928 to 1932 he was rector of Hadleigh in Suffolk and dean of Bocking. An important figure in the Faith and Order Movement, he became dean of York in 1932. He died in May 1941.

Batty, Basil Staunton. Bishop.
Batty was ordained in 1896, and thereafter had a succession of London parishes. He became first bishop of Fulham in 1926, a suffragan of the bishop of London with responsibility for the chaplaincies of North and Central Europe. Honorary assistant bishop of London from 1946, he died in March 1952.

Bell, George Kennedy Allen. Bishop.
Born in 1883, Bell was a student at Oxford before becoming chaplain to the archbishop of Canterbury, Randall Davidson in 1914. In 1924 he became dean of Canterbury, and in 1929 bishop of Chichester. His parallel career lay in his role as the leading English authority in the Life and Work movement and he was chairman of its standing committee when Hitler came to power. Immersed in a succession of controversial affairs, he remained bishop of Chichester until his retirement in 1957, and was made an honorary president of the new World Council of Churches in 1954. He died in 1958.

Dawson, Geoffrey. Journalist.
Born in 1874, Dawson passed his early years gaining journalistic experience in South Africa, working as private secretary to Lord Milner and becoming editor of the Johannesburg Star from 1905 to 1910. In England he became editor of the *Times* newspaper. He died in November 1944.

Don, Alan C. Canon.
Don worked as chaplain and secretary to Archbishop Lang from 1931 to 1941. He also served during these years as chaplain to the king, 1934—36, and chaplain to the Speaker of the house of commons, 1936—46. Afterwards Don became canon of Westminster and rector of St Margaret's, Westminster. He was sub-dean of Westminster Abbey from 1941 to 1946, and appointed dean in 1946. He died in May 1966.

Douglas, John. Canon.

Honorary canon at Southwark Cathedral and deputy vice-chancellor of the University of London, Douglas was an authority on the Eastern Church. In 1933 he became honorary general secretary of the Archbishop of Canterbury's Council on Foreign Relations.

Duncan-Jones, Arthur Stuart. Dean.

Born in 1879, Duncan-Jones was a student and then chaplain, fellow and dean of Caius College, Cambridge. In 1912 he became vicar of Blofield in Norfolk and then vicar of Louth in Lincolnshire. In 1916 he became vicar of St Mary's, Primrose Hill, in London, and afterwards vicar of the fashionable parish of Knightsbridge. In 1929 he was appointed dean of Chichester. Duncan-Jones was deeply committed to foreign affairs and an important figure at the Council of Foreign Relations. He died in 1955.

Ebbutt, Norman. Journalist.

Born in 1894, Ebbutt joined the staff of the *Times* in 1914. In September 1925 he was appointed its second correspondent in Berlin, and in 1927 he became chief correspondent. His critical accounts of affairs in the Third Reich proved unpopular with the authorities there, and he was expelled in 1937.

Fox, Henry Watson. Author.

Author of *Christianity and politics* (1925) and *Loyalties to church and state* (1935), Fox was an important figure in the Council on Foreign Relations, and also much involved with the World Alliance.

Headlam, Arthur Cayley. Bishop.

Born in 1862, Headlam acquired a formidable reputation as a theologian at Oxford and Cambridge, becoming professor successively at King's College, London, and Oxford. In 1923 he became bishop of Gloucester, and remained there until his retirement in 1945. He died in January 1947.

Henderson, Sir Neville. Diplomat.

Henderson held a succession of diplomatic posts in St Petersburg, Tokyo, Rome, Paris, Constantinople, Cairo and Belgrade before becoming ambassador to the Argentine Republic and Minister to Paraguay from 1935 to 1937. In 1937 he was appointed ambassador to Berlin, and he remained there until the outbreak of war in September 1939. He died in December 1942.

Lang, Cosmo Gordon. Archbishop.

Born in 1864, Lang had a distinguished career at Oxford before making his name in the Church of England as vicar of Portsea from 1896 to 1901. In 1901 he was appointed bishop of Stepney, and in 1908 he became archbishop of York. From here his elevation to Canterbury was not difficult to predict, and he followed Randall Davidson in 1928. He retired to make way for Archbishop Temple in 1942, but outlived his successor and died in December 1945.

Macdonald, A.J.

Born in 1887, Macdonald was made vicar of St Dunstan-in-the-West, London, in 1930 and held a number of related positions in the heart of London. Author of a number of works, he was familiar with Germany and visited the country often. In 1943 he was appointed rural dean of the City of London. He retired in 1957, and died in February 1959.

Oldham, J.H. Ecumenist.

Born in 1874, Oldham was the executive secretary of the World Missionary Conference at Edinburgh in 1910. From 1911 he was secretary of its continuing committee and then, in 1921, secretary of the International Missionary Council which succeeded it. Oldham was present at the Stockholm conference in 1925 and in 1934 he became the chairman of the research committee for Life and Work. He was chairman of the research commission which prepared the Oxford conference on Church, Community and State in 1937. At Utrecht in 1938 he was an important force in the drafting of the constitution for the new World Council of Churches. He died in 1969.

Phipps, Sir Eric. Diplomat.

Born in October 1875, Phipps served as envoy extraordinary and minister pleni-potentiary in Vienna from 1928 to 1933. He became ambassador in Berlin in 1933, and remained there until his appointment to the embassy in Paris in 1937. In 1939 he left Paris to return to England. He died in August 1945.

Rouse, Ruth. Youth leader and ecumenist.

From 1905 to 1924 Rouse was a secretary of the World's Student Christian Federation. In 1925 she was appointed editorial and education secretary to the missionary council to the Church Assembly, and in 1938 she became president of the world's Young Women's Christian Association, a post she held until 1946. From 1948 to 1954 she worked as editorial secretary to the committee appointed to write the history of the ecumenical movement. The fruit of these labours, which she edited with Stephen Neill, was published in 1954.

Rumbold, Sir Horace. Diplomat.

Born in February 1869, Rumbold held a series of posts in the diplomatic corps in Berlin, Switzerland, Poland, Constance and Madrid before his appointment as British ambassador in Berlin in 1928. He left Germany in August 1933. In December 1935 he was the British representative at the Geneva conference to advise the council of the League of Nations on the refugee crisis. He died in May 1941.

Temple, William. Archbishop.

Born the son of Frederick Temple (archbishop of Canterbury 1897–1902), Temple had a brilliant career as a student and fellow at Oxford before becoming headmaster of Repton school. In 1914 he was made rector of St James's, Picca-dilly, and then in 1919 a canon of Westminster. He became bishop of Manchester in 1921, and in 1924 organized the celebrated Conference on Christian politics, economics and citizenship (C.O.P.E.C.) at Birmingham. His commitment to social and political affairs won him a reputation throughout the church. In 1929 he was appointed archbishop of York and in 1942 he was translated to Canterbury. He died on 26 October 1944.

GERMANY

Asmussen, Hans. Lutheran pastor, theologian and liturgist.
Born in 1898, Asmussen was the co-author of the Altona Declaration in 1932, a leading member of the Barmen synod 1934, and co-author with Karl Barth and Thomas Breit of the Barmen statement. In May 1941 he was arrested with the entire examining board of the Old Prussian Council of Brethren. Later in the war he became involved with Carl Goerdeler, former mayor of Leipzig and resistance leader, who asked for a report on the church's views on economic matters, summer 1942.

Barth, Karl. Theologian.
Born in 1886, Barth was successively professor of Reformed theology at the University of Göttingen 1921–5, professor for dogmatics and New Testament exegisis at the University of Münster 1925–30, professor of systematic theology at the University of Bonn 1930–5, and professor of systematic theology at Basle from 1935. His crucial significance in the church struggle in the Third Reich rested with his substantial authorship of the Barmen Declaration (1934) and his book *Theologische Existenz Heute*. Barth died in 1968.

Bodelschwingh, Friedrich von. Pastor.
Pastor and famous Christian social worker at the Bethel settlement. Bodelschwingh was nominated by Kapler's committee in May 1933 to be the new *Reichsbischof* of the *Reichskirche*. After his defeat by Müller he retreated from the foreground of church affairs.

Böhm, Hans. Lutheran pastor.
Based at Berlin-Zehlendorf, Böhm was appointed a member of the new provisional executive committee for the Provisional Church Administration, with Niemöller and Martin Albertz in 1936.

Bertram, Adolf. Cardinal archbishop.
Born in 1859, Bertram was ordained in 1881 and consecrated bishop of Hildersheim in 1906. He was appointed archbishop of Breslau in 1914, and made cardinal in 1919. For many years he served as the chairman of the conference of German bishops at Fulda. He died in 1945.

Bonhoeffer, Dietrich. Theologian and pastor.
Born in 1906, Bonhoeffer was a student of theology in Berlin in 1923–7, and then university chaplain there from 1931 to 1933. In 1933 he became pastor of the German congregation at Sydenham in London, and he remained there until his return to Germany in 1935. Between 1935 and 1941 Bonhoeffer was the director of an illegal preachers' seminary at Finkenwalde, Pomerania. By 1942

he was involved with resistance circles, and in May 1942 he met Bishop Bell in Sweden and asked him to forge a link between his group and the British government. He was arrested on suspicion of political conspiracy in 1943, and murdered at Flossenbürg on 9 April 1945.

Breit, Dr Thomas. Lutheran pastor.
Lutheran. Senior church councillor in Bavaria. Member of the executive committee for the Confessing Church in October 1934, he was appointed a member of the new Provisional Church Government (*Vorläufige Leitung*) of the Evangelical Church on 22 November 1934. Later he was arrested and detained with Marahrens in Darmstadt on seeking to demonstrate sympathy for four Hessian pastors in concentration camps. Breit was chairman of the Luther Council (*Lutherrat*), appointed in 1936, and a co-signatory of a statement released on 29 August 1937 affirming the right to preach the Gospel.

Deissmann, Adolf. Theologian and ecumenist.
Deissmann was a professor at the University of Berlin. He had played a prominent part at the Life and Work conference at Stockholm in 1925 and the Faith and Order conference at Lausanne in 1927. From 1930 to 1931 he was rector of Berlin University.

Dibelius, Otto. Superintendent.
Born in 1880, Dibelius was ordained in 1907. He was general superintendent of Berlin from 1925 to 1933. Briefly suspended in the summer of 1933, he was soon restored to office. In June 1937 Dibelius stood trial for breaching the Conspiracy Law and was acquitted. In 1947 he became bishop of Berlin and Brandenburg. He also became chairman of the central committee of the Evangelical Church in Germany and a president of the World Council of Churches. He died in 1967.

Dieckhoff, Hans-Heinrich. Diplomat.
Born in 1884, Dieckhoff was responsible for the Anglo-American department in the foreign ministry in the 1930s and was briefly state secretary between 1936 and 1937. Brother-in-law of Joachim von Ribbentrop, he accepted the post of ambassador in Washington in 1937 partly to avoid working under him. He was recalled to Berlin in November 1938. In May 1943 he was appointed ambassador in Madrid, but he was dismissed the following year. He died in 1952.

Diestel, Max. Superintendent.
Superintendent in Berlin, Diestel was an important figure in the ecumenical world, a leading member of the World Alliance, and a patron of Dietrich Bonhoeffer.

Fabricius, Cajus. Theologian.
Born in 1884, Fabricius was professor of systematic theology at Berlin in 1921 and professor of systematic theology at Breslau from 1935 to 1943. He joined the National Socialist Party in 1932. His work sought to define 'positive Christianity' in the Third Reich, but in time he was disillusioned by the values of the Hitler regime, leaving the party in 1940. He died in 1951.

Faulhaber, Michael. Cardinal Archbishop.
Born in 1869, Faulhaber was ordained in 1892. From 1903 to 1910 he was
professor of Old Testament exegesis at Strasbourg, and the bishop of Speyer
from 1910 to 1917. In 1917 he became archbishop of Munich, and he was made
cardinal in 1921. He died in 1952.

Fezer, Professor Karl. Theologian.
Professor at Tübingen. A 'moderate' member of the *Deutsche Christen*, Fezer
was invited by Kapler's committee of three to make recommendations for the
drafting of the new constitution of the German Evangelical Church in the summer
of 1933. He was appointed a provisional administrator of the church after Müller
was elected *Reichsbischof* and members of the Supreme Church Council
resigned, until the meeting of the national synod at the end of September.
Visited England with Hossenfelder in October 1933, invited by the Oxford Group
Movement. He resigned from the *Deutsche Christen* movement in the autumn
of 1933 and receded into the background of the dispute.

Frick, Wilhelm. Politician.
Born in 1877, Frick was a Munich lawyer and an early convert to the National
Socialist Party. He participated in the Munich *Putsch* in 1923, and was
imprisoned for fifteen months. In 1924 he became a deputy for the party in the
Reichstag. Frick was Reich minister of the interior from 1933 to 1943. He was
tried before the war crimes tribunal at Nuremberg in 1945–6 and executed in
1946.

Galen, Clemens August Graf von. Cardinal Bishop.
Born in 1878, Galen was ordained in 1904 and thereafter had pastorates in Berlin
and Münster. He was made bishop of Münster in 1933, and later became famous
abroad for his outspoken opposition to the so-called 'euthenasia' programme of
the Hitler regime. He was made cardinal in 1945, and died shortly after the end
of the war.

Gogarten, Professor Friedrich. Theologian.
Born in Dortmund in 1887, Gogarten was a pastor in Stelzendorf, Thuringia, in
1917 and then in Dorndorf in 1925. He founded the journal *Zwischen den Zeiten*
with Karl Barth and Eduard Thurneysen in 1922. A leading light in the new
dialectical theology, Gogarten was lecturer in systematic theology at Jena from
1927. A 'moderate' member of the *Deutsche Christen* he resigned from the
movement in the autumn of 1933 because of its antisemitism, although he still
supported National Socialism in 1937.

Göring, Hermann. Politician.
Born in 1893, Göring was commander-in-chief of the Luftwaffe, prime minister
of Prussia, and the second authority only to Hitler himself. An ace pilot in the
Great War, and an early convert to the National Socialist movement, Göring
became president of the *Reichstag* after the elections of July 1932. When Hitler
became chancellor on 30 January 1933, Goering became Prussian minister of
the interior and commander-in-chief of the Prussian police and the Gestapo. An

important force in the 'co-ordination' of German political and social life in 1933, Göring was appointed commander-in-chief of the airforce in March 1935 and, in 1936, he became plenipotentiary for the four year plan. Now he became a major force in the persecution of the Jews and in the *Anschluss* with Austria in March 1938. On the outbreak of war he became Hitler's designated successor, and in June 1940 he was appointed Reich marshal. His failure to win air supremacy over Britain did much to discredit him in that year. His influence waned, and he was arrested by Allied soldiers on 9 May 1945. He was sentenced to death at Nuremberg in October 1946, but escaped execution by taking poison.

Hanfstängel, Ernst. Businessman.

Born in 1887, he spent his early years in the United States. After returning to Germany at the end of the Great War he met Hitler and became a patron of the National Socialist movement. Hanfstängel participated in the Munich putsch in 1923. In 1931 he was appointed foreign press chief of the party. After 1933 he fell out of favour with the new regime, and in 1937 he travelled to Britain and then the United States. During the Second World War he advised President Roosevelt on German affairs. Afterwards he returned to Germany and died in Munich in 1975.

Heckel, Theodor. Pastor.

Born in 1894, Heckel was ordained in 1921. He was appointed head of the Evangelical Church's foreign relations department in 1934 and there faced difficulties in his relations with the ecumenical movements. Later he was responsible for aid for interned people and prisoners of war. He became dean of Munich in 1950, and held the position until 1964. In 1961, meanwhile, he became a member of the Bavarian senate. He died in 1967.

Hess, Rudolf. Politician.

Born in 1884, Hess joined the National Socialist party in January 1920, and between 1925 and 1932 he served as Hitler's private secretary. In December 1932 he was appointed chairman of the central political commission of the party, and soon he was an S.S. General. On 21 April 1933 Hess became deputy leader and later that year, on 2 December, Reich minister without portfolio. In February 1938 he became a member of the ministerial council for Reich defence, and in 1939 he was designated successor to Hitler and Göring. In May 1941 he flew to Britain to pursue, quite on his own, a peace initiative with the British government. He was tried at Nuremberg in 1946 and sentenced to life imprisonment. He passed the remainder of his life in Spandau prison in Berlin, dying in 1987.

Himmler, Heinrich. Politician.

Born in 1900, Himmler joined the National Socialist Party in 1925. From 1926 to 1930 he was deputy *Gauleiter* of Lower Bavaria. He became *Reichsführer* of the S.S. in 1929, commander of the political police in Bavaria in 1933, and commander of all German police in 1934. During the war Himmler's responsibilities multiplied, commanding the S.S. and the *Waffen-S.S.* divisions, and governing the occupied territories. In August 1943 he was appointed minister of the interior. Above all he assumed a central responsibility for the destruction of

European Jewry, the 'Final Solution'. Captured at the end of the war, he committed suicide on 23 May 1945.

Hindenburg, Paul von. Soldier and politician.

Born in 1847, Hindenburg served as general field marshal during the Great War and there acquired a powerful reputation. He was elected president of the Weimar Republic in 1925, and defeated Hitler to be re-elected in April 1932. He was persuaded to appoint Hitler chancellor nine months later. Elderly and weak, he did little to contest the creation of a totalitarian state in the year that followed, although he intervened significantly in the church struggle. He died in August 1934.

Hirsch, Emanuel. Theologian.

A leading member of the *Christliche-deutsche Bewegung*, founded in 1930. Often an opponent of Barth, whom he met at Göttingen in the early 1920s, he lent his academic authority to the *Deutsche Christen*.

Hossenfelder, Joachim. Pastor.

Born in 1899, Hossenfelder was ordained in 1923. A leader of the Thuringian *Deutsche Christen*, he became Reich leader of the *Glaubens bewegung Deutsche Christen* in 1932. He was appointed bishop of Brandenburg by the general synod of Prussia in September 1933, but was later forced to resign as Reich leader of the *Deutsche Christen* and the National Spiritual Ministry.

Jäger, August. Lawyer.

Jäger joined the National Socialist Party in March 1933. In June of that year he was appointed commissioner for the Prussian Evangelical Church, but his coercive approach soon lost him support and he was forced from authority. In 1939 he became administrator and deputy governor of Warthegau. He was executed in Poland in 1945.

Jacobi, Gerhard. Pastor.

Born in 1891, Jacobi made his name as the pastor of the *Kaiser-Wilhelm-Gedächtniskirche* and head of the Berlin synod. Host of the 'Young Reformation Movement', his home was the centre of debate among pastors who went on to lead the Confessing Movement, of which he was himself a leading light. He was a member of the working committee of the Barmen synod, and, afterwards, a member of the Council of Brethren of the Prussian Union. Kerrl brought pressure on the Prussian Church Committee to have him dismissed in December 1935 after allegations that he had one Jewish grandparent. Jacobi was arrested in June 1937, tried 2 July 1937 and acquitted. After the war he became the protestant bishop of Oldenburg.

Kapler, Hermann.

Kapler was elected president of the *Kirchenausschuss*, the executive committee of the *Kirchenbund*, in January 1925. A key figure in negotiations for a treaty between the Prussian church and the Weimar state, he was also a friend of the chancellor, Gustav Stresemann. His own sympathies for the Weimar Republic did much to foster a working relationship between the churches and the new state. Kapler led the committee of three which drafted a constitution for a new united church in 1933. He resigned as president soon after, on 21 June 1933.

Karow, Dr. Bishop.
General superintendent of Berlin, Karow was appointed bishop of Berlin by the general synod of the Old Prussian Union in September 1933.

Kerrl, Hanns. Politician.
Born in 1887, Kerrl was a student of law, and then a member of the Prussian provincial parliament. He joined the National Socialist Party in 1925, and was later president of the Prussian *Landtag* and Prussian minister of justice from April 1933 to June 1934. Between 1934 and 1935 he was minister without portfolio, responsible for town and country planning, before becoming minister for church affairs in July 1935. He died in Paris in 1941.

Koch, Karl. Pastor.
Pastor of Bad Oeynhausen and chairman of the 'Gospel and Church' group, Koch was shouted down at the 'Brown Synod' in August 1933. A leading light in the Confessing Church, he was chairman of the synod of Dortmund of 16 March 1934 which set up an independent 'constitutional' church of Westphalia, and he was elected president of it. He presided over the Barmen synod of 29–31 May 1934. In August 1934 he and Dietrich Bonhoeffer were appointed as consultative members of the Council of Life and Work at Fanö. In November 1934 Koch was made president of the Provisional Church Government of the Confessing Church. In August 1935 he, Bonhoeffer and Marahrens refused to attend the Life and Work conference at Chamby-sur-Montreux because Heckel and representatives of the *Reichskirche* were also present. Abroad, Koch was one of the most widely admired leaders of the Confessing Church.

Krause, Reinhold. Pastor.
Member of the Brandenburg provincial synod and the Prussian Land synod, and leader of the Greater Berlin district of the Faith Movement. Krause organized the grand rally of 20,000 members of the *Deutsche Christen* movement at the *Sportspalast* in Berlin on 13 November 1933. The main speaker of the evening, he urged that a *Volkskirche* must repudiate the Old Testament and press forward with the 'Non-Aryan Paragraph' in the church and create a separate church for protestants of 'alien blood'. In the furore that followed Müller dismissed Krause from his responsibilities.

Künneth, Walther. Pastor.
Member successively of the *Junge Reformatische Bewegung*, the *Pfarrernotbund* and then the Confessing Church, Künneth ran a church centre in Spandau, Berlin. He was a friend of Martin Niemöller. It was to Künneth that Niemöller spoke on the telephone before the conference with Hitler on 25 January 1934.

Krummacher, Gottfried-Adolf. Theologian.
A Land leader of the Faith Movement in the Rhineland, Krummacher was a close friend of the leader of the German Labour Front, Robert Ley. He was appointed *Landrat* of *Gummersbach* and *Gau Führer* in the West in 1933.

Ley, Robert. Politician.

Born in 1890, Ley joined the National Socialist movement in 1924 and was promptly made *Gauleiter* in the Rhineland. He became a member of the *Reichstag* in 1930, and was appointed Reich organization leader in November 1932. A particularly notorious antisemite, he was responsible for the co-ordination of the trades unions into the German Labour Front in May 1933. He led this body, the largest in the Third Reich, until 1945, and also oversaw the *Kraft durch Freude*, or 'Strength through Joy' movement, which organized leisure and holidays in Germany. During the war Ley added to his responsibilities housing and the education of the new National Socialist *élite* at the *Ordensburg* schools. He was captured by American soldiers at the end of the war, and committed suicide on 24 October 1945.

Lietzmann, Professor Hans. Church historian and theologian.

Born in 1875, Lietzmann was a student and a lecturer at the universities of Jena and Bonn. Lietzmann succeeded Adolf Harnack to a chair at Berlin. A distinguished scholar, he was one of a group of prominent theologians who contested the 'Aryan Paragraph' in the church in a joint statement in November 1933. He died in 1942.

Lilje, Hanns. Pastor and ecumenist.

Born in 1899, Lilje was appointed general secretary of the German Student Christian Movement in 1924. A leading light in the *Junge Reformatische Bewegung*, he was also the editor of its journal, *Junge Kirche*. In February 1937 Lilje was appointed head of the Gremium, a temporary committee representing the Lutheran, Reformed and United churches, to direct affairs in the churches after Hitler's call for fresh elections in February 1937 and the end of the Reich church committee. In 1944 Lilje was tried by a people's court for 'inner resistance' against the state. He survived the last months of the war and was later bishop of the Evangelical Lutheran Church in Hanover from 1947 until his retirement in 1971. Between 1955 and 1969 Lilje was presiding bishop of the United Evangelical Lutheran Church in Germany. Between 1947 and 1970 he was a member of the executive committee of the Lutheran World Federation; he served as president between 1952 and 1957. His stature as an ecumenical leader was recognized when he was appointed president of the World Council of Churches in 1968. He retired in 1975 and died in 1977.

Marahrens, August. Lutheran bishop.

The Lutheran bishop of Hanover, Marahrens was a member of Kapler's group chosen to draft the new constitution at Loccum in May 1933. He was present at the meeting with Hitler on 25 January 1934, and conceded his loyalty to Müller afterwards. Later he withstood the pressure of the *Deutsche Christen* who wished to see Hanover incorporated into the *Reichskirche*, successfully appealing to his pastors for support.

Meiser, Hans. Lutheran bishop.

Born in 1881, Meiser was ordained in 1905 and afterwards had parishes in Munich. He was elected bishop of the Evangelical Lutheran Church in Bavaria in 1933. Meiser supported the nomination of Ludwig Müller as *Reichsbischof* in May 1933 at Eisenach. Removed from office by decree in October 1934 and placed under house arrest he was released and reinstated as bishop after Jäger's resignation later that month. A member of the central committee of the World Council of Churches in 1948, Meiser retired in 1955.

Muhs, Hermann. Politician.

Born in 1894, Muhs joined the National Socialist Party in 1929. He was appointed *Gauleiter* of South Hanover-Brunswick in 1932, and then state secretary to the ministry of church affairs in 1937. After Kerrl's death in 1941 Muhs was responsible for the ministry of church affairs until 1945.

Müller, Ludwig. Bishop.

Born in 1883, Müller was a naval chaplain from 1914 to 1926 and army chaplain in Königsberg from 1926 to 1933. A personal friend of Hitler, in 1933 he was appointed bishop of the Prussian Evangelical Church and then bishop of the Reich Evangelical Church. He was displaced after the establishment of Kerrl's church ministry in September 1935. He died in 1945.

Neurath, Constantin Freiherr von. Diplomat.

Born in 1873, Neurath entered the diplomatic service as a young man. Between 1903 and 1908 he was vice-consul in London, and then a councillor in the German foreign office. By 1930 he had served as ambassador to Copenhagen and Rome. Between 1930 and 1932 he was ambassador in London, and returned to Berlin to become foreign minister in Papen's government in June 1932. He joined the National Socialist Party only in 1937, but lost office on 4 February 1938. Until 1945 he had only nominal status as Reich minister without portfolio. On 18 March 1939 he was appointed Reich protector of Bohemia and Moravia. He was replaced by Heydrich. Arrested at the end of the war, Neurath was sentenced to fifteen years in prison. Released in 1954, he died in August 1956.

Niemöller, Martin. Pastor.

Born in 1892, Niemöller sailed with the German navy from 1910 to 1918. In 1924 he was ordained, and between 1931 and 1937 he was pastor in Dahlem, an affluent suburb of Berlin. He was arrested in 1937 and tried for 'abuse of the pulpit' in 1938. After a virtual acquittal he was imprisoned in Sachsenshausen and Dachau until 1945. After the war he was leader of the German Evangelical Church's foreign office until 1956, and church president of Hessen from 1948–1962. He was appointed a president of the World Council of Churches in 1961. He died in 1984.

Oberheid, Heinrich. Bishop.

Oberheid was the *Deutsche Christen* bishop of Köln-Aachen. He served Ludwig Müller as his assistant in 1933 and he was appointed Müller's chief of staff in March 1934.

Papen, Franz von. Politician and diplomat.

Born in 1879, Papen spent his early years in military affairs. Between 1920 and 1932 he was a member of the Catholic Centre Party and served on the Prussian legislature. Politically, he was an authoritarian nationalist with a strong bias towards militarism. His good connexions assured him a successful political career, and on 1 June 1932 he became chancellor. His tenure of office did much to destroy the democratic conventions of the Weimar Republic, not least his lifting of the ban against the violent *Sturmabteilung* (S.A.) wing of the National Socialist Party. After he lost power in December 1932, Papen was instrumental in the negotiations which made Hitler chancellor on 30 January 1933. On the same day he was himself made vice-chancellor, a position he held until 3 July 1934. On 17 June 1934 he had made a speech at Marburg which appeared to criticize the new regime, and this received international attention. He continued, however, to work with the National Socialist state, and in 1936 he became ambassador to Vienna, proceeding to work for the *Anschluss* of Germany and Austria. Between 1939 and 1944 he was ambassador to Ankara. At the end of the war he was arrested and then acquitted at Nuremberg. In 1947 he was put on trial a second time, and this time sentenced to eight years in prison. He died in May 1969.

Preysing, Konrad, Graf von. Roman Catholic bishop.
Born in 1880, Preysing was ordained in 1909 and then became canon of Munich. He was appointed bishop of Eichstätt, Bavaria, in 1932, and then bishop of Berlin in 1935. Made Cardinal in 1946, he died in 1950.

Rehm, Wilhelm. Pastor.
Head of the *Deutsche Christen* in Württemberg, Rehm succeeded Christian Kinder as head of the Reich movement in November 1935. He published a pamphlet, *For a Jewish-Free German Evangelical Church*. By 1937 his wing of the *Deutsche Christen* movement was declining, but Rehm refused to ally his forces with the radical sections of the movement. In July 1937 he attached the title 'Reformation Reich Church' to his movement.

Rendtorff, Heinrich. Bishop.
In April 1933 Rendtorff declared publicly that he would join the National Social-ist party. As bishop of Mecklenburg in May 1933 he nominated Müller as the *Deutsche Christen* candidate for *Reichsbischof* at Eisenach. He resigned as bishop on 6 January 1934.

Reventlow, Count Ernst zu.
A historian, Reventlow was elected to a seat in the *Reichstag* in 1924. He joined the National Socialist party in 1927. A leader of the German Faith Movement, Reventlow participated in the conference of the Nordic religious groups which formed the Working Association of the German Faith Movement (*Arbeitsgemei-neschaft der Deutschen Glaubensbewegung*) at Eisenach in July 1933. In May 1934 the name of the movement was changed to the German Faith Movement, and Reventlow became its deputy Führer. He spoke at a meeting of the movement in the *Sportpalast* in Berlin in April 1935.

Ribbentrop, Joachim von. Politician and diplomat.
Born in 1893, Ribbentrop travelled, learnt languages, served in the army and then spent a brief period as military attaché in Istanbul before becoming a successful businessman. He joined the National Socialist Party in May 1932 and

soon became a member of the *Reichstag*, a colonel in the S.S. and a friend of Hitler himself. In June 1935 he negotiated the Anglo-German naval agreement, and then, on 24 July 1936, he was appointed ambassador to London. In November 1936 he was involved in the creation of the anti-Comintern pact with Italy and Japan. On 4 February 1938 he became Reich foreign minister, and on 23 August 1939 he negotiated the Nazi-Soviet pact which facilitated the German invasion of Poland. His political influence declined during the war. In June 1945 he was arrested by British troops, tried at Nuremberg, and executed in October 1946.

Rieger, Dr Julius. Pastor.
Born in 1901, Rieger studied theology in Berlin, Bethel and Berne. In 1930 he became pastor of the German Lutheran congregation at St George's Church in London. He remained here until 1953, when he was appointed superintendent in Berlin-Schöneberg.

Ropp, Baron von der.
A constant propagandist for the National Socialist regime, von der Ropp frequently visited Britain to plead the case for his government and for the *Deutsche Christen* movement. He was a founder member of the Anglo-German Brotherhood, a barely significant group of National Socialist sympathizers, but enjoyed the patronage of eminent friends, both in Britain and Germany. His credibility was tainted when Bell was informed that he was formerly an agent for the German secret service.

Rosenberg, Alfred. Architect and politician.
Born in 1893, Rosenberg joined the National Socialist Party in 1921. He became editor of the party newspaper *Völkische Beobachter* from 1921 to 1924. In 1934 he was appointed Hitler's delegate for cultural and educational supervision and the training of the party. Rosenberg was tried, sentenced and executed at Nuremberg in 1945–6. Author of *Der Mythos der seelisch-geistigen Gestaltenkämpfe unserer Zeit* (1930).

Rust, Bernhard. Educationalist and politician.
Born in 1883, Rust joined the National Socialist Party in 1922 and in 1925 became *Gauleiter* of Hanover-Braunschweig. In 1930 he became a deputy in the *Reichstag*. He was appointed Prussian minister of education, science and popular culture in February 1933, and appointed Reich minister of education in 1934. He was responsible for the purging of the universities thereafter. Rust committed suicide in May 1945.

Sasse, Martin. Bishop.
Appointed bishop of the Evangelical Church of Thuringia 1934. In November 1938 he and state minister Freyberg of Anhalt had protested against a directive from the National Socialist Teachers' Organization to ban religious education classes. This succeeded. In May 1939 Sasse and Bishop Schultz of Mecklenburg wrote a memorandum to complain of the anti-Christian influences fostered and promoted by the state. He died in 1941.

Schimanowsky, Herr. Politician.

Once a pastor, Schimanowsky left the church. He was responsible for the police department of the ministry of church affairs, and was widely feared for his aggressive approach to controversy and dissent.

Schirach, Baldur von. Politician.

Born in 1907, Schirach joined the National Socialist Party in 1925. He was appointed Reich youth leader of the party in 1929, and, after Hitler came to power, leader of German Youth from 1933 to 1939. In 1940 he became *Gauleiter* and governor of Vienna. He was arrested after the war, tried by the war crimes tribunal at Nuremberg in 1946, and sentenced to twenty years' imprisonment. He was released from Spandau prison in Berlin in 1967.

Schöffel, Simon. Lutheran bishop.

Bishop of Hamburg, Schöffel was one of the three Lutheran bishops to vote against the nomination of Bodelschwingh for the position of *Reichsbischof* at the council of the German Evangelical Church Confederation in May 1933. Müller appointed him a member of his Spiritual Ministry at the first national synod at Wittenberg in September 1933. He resigned when Müller asked him to share the supervision of the Lutheran churches with the bishop of Saxony, Friedrich Coch, in November 1933. Schöffel was one of three church leaders to visit Müller and offer their support after the conference with Hitler in January 1934 (the other two being Marahrens and Jakob Kessler, president of the church of the Palatinate).

Schönfeld, Hans. Ecumenist.

Schönfeld worked at the Evangelical Church's external affairs office under Bishop Heckel. He represented the 'Reich Church Group' at Chamby, August 1936, and later worked at the research department of the Ecumenical Council, Geneva. Broken by the strains brought by the war, and his own involvement with resistance circles in Germany, he died in 1954.

Schulenberg, Fritz-Dietlof, Count von der.

Born in 1902, he joined the National Socialist Party in 1932 but was soon disillusioned by its corruption in government. In 1937 he was appointed deputy police president in Berlin, and he began to gather other like-minded colleagues in various departments of administration and government. By 1938 he was heavily involved with a plan to overthrow the Hitler regime; by the spring of 1939 his determination to resist was fortified by the persecution of the Jews and the threat of war. After September 1939 he was expelled from the National Socialist Party for being 'politically unacceptable'. As the war progressed Schulenberg became deeply involved with resistance circles in the military and civilian spheres, working with Ludwig Beck, Claus von Stauffenberg, Henning von Tresckow, Johannes Popitz and Julius Leber, and devising a new constitution for a post-National Socialist Germany. In July 1944 he was a major figure in the final attempt to assassinate Hitler and destroy his regime. After its failure he was tried and executed on 19 August 1944.

Schultz, Walther. Bishop.

Deutsche Christen leader of Mecklenburg. After Rendtorff resigned as bishop of Mecklenburg-Schwerin in January 1934, Schultz became bishop of the new Mecklenburg Land church in May 1934. In December 1937 he protested to the government when Himmler banned the combination of the cross and the swastika. This did not succeed. In May 1939 he and the bishop of Saxony, Martin Sasse, protested against anti-Christian propaganda promoted by the state. Copies of their complaint were confiscated. During the war he was a member of the Spiritual Confidential Council, which was constituted two days before the outbreak of hostilities to advise Werner on the German Evangelical Church.

Siegmund-Schultze, Professor Friedrich. Ecumenist.

Siegmund-Schultze was an influential Christian social worker, a leading member of the World Alliance for Friendship between the Churches and editor of its German journal, *Sas Eiche*. His pacifism made him a controversial figure in Germany, and he soon left after Hitler came to power. He spent the war in Zurich, and was in touch with Bell in England and members of resistance movements in Germany itself in that period.

Sproll, John Baptist. Bishop.

Born in 1870, Sproll was ordained in 1895, thereafter serving in Württemberg parishes. In 1912 he was appointed coadjutor and then, in 1915, suffragan bishop of Rottenburg. He became bishop of Rottenburg in 1926. In the Third Reich he was personally attacked and, in 1938, banned from Württemberg. Sproll only returned in 1945, and he died in 1949.

Stange, Erich. Youth leader.

Stange was the head of the *Evangelische Jugend Deutschlands*, the youth organization of the German protestant churches, which had over 7,000 members in 1933. He fought to preserve the independence of the movement during the first year of the Hitler regime, but in July Müller assumed responsibility over the organization. On 21 December Müller informed Hitler that Stange had been dismissed and that the Evangelical youth movement had been absorbed by the *Hitler Jugend*.

Thadden-Trieglaff, Dr Reinhold von.

Based in Pomerania, Thadden was with Paul Humburg the co-chairman of the evangelical weeks programme. The first of the series was held in August 1935 in Hanover, and proved popular. Soon the idea also became controversial, and between January and August 1937 six evangelical weeks were banned.

Tillich, Paul. Theologian.

Born in 1886, Tillich studied theology at Berlin, Tübingen and Halle. An army chaplain in the Great War, he became professor of theology at Marburg in 1924, then at the technical *Hochschule* at Dresden and then professor of philosophy at Frankfurt. Because of associations with socialists, he left Germany in 1933 and moved to the United States. He was appointed professor of philosophical

theology at the Union Theological Seminary in New York. In 1955 he was
appointed to a chair at Harvard University.

Wahl, Hans. Pastor.

A jurist in the German Federation office, Wahl visited Bell in London with
Heckel and Krummacher in February 1934. In the *Kirchenbundesrat* he was
involved with the 'Jewish Question'. He accompanied Heckel and Schreiber to
the Life and Work conference at Novi Sad in 1933.

Weber, Dr. Otto. Reformed Pastor.

Weber, from Elberfeld, was appointed member of Müller's Spiritual Ministry
in 1933. He resigned on 22 December 1933. Later he was a member of the
Spiritual Confidential Council of the Evangelical Church during the war.

Weissler, Dr Friedrich.

Head of the chancellory office of the Second Provisional Government of the
Confessing Church, Weissler was implicated in the leaking of the May 1936
memorandum to Hitler. He was arrested on 6 October 1936 and died in Sachsenhausen concentration camp on 19 February 1937. His death provoked an international outcry.

Werner, Dr Friedrich.

Born in 1902, Werner was a lawyer in the Prussian church commission and a
leading supporter of the *Deutsche Christen*. On 24 June 1933 he was appointed
president of the supreme church council of Prussia, and later a member of
Müller's Spiritual Ministry. On 20 April 1938 it was Werner who decreed that
the pastors of the churches of the Old Prussian Union should take an oath of
loyalty to Hitler, thereby precipitating a new crisis in the church struggle.

Wienecke, Friedrich. Pastor.

A pastor at Soldin cathedral and a founding member of the *Glaubens-bewegung
Deutsche Christen*. It was Wienecke who combined the cross and the swastika.

Wurm, Theophil. Bishop.

Born in 1868, Wurm was appointed church president of Württemberg in 1929
and bishop of Württemberg in July 1933. He was dismissed and then reinstated
in 1934. After the war Wurm became chairman of the reconstituted Evangelical
Church in Germany in 1945. He retired in 1949 and died in 1953.

Zöllner, Wilhelm. Lutheran Superintendent.

General Superintendent of the Provincial Church of Westphalia before Hitler
came to power, Zöllner was a respected church leader with a reputation for
ecumenical commitment. In 1927 he went to the Faith and Order conference at
Lausanne as an unofficial representative of the German Evangelical Church
Confederation. In April 1933 he appealed to all Lutherans to endorse the unification of the church. In February 1936 he came out of retirement to accept the
chairmanship of the new Reich Church Committee, but when this failed he
departed from public life again in the following February and his influence
ended.

THE INTERNATIONAL ECUMENICAL MOVEMENTS

Ammundsen, Valdemar. Bishop.
Ammundsen was bishop of Haderslev in Denmark, vice-chairman of the international committee of the World Alliance and also the chairman of its management committee. He worked closely with Bell throughout this period.

Forell, Birger. Pastor.
Chaplain to the Swedish embassy in Berlin, Forell provided much valuable information about the crisis in the German churches to Bishop Bell between 1933 and 1939.

Keller, Adolf. Professor.
Keller, who held academic posts at Zurich and Geneva, was widely admired beyond his native Switzerland as an ecumenist and writer on European protestantism. Two of his books, *Church and state on the European continent* (1936) and *Religion and the European mind* (1934) proved particularly popular in England, where he was well known to church leaders.

Koechlin, Dr Alphons. Pastor.
Swiss pastor, based at Basle, and eminent ecumenist, Koechlin corresponded regularly with Bishop Bell during the National Socialist period. He attended the Dahlem Confessing synod in October 1934 on behalf of Life and Work, and, again at Bell's invitation, visited Marahrens and Koch in Germany in May 1938. Not only a source of information, Forell also provided a guiding hand when Bell needed advice on ecumenical ventures and German affairs.

Monod, Wilfrid. Pastor.
A widely respected figure in the French churches, Monod was the leading ecumenist of his generation in that country and president of the continental section of Life and Work. He favoured a stern response to National Socialism, and to Germany at large, between the wars, and launched a barrage of protests at Heckel when he attacked the 1925 Stockholm declarations at Novi Sad in 1933. He died during the German occupation of France.

Mott, John Raleigh. American methodist and ecumenist.
Mott was born in 1865. As a young man he held a number of important positions in the international Christian youth organizations. Particularly drawn to missionary work, Mott chaired the committee which created the international missionary conference in Edinburgh in 1910. This was a landmark in the history of ecumenism.

Visser 't Hooft, Wilhelm A.
Born in 1900, Visser 't Hooft became general secretary of the World Student Christian Federation in 1932. In 1935 he was chairman of the steering committee for the World Conference of Christian Youth at Amsterdam. In 1948 he was appointed first general secretary of the World Council of Churches, a

position he held until 1966 when he retired. He was elected honorary president of the World Council of Churches at Uppsala in 1968. He died in July
1985.

SELECTIVE BIBLIOGRAPHY

PUBLISHED WORKS

Proceedings

Chronicle of the convocation of Canterbury, London, 1933—9.
Proceedings of the church assembly, London, 1933—9.

Books and articles

Barnes, Kenneth, *Nazism, liberalism and Christianity: protestant social thought in Germany and Great Britain 1925—1937*, Kentucky, 1991.
Barnett, Victoria, *For the soul of the people: protestant protest against Hitler*, New York, 1992.
Bell, G.K.A., *Randall Davidson, archbishop of Canterbury*, London, 1952 edn.
——, *The church and humanity*, London, 1946.
——, *The kingship of Christ*, London, 1954.
Bell, G.K.A. and Adolf Deissmann (ed.) *Mysterium Christi: Christological studies by British and German theologians*, London, 1930.
Bentley, James, *Martin Niemöller*, London, 1984.
Bergen, Doris, *The twisted cross: the German Christian movement in the Third Reich*, North Carolina, 1996.
Bethge, Eberhard, *Dietrich Bonhoeffer: theologian, Christian, contemporary*, London, 1970.
Boyens, Armin, *Kirchenkampf und Ökumene 1933—1939: Darstellung und Dokumentation*, Munich, 1969.
Busch, Eberhard, *Karl Barth: his life from letters and autobiographical texts*, transl. John Bowden, London, 1976.
Carpenter, S.C., *Duncan-Jones of Chichester*, London, 1956.
Chadwick, Owen, *Hensley Henson: a study in the friction between church and state*, Oxford, 1983.
——, 'The English bishops and the Nazis', *Annual Report of the Friends of Lambeth Palace Library* (1973).
Chandler, Andrew, 'A question of fundamental principles: the Church of England and the Jews of Germany 1933—1937', *Leo Baeck Institute Yearbook*, XXXVIII (1993), 221—61.
——, 'Lambeth Palace, the Church of England and the Jews of Germany and Austria in 1938', *Leo Baeck Institute Yearbook*, XL (1995), 225—47.
——, 'The death of Dietrich Bonhoeffer', *Journal of Ecclesiastical History*, XLV (1994), 448—59.
Cochrane, Arthur, *The church's confession under Hitler*, Philadelphia, 1962.
Conway, John S., *The Nazi persecution of the churches*, London, 1968.
——, 'The attitudes of English speaking churches to developments in German protestantism', *Kirchliche Zeitgeschichte*, 6 Jahrgang, Heft 1 (1993), 147—59.
Dibelius, Otto, *In the service of the Lord*, London, 1964.
Duncan-Jones, A.S., *The struggle for religious freedom in Germany*, London, 1938.

Ericksen, Robert, *Theologians under Hitler: Gerhard Kittel, Paul Althaus and Emanuel Hirsch*, New Haven, 1985.

Forstman, Jack, *Christian faith in dark times: theological conflicts in the shadow of Hitler*, Kentucky, 1992.

Gutteridge, Richard, 'The churches and the Jews in England 1933–1945', in *Judaism and Christianity under the Impact of National Socialism*, ed. Otto Dov Kulka and Paul Mendes-Flohr (Jerusalem, 1987).

Hastings, Adrian, *A history of English Christianity 1920–1985*, London, 1986.

Helmreich, Ernst, *The German churches under Hitler: background, struggle epilogue*, Detroit, 1979.

Hildebrandt, Franz (ed.), *And other pastors of thy flock*, Cambridge, 1942.

Hoover, A.J., *God, Germany and Britain in the Great War: a study in clerical nationalism*, New York, 1989.

Hope, Nicholas, *German and Scandinavian protestantism 1700–1918*, Oxford, 1995.

Jasper, R.C.D., *George Bell, bishop of Chichester*, London, 1967.

——, *Arthur Cayley Headlam, life and letters of a bishop*, London, 1960.

Lindt, Andreas (ed.), *George Bell, Alphons Koechlin: Briefwechsel 1933–1954*, Zurich, 1962.

Lockhart, J.G., *Cosmo Gordon Lang*, London, 1949.

Micklem, Nathaniel, *The box and the puppets (1883–1953)*, London, 1957.

Norman, E.R., *Church and society in England 1770–1970: a historical study*, Oxford, 1976.

Rieger, Julius, *The silent church: the problem of the German confessional witness*, London, 1944.

Robbins, Keith, 'Martin Niemöller, the German church struggle and English opinion', *Journal of Ecclesiastical History*, XXXI (1970), 149–70.

——, 'Dorothy Buxton and the German church struggle', in *Church, society and politics*, ed. Derek Baker (Oxford, 1975), pp. 419–33.

Robertson, Edwin, *Unshakeable friend: George Bell and the German churches*, London, 1995.

Rouse, Ruth, and Stephen Neill (ed.), *A history of the ecumenical movement 1517–1948*, London, 1954.

Rupp, Gordon, *The righteousness of God*, London, 1953.

——, *Martin Luther. Hitler's cause - or cure?*, London, 1945.

——, *I seek my brethren: Bishop George Bell and the German churches*, University of East Anglia, Mackintosh Lecture, 1975.

Rusama, Jaakko, *Unity and compassion: moral issues in the life and thought of George K.A. Bell*, Helsinki, 1986.

Sachs, William, *The transformation of Anglicanism: from state church to global communion*, Cambridge, 1993.

Slack, Kenneth, *George Bell*, London, 1971.

Scholder, Klaus, *A requiem for Hitler and other new perspectives on the German church struggle*, London, 1989.

——, *The churches and the Third Reich*, transl. John Bowden, 2 vols., London, 1987–8.

Schwarz, Angela, *Die Reise ins Dritte Reich. Britische Augenzeugen im nationalsozialistischen Deutschland (1933–1939)*, Göttingen, 1993.

Simon, Ulrich, *Sitting in judgement 1913–1963*, London, 1978.

Visser 't Hooft, W.A., *Memoirs*, London, 1973.

Ward, W.R., *Theology, sociology and politics: the German protestant social conscience 1890–1933*, Berne, 1979.

Wilkinson, Alan, *Dissent or conform? War, peace and the English churches 1900–1945*, London, 1986.

Wright, J.R.C., *'Above Parties'; The political attitudes of the German protestant church leadership 1918–1933*, Oxford, 1974.
Zabel, James, *Nazism and the pastors: a study of the ideas of three 'Deutsche Christen' groups*, Missoula, 1976.
Zipfel, Friedrich, *Kirchenkampf in Deutschland 1933–1945*, Berlin, 1965.

UNPUBLISHED MATERIAL

Chandler, Andrew, 'The Church of England and Nazi Germany 1933–1945', Ph.D. dissertation, University of Cambridge, 1991.
Hampson, Daphne, 'The British response to the German church struggle 1933–1939', D.Phil. dissertation, University of Oxford, 1973.
Walker, Peter K., 'Bishop Bell of Chichester', typescript in the possession of the author.

INDEX

Abdication crisis 105, 136
Abyssinia 103
Act of Uniformity 5
Althaus, Paul 16
Ammundsen, Bishop 127, *175*
Anglo-continental society 11
Anglo-German movement for friendship
  between the churches 2
Anschluss of Germany and Austria 142, 144, 152
Archbishop of Canterbury's Council on Foreign
  Relations 11, 14, 15, 22, 24, 33, 34, 39,
  45, 50, 51, 53, 56, 58, 66, 69, 72, 95, 102,
  139, 141
Arning, Herr 107
'Aryan Paragraph' 17, 42, 43, 62, 63, 65, 68,
  78, 79, 81
Asmussen, Hans 125, 144, 147, *162*
Athenaeum 77, 89
Attolico, Bernhard 103
Augsburg, confession 29, 46, 73, 75, 84, 102,
  106
Augsburg, synod 1935 9, 94
Augsburg, treaty 6
Augustine 85
Baden, church of 18, 59, 60, 82, 94
Baldwin, Stanley 14
Banasch, Monsignor 83, 84
Banke, Herr 116
Bares, Bishop 83
Barker, Ernest 145
Barmen, synod 1934 18, 21, 68, 82, 84, 87,
  88, 131, 133
Barnes, Bishop 25
Barth, Karl 9, 10, 28, 32, 46, 71, 86, 130, 132,
  150, 152, 154–5, 155–7, *162*
Barth, Markus 154, 155
Bate, H.N. 45, 51–2, 82, 83–8, *159*
Batty, Bishop 20, 22, 26, 34, 50, 52, 72–4,
  74–5, 75–7, 81, 88, 101, 101–2, 102–3, 106,
  159
Bäuerle, Herr 108
Bavaria, church of 18, 19, 69, 70, 82, 89, 90,
  104, 106, 110, 125
Beazley, Sir Raymond 23
Beethoven, Ludwig van 12
Bell, Bishop 1–4, 6, 8, 9, 10, 13, 14, 15, 20,
  22, 23, 24, 25, 26, 27, 28, 29, 30, 32, 33,
  34, 39, 41, 42, 43, 50, 68, 69, 70, 71, 77–81,
  82, 89–92, 92–3, 94, 99–101, 105, 119,
  121–33, 135–6, 139–40, 143, 144, 153,
  154, *159*

Bell, Henrietta 4, 100
Berber, Professor 107
Berlin, university of 57, 117, 122, 130
Bernstorff, Count 108
Bertholet, Professor 108
Bertram, Cardinal 129, *162*
Beta, Pfarrer 83, 84
Bethel settlement 139
Beyer, Professor 109
Birnbaum, Herr 70
Bismarck, Count Otto von 7, 132
Bismarck, Count Otto Christian von 30
Blomberg, General 142
Bodelschwingh, Friedrich von 2, 16, 30,
  41, 42, 48, 53, 55, 62, 79, 91, 99, 125,
  162
Bodelschwingh, Gustav von 132, 136
Böhm, Hans 109, 128, 136, 144, 145, 146,
  147, *162*
Böhme, Jakob 130
Bolshevism 12–13, 15, 56, 57, 89–92, 93,
  113, 115, 150, 152
Bonhoeffer, Dietrich 15, *162–3*
Bornkaum, Professor 109
Breit, Thomas 124, 135–6, 145, *163*
Brocket, Lord 26
Brutschke, Pfarrer 108
Bucer, Martin 1
Buchman, Frank 26, 42
Bunyan, John 8
Burchard-Motz, Dr 107, 109
Burroughs, Bishop 26
Butler, Samuel 10
Buxton, Dorothy 25, 33
Calvin, John 6, 13
Canterbury diocesan conference 66, 67
Canterbury, conference 1927 10
Carlyle, Thomas 8
Cecil, Lord 89
Chamberlain, Neville 14, 143
Chichester, conference 1931 10
Christian socialism 5–6
Christian social union 5
Church Assembly 5, 11, 14, 23, 27–9, 39, 94,
  153
Church House, Westminster 77
Church Quarterly Review 3
Church Times 12, 13
Cole, Henry 8
Coleridge, S.T. 8
Collyer, Miss 122

Cologne, English church in 20
Concentration camps 11, 91
Concordat between Germany and the
  Vatican 41, 42, 86, 119
Confessing (or 'Confessional') Church 18,
  21, 23, 95, 96, 99, 101, 102–3, 106, 107,
  110, 111, 116, 120, 121–2, 122, 124, 134,
  135, 136, 140, 149, 152, 153
Convocation of Canterbury 5, 20, 27–9, 68,
  82
Copernicus 99
Council of Brethren (*Bruderrat*) of the
  Confessing Church 18, 19
Council on Foreign Relations (see Archbishop
  of Canterbury's Council on Foreign Relations)
Cragg, Roland 14, 34, 48, 74, 84, 87
Cranmer, Thomas 1, 8
Creighton, Bishop 8
Dahlem, synod 1934 70, 126
Dark, Sidney 13
Davidson, Archbishop 2, 3, 4, 89, 90, 157
Dawson, Geoffrey 75, *159*
Deedes, Sir Wyndham 91
Deissmann, Adolf 2, 10, 13, 46, 49, 51, 73,
  75, 108, 128, *163*
Der Stürmer 69, 127
Deutsche Christen ('German Christians') 16,
  17, 18, 21, 22, 23, 26, 30, 40, 41, 42, 43,
  49–50, 51, 57, 58, 61, 62, 63, 64, 65, 72,
  73, 74, 75, 78, 82, 91, 94, 95, 100, 106, 109,
  112, 118, 119, 125, 127, 128, 131, 140, 148,
  149, 150, 153
Dibelius, Martin 9
Dibelius, Otto 19, 39, 49, 51, 61, 63, 128–30,
  133, 144, 145, 146, 147, 149, 150, *163*
Dieckhoff, Hans Dietrich 108, *163*
Diesel, Dr 108
Diestel, Max 131, 144, *163*
Ditter, Herr 101
Dodd, C.H. 10
Don, Alan C. 12, 51, 52, *159*
Döring, Pfarrer 108
Dortmund, synod 1934 68
Douglas, Canon John 24, 102, *160*
Dryander, Dr Ernst 2
Duncan-Jones, A.S. 6, 14, 21, 22, 28–9,
  47–8, 51, 52–8, 69, 101, 140, 141, 142,
  160
Durckheim, Count 98, 133, 136
Eastern churches committee of the Church of
  England 11
Ebbutt, Norman 14, 47–8, 88, *160*
Eckhardt, Dr 87
Eckhardt, Meister 130
Edinburgh, conference 1910 1, 2, 3
Edinburgh, conference 1938 128, 133, 135,
  147
Eger, Herr 87
Ehrhardt, Arnold 154, 155
Einstein, Albert 12

Eisenach, first Evangelical Church conference
  1852 6
Eisenach, conference 1928 10
Enabling Law 40, 119
Evangelical Weeks 95, 121, 124–5, 133
Evangelical youth organizations 17
Fabricius, Cajus 23, 149, 150, *163*
Faith and Order (see also Edinburgh conference
  1938) 1, 4, 135, 146
Fanö, conference of 1933 70, 82, 88, 127
Faulhaber, Cardinal 76, 129, *164*
Feronce, Baron Dufour von 108
Fezer, Karl 42, 46, *164*
Forell, Birger 15, 67, 84, 127, 154, *175*
Formgeschichte (Form criticism) 9, 10
Fox, H.W. 30, 60–1, *160*
Free churches of Great Britain 30
Free churches of Germany 111
Frick, Wilhelm 17, 40, 41, 55, 56, 70, 71, 78,
  95, 119, 120, *164*
Fricke, Herr 108
Friedenthal, Fraulein 130, 137–9
Friedrich-Stammer Gesellschaft 107
Fritsch, Werner Freiherr von 142, 155
Froude, J.A. 8
Fuchs, Ernst 122
Fulda, conference 1937 129
Galen, Bishop Count von 114, 129, *164*
Garbett, Bishop 26
Gerber, Professor 109
Gerll, Dr 97, 98
German Church Federation
  (*Kirchenbund*) 16, 17, 40, 41
German Faith Movement 18, 42, 65, 75–7,
  87, 90, 94, 104
German Labour Front 15
Gerstenmaier, Eugen 116
Gestapo 43, 69, 104
Gillie, Mr 47, 58
Gleichschaltung 15–16, 62
Glick, David 132
Goebbels, Josef 23, 40, 116, 120
Goethe, Johann Wolfgang von 12, 130
Gogarten, Professor Friedrich 87, *164*
Gore, Bishop 5
Göring, Hermann 17, 68, 75, 78, 80, 82,
  164–5
Gospel and Church group 17, 42, 60, 60–1
Gottfriedsen, Herr 108
Göttingen, university of 26
Greek Orthodox church in Berlin 115
Grey, Sir Edward 2
Gros, Wilhelm 132
Grossmann, Pastor 54, 55, 94
Grotsche, Dr 83
Guardian, The 12, 13, 101
Guardini, Professor 83, 84
Gustav Adolf Verein 109
Gutteridge, Richard 8
Hamilton Baynes, A. 28

Hampson, Daphne 33
Hanfstängel, Ernst 47, *165*
Hanover, Lutheran church of 7, 19, 69, 70,
    89, 104, 106, 110, 117, 125
Hare, Julius 8
Harnack, Adolf 2, 57
Hauer, Professor 104
Hauk, Pastor 48
Headlam, Bishop 3–4, 8, 9, 10, 11, 14, 22,
    23, 24, 25, 29, 30, 34, 43, 48, 50, 52, 61,
    66, 73, 134–5, 140, 140–1, 142, 149, *160*
Headlam-Morley, Agnes 149
Heckel, Theodor 27, 42, 44, 68, 70, 77–81,
    109, 115–16, 117, 122, 131, 144, 145, 146,
    151, 165
Heidelberg, university of 26, 153
Heiler, Professor 83–7
Heine, Heinrich 12
Henderson, Arthur 89
Henderson, Sir Neville 148–9, *160*
Henrich, Pastor 125
Henson, Bishop 8, 9, 10, 13, 23, 26, 34, 142
Hermsdorf, conference 1934 82, 83–8
Hess, Rudolf 30, 94, 97–8, 100, 127, *165*
Hess, Frau 97–8
Hesse, Dr 16, 40
Hildebrandt, Franz 154–5, 156
Himmler, Heinrich 69, 104, 151, *165–6*
Hindenburg, Paul von 17, 30, 41, 50, 55, 68,
    69, 78–9, *166*
Hirsch, Professor Emanuel 16, 87, *166*
Hitler, Adolf 11, 12, 13, 15, 17, 18–19, 21,
    23, 24, 25–6, 30, 39, 41, 46, 50, 51, 55,
    55–6, 57–8, 59, 62, 68, 70, 78–9, 88, 89,
    90, 91, 93, 94, 97, 98, 99, 100, 104, 106–7,
    113, 114, 118, 119, 120, 122, 126, 127, 128,
    130, 131, 132, 134, 135, 138, 140, 142, 143,
    148, 151, 152, 153, 155
Hitler Youth (*Hitler Jugend*) 17, 64, 108, 110,
    116, 138, 150, 151, 153
Hoesch, Leopold von 13, 30, 46
Hooker, Richard 10
Horstmanbunde, Pastor 127
Hoskyns, Sir Edwyn 9, 10, 26
Hossenfelder, Joachim 17, 26, 41, 43, 46, 50,
    53, 63, 64, 65, 66, 67, 72, 77, 106, *166*
Huber, Max 146
Huguenot church 111
Inge, W.R. 13
Innere Mission 63
Jacobi, Gerhard 54, 55, 101, 106, *166*
Jäger, August 17, 18, 41, 49, 69, 70, 82, 86,
    88, 110, 128, *166*
Jews, baptism of 102
Jews, persecution of 11, 23, 25, 27, 45, 46,
    47, 51, 51–2, 61, 95, 113, 142, 143, 152
Kagerah, Pastor 149–50
Kaiser Wilhelm Gedächtniskirche 48, 50,
    54–5
Kant, Emanuel 12

Kapler, Hermann 16–17, 40, 41, 46, 47, 49,
    166–7
Karow, Bishop 49, 73, 75, *167*
Keller, Professor Adolf 50, 52, 121, 122, 123,
    130, 131, 133, *175*
Kerrl, Hanns 18, 19, 20, 24, 95, 96, 98–9,
    100, 101, 102, 103, 104, 105, 106, 109, 110,
    112, 113, 114, 116, 117, 118, 119, 120, 124,
    125, 129, 136, 139, 142, 143, 147, 149, *167*
Kidd, Canon 28
Kirchentage 6
Kirston, J. 107
Koch, Pastor of Breslau 83, 85
Koch, Praeses Karl 68, 90, 99, 100, 122,
    126–8, 132, 135–6, *167*
Koch, Werner 105
Koechlin, Alphons 15, 144, *175*
Korf, Graf von 149
Krause, Reinhold 17, 43, 72, 77, *167*
Krummacher, Gottfried Adolf 66, 77–81,
    109, 116, *167*
Künneth, Walther 78, *167*
Lambeth conference, sixth 4
Lambeth conference, seventh 4
Lang, Archbishop 4, 11, 12, 13, 14, 15, 20,
    21, 22, 24, 26, 27, 29, 30, 33, 34, 40, 41,
    45, 46, 47, 51, 52, 66, 67, 68, 69, 71, 72, 74,
    82, 88, 89, 92–3, 94, 101, 105, 133, 135–6,
    139–40, 140–1, 142, 143, 149, 153, *160*
Lange, Pastor 128
Langenhahn, Freiherr von 108
Lausanne, conference 1927 4, 128
League of Nations 3, 43, 126
Leeper, Alan 14
Leffler, *Oberregierungsrat* 106, 109, 117
Ley, Robert 15, 40, 127, 151, *168*
Lietzmann, Professor 149, *168*
Life and Work movement 1, 4, 30, 39, 40, 42,
    68, 70, 80, 81, 82, 88, 95, 98, 104–5, 128,
    144, 146
Lilje, Hanns 47, 99–101, 106, 108, 121–2,
    124, 131, 133, 136, 144, 168
Loccum, manifesto of 16, 40
Londonderry, Lord 26
Loveday, Arthur 29
Lübeck 19, 119
Lund, Bishop 4
Lunt, Bishop 25
Lunt, Canon Ronald 25
Luther, Martin 7, 8–9, 43, 58, 73, 111, 130,
    150
Lutheran Council 122, 124, 125, 133, 136,
    139, 144, 147
Macdonald, A.J. 11, 22, 23, 34, 58–60,
    107–18, 130, 139, 140–1, *161*
Marahrens, Bishop 16, 19, 20, 32, 40, 55, 96,
    99–101, 110, 116, 121, 122–3, 124, 125,
    131, 133, 135–6, 143, 144, 146, 147, 149,
    151, *168*
Marburg, university of 43, 51, 65

Martin, Archdeacon 28
Martin, Professor 122
Maurice, F.D. 5
Mecklenburg, church of 19, 88, 104
Meisel, Admiral 55
Meiser, Lutheran Bishop 18, 20, 44, 68, 70,
    79, 82, 96, 110, 121, 122, 124, 125, 128,
    133, *143, 168–9*
Memel 126, 153
Mercier, Cardinal 4
Michael, Dr 88
Micklem, Nathaniel 10
Ministry of Church Affairs 95, 100, 101, 112,
    114, 116, 117, 118, 119, 125, 142
Mit Brennender Sorge (Papal encyclical
    1937) 119, 129
Modernism 57, 61, 112
Mommsen, Theodor 113
Monod, Wilfid 66, *175*
Mott, J.R. 47, *175*
Mozley, J.K. 9–10
Muhs, Hermann 20, 119, 121, 125, 128, 129,
    136, *169*
Müller, Eberhard 124, 125
Müller, Ludwig 16–20, 22, 26, 27, 40, 41,
    42, 43, 49, 51, 53, 55, 61, 62, 63, 64, 65,
    67, 68, 69, 70, 72, 73–4, 75, 77, 80, 81, 82,
    86, 88, 90, 93, 94, 95, 106, 132, 134, *169*
Mussolini, Benito 13, 126, 129, 153
'Muzzling order', 4 January 1934 17, 18, 68
National Socialism 15, 21, 87, 90, 99, 113,
    114, 116, 123, 129, 130, 148, 150
Neurath, Baron von 31, 79, 121, *169*
New Reformation movement (*Neue
    Reformatische bewegung*) 55
Niemöller, Martin 17, 19, 20, 24, 25, 30, 32,
    73, 75, 77–9, 91, 96, 104, 106, 107, 109,
    111–12, 118, 120, 123–4, 132, 136, 139,
    140, 141, 142, 148, 154–5, 155–7, *169*
Niemöller, Else 144, 148
'Non-Aryan Christians' 45, 52, 136, 137–9,
    140
Novi Sad, conference 1933 42, 66
Nubel, Dr 147
Nygren, Professor Anders 84, 85, 86
Oberammergau, passion play 91
Oberheid, Heinrich 86, *169*
Oeynhausen, synod 1936 104, 127
Old Prussian Union, churches of 6, 17, 41,
    42, 49, 60–1, 62, 65, 94, 95, 142, 143, 148
Oldham, J.H. 69, 70, 146, *161*
Orsenigo, Monsignore Cesare 83
Osiander, Andreas 1
Ossietzky, Carl von 122
Ottmer, Pastor 107
Oud Wassenaar, conference 1919 3
Oxford, conference 1937 19, 98, 104–5, 116,
    120, 122–3, 126, 128–9, 133, 135, 144, 145,
    146, 147
Pacelli, Cardinal Eugenio 129

Papen, Franz von 69, 89, 90, *169–70*
Parsch, Dr 83, 84
Pastors' Emergency League
    (*Pfarrernotbund*) 17, 42, 68, 72, 73, 75,
    77–8, 78–9, 87, 110
Paulusbunde 130, 137–9
Phipps, Sir Eric 31, 72, 121, 136, *161*
Pinsk, Dr 83
Poland 153
Pollock, Bishop 28
'Positive Christianity' 15, 23, 101–15, 125,
    130
Prange, Dr 83
Preysing, Bishop Graf von 129, *170*
Pribilla, Father Max 83
Provisional Church Government of the
    Confessing Church 18, 19, 70, 94
Provisional Church Government of the
    Confessing Church (second) 19, 104, 125,
    126–7, 128, 129, 131, 132, 133, 139, 143
Raeder, Admiral 155
Rath, Ernst vom 143
Raven, Charles 10
Record, The 12, 13
Rehm, Wilhelm 106, 128–30, 131, *170*
Reich Church Committee 19, 101–2, 105,
    106, 119, 124, 125, 128, 136
Relton, Dr 28
Rendtorff, Heinrich 61, *170*
Rengsdorf, conference 1933 39
Reventlow, Count Ernst zu 76, 104, *170*
Ribbentrop, Joachim von 26, 30, 31, 89–92,
    92–3, 95, 99, 105, 121, 123, 133, 134–5,
    136, 142, 149, 153, *170–1*
Ribbentrop, Frau von 91
Rieger, Julius 21, 109, *171*
Ritter, Pastor 83, 84, 85, 86
Röhm, Ernst 127
Roman Catholic Church 16, 56, 56–7, 79,
    83–8, 93, 101, 115, 116, 126, 127, 128, 129,
    134
Ropp, Baron von der 108, 109, 130, *171*
Rose, Pastor 148
Rosenberg, Alfred 23, 97, 98–9, 99, 120, 125,
    131, 148, 150, 151, *171*
Rosenmüller, Herr 83
Rothe, Pastor 107
Rouse, Ruth 61–7, 67, *161*
Rupp, Gordon 8
Rust, Bernhard 17, 41, 54, 55, 68, 139, 153,
    171
S.A. (*Sturmabteilung*) 62, 63, 69, 98, 129, 138
Saar plebiscite 31, 94
Sachsenberg, concentration camp 148
Sasse, Martin 171
Saxony, church of 19, 104, 106
Schäfer, Paula 83
Schäffer-Bernstein, Baroness von 109
Schairer, Hof Prediger 97
Schimanowsky, Herr 121, 125, 136, *172*

Schirach, Baldur von   44, 116, *172*
Schleswig-Holstein, church of   7, 121
Schöffel, Simon   61, *172*
Schönfeld, Hans   22, 147, *172*
Schulenberg, Count von der   48, *172*
Schultz, Bishop   129, 149, *173*
Schulz, Georg   87
Scott Holland, Henry   2, 5
Seeberg, Professor   130, 136
Seyferth, Herr   108
Shepherd, Archdeacon   28
Sheppard, 'Dick'   14
Siegmund-Schultze, Professor Friedrich   133,
   146, *173*
Simon, Sir John   30
Simon, Paul   83
Simons, Dr   108
Søderblom, Archbishop   3
Spender, J.A.   155
Sproll, John Baptist   *173*
Spiero, Dr   130, 137−9
Sportpalast, meeting of 1933   17, 43, 44, 72,
   73, 74, 75, 77, 78
S.S. (*Schutzstaffeln*)   98, 129, 138
Stählin, Professor   83−4
Stahn, Dr   108
Stalin, Josef   13
Stange, Erich   56, *173*
Stimmen der zeit   83
Stöcker, Adolf   7, 109
Stockholm, conference 1925   4, 42, 98
Streeter, Professor B.H.   10
Streicher, Julius   127
Strong, Bishop   28
Student Christian Movement   82
Stuttgart   124
Sudeten crisis   20, 143, 149−50
Sweden, church of   67, 70, 107
Tacitus   76
Temple, Archbishop   1, 2, 6, 10, 13, 23, 26,
   82, 91, *161−2*
Thadden-Trieglaff, Baron von   124−5, 144,
   173
Theology   11
Tillich, Ernst   127
Tillich, Paul   105, 146, *173−4*
Times, The   14, 25, 26−7, 27, 41, 47, 58, 66,
   67, 69, 75, 81, 87, 88, 94, 105, 116, 119,
   133, 136, 142, 143
Tissington Tatlow, Canon   2
Todt, Rudolf   7

Ulm, synod 1934   28, 69, 82, 125
Utrecht, conference 1938   142, 145, 147
Vatican, the (see also Concordat)   86
Versailles, treaty of   11, 94
Visser 't Hooft, Dr W.A.   82, 146, *175*
Völkischer Beobachter   86
Wahl, Hans   68, 77−81, 108, 109, 122, 131,
   144, *174*
Walter, Bruno   12
Walter, John   48
Weber, Otto   61−2, 63, *174*
Weigall, Sidney   89
Weimar Republic   7, 59
Weissler, Friedrich   19, 105, 119, 127, *174*
Wendland, Heinz-Dietrich   116
Werner, Friedrich   19, 20, 53, 63, 119, 120,
   142, 153, *174*
Wesley, John   8
Westcott, Bishop   5
Westcott House   149
Westphalia, church of   60−1, 68, 82, 89, 128
Wichern, Johann   7
Wienecke, Friedrich   106, *174*
Wilhelm II   2, 7, 101
Winterhelfe   108, 116, 116−17
Winthrop Young, Geoffrey   91
Winzer, Father   83
Wittenberg, first German national synod   17,
   43, 62, 65
Wittenberg, university of   117
Wobbermin, Professor   108, 149, 150
Woods, Bishop   25
Woodward, Bishop   13
World Alliance for Promoting International
   Friendship through the Churches   2, 3
World Council of Churches   146
Wurm, Bishop   18, 20, 44, 68, 70, 79, 106,
   110, 125, 143, *174*
Württemberg, church of   18, 19, 61, 65, 69,
   82, 89, 90, 104, 106, 110, 125
Y.M.C.A. (Young Men's Christian
   Association)   47, 56, 64
Young Reformation Movement (*Junge
   reformatische bewegung*)   65, 88
Y.W.C.A. (Young Women's Christian
   Association)   61, 62, 63, 64
Zimmern, Sir Alfred   155
Zöllner, Wilhelm   19, 23, 24, 95, 106, 109,
   110, 114, 115, 117, 119, 122, 124, 125, 126,
   127, 128, 129, 131, 132, 133, 135−6, 139,
   140, 148, 149

PUBLICATIONS

1. VISITATION ARTICLES AND INJUNCTIONS OF THE EARLY STUART CHURCH. VOLUME I. Ed. Kenneth Fincham (1994)
2. THE SPECULUM OF ARCHBISHOP THOMAS SECKER: THE DIOCESE OF CANTERBURY 1758–1768. Ed. Jeremy Gregory (1995)
3. THE EARLY LETTERS OF BISHOP RICHARD HURD 1739–1762 Ed. Sarah Brewer (1995)
4. BRETHREN IN ADVERSITY: BISHOP GEORGE BELL, THE CHURCH OF ENGLAND AND THE CRISIS OF GERMAN PROTESTANTISM 1933–1939. Ed. Andrew Chandler (1996)

Forthcoming Publications

THE BRITISH DELEGATION AND THE SYNOD OF DORT. Ed. Anthony Milton

VISITATION ARTICLES AND INJUNCTIONS OF THE EARLY STUART CHURCH. VOLUME II. Ed. Kenneth Fincham

THE HISTORIC CANONS OF THE CHURCH OF ENGLAND. Ed. Gerald Bray

THE DIARY OF AN OXFORD PARSON: THE REVEREND JOHN HILL, VICE-PRINCIPAL OF ST EDMUND HALL, OXFORD, 1805–1808, 1820–1855. Ed. Grayson Carter

THE 1669 RETURN OF NONCONFORMIST CONVENTICLES. Ed. David Wykes

PROPHESYINGS, CONFERENCES AND EXERCISES IN THE ELIZABETHAN AND JACOBEAN CHURCH OF ENGLAND. Ed. Patrick Collinson

ANGLO-CATHOLIC COMMUNICANTS' GUILDS AND SOCIETIES IN THE LATE NINETEENTH CENTURY. Ed. Jeremy Morris

THE DIARIES OF BISHOP BEILBY PORTEUS. Ed. Andrew Robinson

THE CORRESPONDENCE OF THEOPHILUS LINDSEY. Ed. G.M. Ditchfield

A CHURCH OF ENGLAND MISCELLANY

Suggestions for publications should be addressed to Dr Stephen Taylor, General Editor, Church of England Record Society, Department of History, University of Reading, Whiteknights, Reading RG6 2AA.